ASPECT, COMMUNICATIVE APPEAL, AND
TEMPORAL MEANING IN BIBLICAL HEBREW
VERBAL FORMS

LINGUISTIC STUDIES IN ANCIENT WEST SEMITIC

Edited by
Cynthia L. Miller-Naudé and Jacobus A. Naudé

The series Linguistic Studies in Ancient West Semitic is devoted to the ancient West Semitic languages, including Hebrew, Aramaic, Ugaritic, and their near congeners. It includes monographs, collections of essays, and text editions informed by the approaches of linguistic science. The material studied will span from the earliest texts to the rise of Islam.

1. *The Verbless Clause in Biblical Hebrew*, by Edited by Cynthia L. Miller
2. *Phonology and Morphology of Biblical Hebrew*, by Joshua Blau
3. *A Manual of Ugaritic*, by Pierre Bordreuil and Dennis Pardee
4. *Word Order in the Biblical Hebrew Finite Clause*, by Adina Moshavi
5. *Oath Formulas in Biblical Hebrew*, by Blane Conklin
6. *Biblical Hebrew Grammar Visualized*, by Francis I. Andersen and A. Dean Forbes
7. *Time and the Biblical Hebrew Verb*, by John A. Cook
8. *Diachrony in Biblical Hebrew*, edited by Cynthia Miller-Naudé and Ziony Zevit
9. *The Syntax of Volitives in Biblical Hebrew and Amarna Canaanite Prose*, by Hélène M. Dallaire
10. *The Relative Clause in Biblical Hebrew*, by Robert D. Holmstedt
11. *Language Change in the Wake of Empire*, by Aaron Michael Butts
12. *Advances in Biblical Hebrew Linguistics*, edited by Adina Moshavi and Tania Notarius
13. *The Morphophonological Development of the Classical Aramaic Verb*, by Joseph L. Malone
14. *Non-Semitic Loanwords in the Hebrew Bible*, by Benjamin J. Noonan
15. *Judging the Judges*, by Mary L. Conway
16. *Aspect, Communicative Appeal, and Temporal Meaning in Biblical Hebrew Verbal Forms*, by Ulf Bergström

Aspect, Communicative Appeal, and Temporal Meaning in Biblical Hebrew Verbal Forms

ULF BERGSTRÖM

EISENBRAUNS | University Park, Pennsylvania

Library of Congress Cataloging-in-Publication Data

Names: Bergström, Ulf, 1974– author.
Title: Aspect, communicative appeal, and temporal meaning in Biblical Hebrew verbal forms / Ulf Bergström.
Other titles: Linguistic studies in ancient West Semitic ; 16.
Description: University Park, Pennsylvania : Eisenbrauns, [2022] | Series: Linguistic studies in ancient West Semitic ; 16 | Includes bibliographical references and index.
Summary: "Offers a new explanation for the expression of tense and aspect in Biblical Hebrew, demonstrating that the verbal forms have basic aspectual and derived temporal meanings"—Provided by publisher.
Identifiers: LCCN 2021054185 | ISBN 9781646021406 (cloth)
Subjects: LCSH: Hebrew language—Verb. | Hebrew language—Aspect. | Hebrew language—Tense. | Hebrew language—Semantics.
Classification: LCC PJ4645 .B47 2022 | DDC 492.45/6—dc23/eng/20211122
LC record available at https://lccn.loc.gov/2021054185

Copyright © 2022 Ulf Bergström
All rights reserved
Printed in the United States of America
Published by The Pennsylvania State University Press,
University Park, PA 16802–1003

Eisenbrauns is an imprint of The Pennsylvania State University Press.

The Pennsylvania State University Press is a member of the Association of University Presses.

It is the policy of The Pennsylvania State University Press to use acid-free paper. Publications on uncoated stock satisfy the minimum requirements of American National Standard for Information Sciences—Permanence of Paper for Printed Library Material, ANSI Z39.48–1992.

CONTENTS

List of Illustrations..ix
Acknowledgments..xi
List of Abbreviations...xiii
Transliteration Key.. xv

CHAPTER 1. Introduction 1
   1.1. The Problem 1
   1.2. Aim 4
   1.3. What "Meaning" Means 5
      1.3.1. Semantics and Pragmatics 6
      1.3.2. Criteria for Explanatory Semantics 8
   1.4. The Biblical Hebrew Verbal System 13
   1.5. Scope 16
      1.5.1. Source Material 16
      1.5.2. Diachronic Diversity 18
      1.5.3. Prose and Poetry 19
   1.6. Summary 21

CHAPTER 2. Comments on the State of Research 23
   2.1. Tense 23
   2.2. Aspect 29
      2.2.1. Aspect in Classical Grammar 29
      2.2.2. Modern Times 32
      2.2.3. Reference Time, Focused Time, and Deictic Centers 41
      2.2.4. Aspect in Hebraistic Studies 45
   2.3. Modality 49
   2.4. Linguistic Attitude (*Sprechhaltung*) 51
   2.5. The Grammaticalization Approach 53
   2.6. Summary 61

CHAPTER 3. A Theory of Aspect and Tense 64
    3.1. Introductory Note: Nonsemantic Factors Indicating Tense 64
    3.2. *Aktionsart* 66
    3.3. Focused Time and the Definition of Tense and Aspect 69
    3.4. Stage-Based Aspect 71
        3.4.1. Resultative 71
        3.4.2. Progressive 76
        3.4.3. Preparative 79
        3.4.4. Stage-Based Aspect and *Aktionsart*: An Overview 81
    3.5. Stage-Based Versus Limit-Based Analysis of Aspect 84
    3.6. Temporalization 89
    3.7. Summary 94

CHAPTER 4. Progressive and Resultative Verbs in Biblical Hebrew 96
    4.1. *Qotel* 98
        4.1.1. Invariant Progressive *qotel* 98
        4.1.2. Temporalized *qotel* 103
        4.1.3. Nonprogressive and Nominal *qotel* 104
    4.2. *Yiqtol*-L 108
        4.2.1. Invariant Progressive *yiqtol*-L 108
        4.2.2. Temporalized *yiqtol*-L 114
    4.3. *Qatal* 118
        4.3.1. Invariant Resultative *qatal* 119
        4.3.2. Temporalized *qatal* 132
        4.3.3. Adjectival and Verbal Stative *qatal* 141
    4.4. *Yiqtol*-S 142
        4.4.1. Invariant Resultative *yiqtol*-S: *wayyiqtol* 142
        4.4.2. Temporalized *wayyiqtol* 149
        4.4.3. Free-Standing Declarative *yiqtol*-S 151
        4.4.4. Volitive *yiqtol*-S 155
    4.5. Summary 156

CHAPTER 5. Communicative Appeal and the Semantics of the Biblical Hebrew Verb 157
    5.1. The Semiotic Foundations for a Theory of Appeal in Language 158
    5.2. Criteria for Full Communicative Appeal 162
        5.2.1. Imminence 162
        5.2.2. Nonexpectancy 163
        5.2.3. Efficiency 165
    5.3. Communicative Appeal and Verbal Grammar: The Case of the English Progressives 170

5.4. Communicative Appeal in the Biblical Hebrew Verbal System   172
    5.4.1. The Resultative Subsystem   173
    5.4.2. The Progressive Subsystem   176
    5.4.3. The Volitive Subsystem   180
5.5. Summary   186

CHAPTER 6 Conclusion   188

Bibliography 195
Index 209

ILLUSTRATIONS

Figures
1. Andrason's diachronic pathways of *yiqtol*-L   55
2. The nuclear event in the framework of the extended event model   83
3. Typical positions of focused time in relation to the extended and the nuclear event   85

Tables
1. Completed and uncompleted in Greek and Latin   31
2. Imperfective and perfective aspect in Russian   33
3. Evidence for an iterative-continuative-progressive-habitual pathway in verbal forms   57
4. Evidence for an iterative-frequentative-habitual pathway in verbal forms   58
5. Stage-based aspect and appeal in the Biblical Hebrew verbal system   192

ACKNOWLEDGMENTS

Several individuals deserve mention for their help in the process of writing this book, first and foremost Göran Eidevall, who has read and commented extensively on all parts of the work from the very first drafts to the final product. I have also continually received encouraging feedback from Sören Holst. Important revisions and amplifications of the work have been made following reviews by Jan Retsö and John Cook.

Further, I am grateful to Atle Grönn for stimulating e-mail conversations concerning some of the basic issues of the study. A special, heartfelt thanks also goes to Nils B. Thelin, who read my early drafts on aspect theory, and whose detailed and penetrating comments helped me to improve my arguments and think critically about my work.

Throughout working on the project, I had the opportunity to present my drafts at numerous colloquia and conferences where I received much appreciated feedback: the colloquia in the Old Testament/Hebrew Bible and Semitic languages at Uppsala University, the colloquia in the Old Testament/biblical exegesis at Lund University, the University of Helsinki, Åbo Akademi University, and the University of Copenhagen, and, last but not least, the conferences organized within the OTSEM network. Many individuals from these contexts could be named here, but, lest I forget someone, I restrict myself to mentioning only a few people who have given substantial input as respondents to papers and/or as conversational partners: Lotta Valve, Ola Wikander, Bo Johnson, Hugh Williamson, Kevin Cathcart, Andreas Scherer, Mats Eskhult, and Bo Isaksson.

Lastly, I am also indebted to the anonymous reviewer and the series editors, Cynthia Miller-Naudé and Jacobus Naudé, for their helpful comments.

ABBREVIATIONS

Bible Translations
NIV   New International Version
NRSV   New Revised Standard Version

Various Grammatical Terms
AOR   aorist
C   consonant
CC   double consonant
D   deictic center
E   event (time)
F   mutual focus of attention/focused content of the event/focused time
IMPF   imperfect
PFCT   perfect
PLUP   pluperfect
PRS   present
PST   past tense
RES   resultative
S   speech (time)
TAM   Tense, Aspect, Modality

Interlinear Grammatical Glossing
1/2/3   first/second/third person
COH   cohortative
F   feminine
IMP   imperative
INFA   absolute infinitive
INFC   infinitive construct

JUSS	jussive
M	masculine
OBJ	object marker
PASS	passive
PL	plural
PST	past tense
Q	question particle
QOT	active participle, *qotel*
QTAL	suffix conjugation, *qatal*
QUOT	quotative
SG	singular
YQTL	prefix conjugation, *yiqtol*
YQTL-L	long *yiqtol*
YQTL-S	short *yiqtol*, morphologically recognizable
YQTL(S)	short *yiqtol*, reconstructed

An asterisk before an example indicates that it is not normal.

TRANSLITERATION KEY

Consonants		Vowels	
א	ʾ	◌ִ	i
ב, בּ	b, ḇ	◌ִי	î
ג, גּ	g, ḡ	◌ֵ	e
ד, דּ	d, ḏ	◌ֵי	ê
ה	h	◌ֶה	eʰ
ו	w	◌ֶ	æ
ז	z	◌ֶי	ǣ
ח	ḥ	◌ֶה	æʰ
ט	ṭ	◌ָ	ā, o
י	y	◌ָה	â
כ, כּ	k, ḵ	◌ָי	āʸ
ל	l	◌ַ	a
מ	m	◌ַה	aʰ
נ	n	ֹ	ō
ס	s	וֹ	ô
ע	ʿ	ֹה	ōʰ
פ, פּ	p, p̄	◌ֻ	u
צ	ṣ	וּ	û
ק	q	◌ְ	ə
ר	r	◌ֱ	ǣ
שׂ	ś	◌ֲ	ă
שׁ	š	◌ֳ	ŏ
ת, תּ	t, ṯ		

CHAPTER I

Introduction

1.1. The Problem

AT THE CORE OF THE PROBLEM with the Biblical Hebrew verbal forms lies the question of their temporal meanings. The problem is partly a very practical one, especially in poetry, as any comparison between different translations of, for instance, Psalm 18 will reveal. But beyond that, the theoretical problem is even more pervasive, since scholars often disagree on how to analyze the meaning of a form, even when the question of how to translate it into another language may not be an issue. This lack of consensus is visible already in the grammatical terminology used in the literature. Most commonly, the terms used for the forms signify some kind of tense, aspect, or modality (TAM). If we take the so-called *yiqtol*-form as an example,[1] excluding the variant that normally has a proclitic *wa-* appended, we find it described in the literature as "present-future,"[2] "future,"[3] "simultaneous,"[4] "modal-futural,"[5] "modal,"[6] "imperfective,"[7] both imperfective and future,[8] and "non-perfective."[9] Matters are further complicated

---

1. Below, I shall refer to this form as "*yiqtol*-L"; see section 1.4.
2. Blau 1976 §20.1. Another way of referring to the same concept is to use the negative term "nonpast" (e.g., Hetzron 1987, 697).
3. Silverman (1973, 168) terms *yiqtol* "simple future" (as opposed to "*waw* future," i.e., *weqatalti*), but see also p. 175, where he states that this form "always refers to future or present time in its widest sense."
4. Kuryłowicz 1972, 84, §14. More exactly, Kuryłowicz speaks of "simultaneity" as the *value* of *yiqtol*.
5. See Zuber 1986, 16 (in German, the term is *modal-futurisch*).
6. Hatav 1997, 198; Joosten 2012, 39.
7. See, among others, Tropper 1998, 178; Gentry 1998, 15; Cook 2006, 32. The same notion is also referred to by various equivalent terms, such as the French "inaccompli" (M. Cohen 1924, 12) or the English "uncompleted" (Weingreen 1959, §29).
8. Andersen 2000, 50.
9. Waltke and O'Connor 1990, §§29.6e; 31.1.2a. As "nonperfective," the *yiqtol* is the unmarked counterpart of the perfective *qatal*, which is to say that the form becomes imperfective

I

by the existence of various grammatical terms that relate in unclear ways to the TAM categories. For example, in Diethelm Michel's nomenclature, *yiqtol* expresses "abhängige Handlung" ("dependent action"),[10] Péter Kustár through a similar notion calls the form "determiniert" ("determined"),[11] and Wolfgang Schneider (among others) says that its fundamental property is to indicate a certain *Sprechhaltung* ("linguistic attitude"), which characterizes the subtype of discourse that he calls "Besprechen" ("discussion").[12] Harald Baayen follows Schneider but employs the term "focal referential concern" for the same function.[13]

One of the challenges for semantic interpretation is to strike a balance between the descriptive and the explanatory aspects of the analysis. Many scholars would agree that the old classification of *yiqtol* as a future tense is of a rather descriptive kind and that the shift to the aspect-based approach that began to gain prominence in the nineteenth century was an attempt at establishing a terminology with more explanatory reach. Even if the success of this undertaking might be disputed, a reasonable goal for a study of verbal semantics should be to go deeper than to call the form by the same name as its most frequent equivalent in, for example, Greek, Latin, or English. Accordingly, with regard to the many suggested meaning-labels for *yiqtol*, we would like to know how each of them relates to the whole range of temporal meanings that the form is able to express. That is, if the *yiqtol* is an imperfective rather than a future form, does that mean that the imperfective meaning may give rise to the very common future meaning of the form by means of some inferential process? Or, if it is a future, how are the nonfuture meanings of the form to be accounted for? The same type of questions, of course, could be posed with regard to the other forms of the system. We should not accept the answer that the temporal meaning of the forms depends solely on contextual factors and has nothing to do with factors internal

---

when contrasted with the perfective form, even though by itself it is neither perfective nor imperfective.

10. Michel (1960, 254) describes the semantic difference between *yiqtol* and the perfect, or *qatal*, as follows: "Das Perfectum wird zur Wiedergabe einer Handlung gewählt, wenn diese als selbstgewichtig, als absolute angesehen wird [...]. Das Imperfectum wird zur Wiedergabe einer Handlung gewählt wenn diese ihre Bedeutung von etwas ausserhalb der Handlung selbst liegendem bekommt, also relativ ist."

11. Kustár (1972, 44–46) claims that his concept "determiniert," as well as its counterpart "determinierend" (represented by *qatal*), are aspects. His definition of aspect is very far from mainstream, though, and it is difficult to see how it can be functionally related with the other categories in the TAM-complex.

12. The linguistic attitude characteristic of *Besprechen*, or discussion, is a tense and responsive state of mind. Thus Schneider (2001, §48.1): "Besprechende Rede **engagiert** ihn [i.e., the listener]: Sprecher und Hörer haben zu agieren und zu reagieren."

13. Baayen 1997, 247. Both Schneider and Baayen follow Weinrich (1977) in this regard. Other proponents of the same approach are Talstra and Niccacci (see 2.4).

to the forms, because they are, after all, used not randomly but in regular and fairly predictable ways.[14]

A complicating factor, however, is that even the meanings of the grammatical terms are disputed. This is particularly the case with aspect. To begin with, the classical aspect categories *completed* and *uncompleted* have been understood rather differently throughout their history—a fact that explains that the terms "perfect" and "perfective," both derived from the Latin *perfectum* ("completed"), mean different things in modern linguistics. Furthermore, many new aspect categories have been suggested, so that it is very difficult to get a clear idea of how many "aspects" there are, which they are, and how they relate to one another. To mention a few examples from Hebraistic studies, whereas Marcel Cohen works with the classical binary opposition of *accompli* and *inaccompli* (i.e., completed/uncompleted), Frithiof Rundgren counts three hierarchically arranged pairs—namely, *stative:fiens*, *cursive:constative*, and *punctual:neutral*—and Galia Hatav has the *progressive*, the *perfect*, and the *sequential*, and so forth.[15] More examples could be given. The word "aspect" as such is hardly sufficient to explain what linguistic phenomenon is being described in each of these proposed models. To this day, there is no authoritative and universally accepted definition of aspect. In some cases, this leads to confusion of aspect with other grammatical categories. For example, some would say that the typical perfect construction (like the English *I have done*) expresses perfect aspect; others would argue that it expresses the *relative tense* value of *anteriority*.

One of the strongest trends in the Hebraistics of the new millennium is the evolutionary, or grammaticalization approach (2.5). It sees the various meanings of the verbal forms as the result of an evolution that can be reconstructed, so that two or more meanings that can be expressed by the same form at a given time in the history of the language can be ordered in terms of their relative age. The conclusions about the relative age of the meanings are drawn on the basis of comparisons with the corresponding verbal forms in genetically related, and preferably older, languages, as well as comparisons with similar forms in languages of all families, ancient and modern (typological studies). Through such comparisons, a verbal form can be classified as an example of a certain cross-linguistic type, the development of which is known to be fairly predictable. Such

---

14. Answers to this effect have been suggested; see Sperber 1966, 591–92; Hughes 1970, 13; Greenstein 1988, 14. As opposed to those who call *yiqtol* "nonperfective" or "nonpast," these authors do not reckon with stable meanings in other forms of the verbal system, whereby the meaning of *yiqtol* can be defined. See also Baayen (1997, 245) on the *qatal*-form. Zuber (1986, 27) claims that there are two semantically distinct subsystems of verbal forms in Biblical Hebrew. Within each subsystem there are no semantic distinctions; the choice of form is made on purely stylistic grounds.

15. M. Cohen 1924, v, 12; Rundgren 1961, 72; Hatav 1997, 6–8.

studies confirm, for instance, that the stative/resultative and intransitive meaning expressed by the *qatal*-form (e.g., *yāšabtî*, "I am seated") is older than the perfect transitive *qatal* with active meaning (*kātabtî*, "I have written"), which, in turn, is older than the preterite interpretation of the form (*kātabtî*, "I wrote"). Each of these meanings can be likened to stations on a diachronic pathway, along which the verbal forms travel throughout their history—with the important qualification that verbal forms may retain old meanings alongside the new ones (they do not have to leave one station to get to the next, as it were). For Biblical Hebrew, two major pathways leading from some kind of "aspectual" to temporal meanings can be reconstructed. The one is from *resultative* to *past*, the other from *progressive* to *future*.[16] The former track is occupied by *qatal* and *wayyiqtol* (below: *yiqtol*-S), the latter by *qotel* and *yiqtol* (below: *yiqtol*-L).[17]

This outline indicates that the temporal meanings of the Biblical Hebrew verbal forms somehow derive from the aspectual ones. There are still many questions surrounding this development, especially from a theoretical point of view. How are the aspectual meanings of the forms to be defined? How does a certain aspectual meaning favor the development of a certain tense meaning? What is the semantic difference between the forms on the same diachronic pathway?

1.2. Aim

The aim of the present study is to increase the understanding of how the expression of temporal meanings in Biblical Hebrew relates to the semantics of the verbal forms. The overarching aim will be accomplished through a synthesis of the following elements:

1. a definition of aspect and an application of this definition on the progressive and the resultative verbal types
2. an account of how tense meanings are derived from aspectual meanings
3. an application of the general theory to the Biblical Hebrew verbal system
4. an analysis of the semantic difference between the forms that belong on the same diachronic pathway

---

16. In section 3.4 we shall return to the question of what kind of aspect the progressive and the resultative are.
17. This description is very simplified, but it gives a general idea of the facts of main interest for this study. In reality, pathways intertwine so that a given source can have more than one endpoint and vice versa. For some examples of intertwined pathways, see Bybee, Perkins, and Pagliuca 1994, 105, 240–41. See also the discussion in section 2.5 below.

A few comments on each of these four points is in order:

Point 1: A clear, general definition of aspect is necessary in view of the widely differing opinions about what the term refers to and which aspectual categories there are. The definition has to take its point of departure in the classical notion of (un)completedness, and the ways it has been and can be interpreted, especially under the designation of (im)perfectivity (see section 2.2). It is further necessary to find out how the modern grammatical categories progressive and resultative fit with the concept of aspect, as well as to address the question of the distinction between aspect and relative tense (2.1, 2.2.3). The latter question is especially relevant to the debate about the nature of the so-called perfects.

Point 2: Given the fact that originally resultative and progressive forms tend to favor opposite tense meanings, it is to be assumed that something in the semantics of those forms invites the inference of those particular tense meanings. If this is the case, the definition of aspect has to accommodate this circumstance (3.5, 3.6).

Point 3: The classification of the Biblical Hebrew verbal forms in terms of their aspecto-temporal meanings is basically given by the typological scheme provided within the framework of grammaticalization studies, although there is some room for diverging opinions as to how to set up the inventory of Biblical Hebrew verbal forms. The choice made in the present study is dealt with in section 1.4.

Point 4: An important consideration with regard to the question of what constitutes the semantic difference between the forms on the same diachronic pathway is whether we should define that difference in terms of TAM or some other semantic category. An attempt to see the problem from a new angle is made in chapter 5 through a reinterpretation of Weinrich's notion of linguistic attitude (*Sprechhaltung*).

1.3. What "Meaning" Means

A study of the meaning of verbal forms may become a bewildering enterprise if there is no decision about what is meant by "meaning." First of all, the reader should know that the word "meaning" in itself is not used as some kind of technical term in this study; that is, it means no less and no more than it does in everyday language. If more precision is required, either the word will be qualified, or other terms will be used. The following subsection (1.3.1) will treat the concepts of "semantic" and "pragmatic" meaning. This discussion prepares the ground for the discussion in subsection 1.3.2 about how to establish the "basic" semantic meanings of verbal forms.

1.3.1. Semantics and Pragmatics

Language is a tool for communication, functioning within a communicative situation consisting of sender, receiver, and the things referred to. An important consequence of this, famously described by Karl Bühler in his *Sprachteorie*, is that the linguistic expression is many-sided and can only be fully understood in relation to each of these entities. For example, the cry "Wolf!" would, in Bühler's terminology, be interpreted at the same time as an *expression* (*Ausdruck*) of the mind, emotions, etc. of the sender, an *appeal* (*Appell*) to the attention, responsiveness, etc. of the receiver, and a *representation* (*Darstellung*) of the animal that is being denoted.[18] Even though these three functions always co-occur, any one of them may come more or less to the fore depending on what particular speech-act is being performed. For instance, if the utterance "Wolf!" is intended as a warning, the appeal is felt very strongly. The expressive function would be more palpable if the same word were exclaimed by a person with a very strong (positive or negative) sentiment toward the animal, who unexpectedly came across a track of it in the neighborhood. Finally, the same word can be used first and foremost for representation—we may think of a more educational situation, where it is used as an answer to the question "What animal left this track?"

There is a certain asymmetry in the above example, however. We observe that, even though the interpretation of the speech acts containing the word "wolf" varies as to the relative dominance of expressive, representative, and appeal functions, one factor remains stable all the way through—namely, the representation of a particular kind of animal. In a certain sense, then, nouns, like "wolf," conventionalize, or encode representational function. However, not only representation but also expression and appeal can be encoded to various degrees, as in the interjections *yippee* (expression) and *hello* (appeal). A good example of the whole spectrum of functions may be the moods in Latin. Thus, whereas appeal dominates in the imperative (*dice*, "say!"), the balance tips toward the expressive side in the optative subjunctive (*dicas*, "may you say"), and toward the representative function in the indicative (*dicis*, "you say").

Now, most ordinary people would no doubt agree that not only the statement accomplished by the indicative but also the command encoded in the imperative and the wish expressed by the subjunctive are meanings of those same forms. It is equally certain, however, that within the linguistic discipline devoted to

---

18. Bühler 1965, 28–29. The example is mine. Note that the word "expression" is used here in two senses: when it occurs in the phrase "linguistic expression," it refers to the speech-product, whether in terms of a specific utterance or in terms of the linguistic forms that the utterance is consists of (morphemes, words, phrases); when it is used in isolation, it refers to the relation between the speaker and the linguistic expression.

the study of meaning in language—that is, *semantics*—representation is the function that has received by far the most attention. One may point to several reasons for this. First, representation is the dominant function in language.[19] Second, there has been intense activity among semanticists working within the field of truth-conditional semantics, a method that can only be applied to representation.[20] Finally, influential theoreticians have explicitly stated that semantics concerns only the relation between the linguistic expressions and the things they represent.[21] This has been done in an attempt to draw the line theoretically between semantics and the neighboring discipline of *pragmatics*. Thus, everything that concerns the relation between the linguistic utterance and the sender and receiver—that is, the *users* of the linguistic expression—has been assigned to pragmatics. Such a distinction excludes the study of expression and appeal (hence optative and imperative moods) from the province of semantics and confines it to the field of pragmatics.[22] However, according to another distinction very commonly drawn, semantics has to do with *conventional* meaning and pragmatics with *situational* meaning.[23] By conventional meaning is understood a meaning that is encoded, or inherent, in a morpheme, word, or phrase. We may, for convenience's sake, call it a *semantic unit*. Situational meaning is a meaning that is associated with a semantic unit due to conditions in (a) specific context(s). In this view, expression and appeal can and should be treated in semantic analysis, since these functions can be encoded by semantic units and therefore also decoded from such units irrespective of context.

Obviously, we are left here with two incompatible conceptions of semantics and pragmatics. The question is which of them to choose.[24] In my opinion,

19. This point is stressed by Bühler (1965, 30).
20. See Palmer 1981, 42–43; Davis 1991, 7.
21. For historical outlines, see Lyons 1977, 114–17; Recanati 2004, 443–44.
22. The first and one of the most influential scholars to distinguish in this way between semantics and pragmatics was Charles Morris. In his *Foundations of the Theory of Signs* (1938), he stated that semantics is the study of "the relation of signs to the objects to which the signs are applicable," and pragmatics is the study of "the relation of signs to interpreters ["interpreters" corresponds to "sender" and "receiver" above]" (Morris [1938] 1971a, 21–22). The popularity of this simple and catchy formulation seems to have overshadowed the fact that Morris later widened the scope of semantics. In *Signs, Language, and Behavior* he states that "other modes of signification than the designative must be dealt with in semantics." According to the reformulated definition "*semantics* deals with the signification of signs in all modes of signifying" (Morris [1946] 1971b, 302). This is to say that semantics includes other functions than representation (representation corresponds to Morris's "designative mode of signification").
23. Recanati 2004, 445; Trask 1999, 243.
24. Recanati writes about the theoretical impasse arising from these conflicting views: "Some linguistic forms (e.g., *goodbye*, or the imperative mood) have a 'pragmatic' rather than a 'semantic' meaning: they have use conditions but do not 'represent' anything and hence do not contribute to the utterance's truth conditions. Because there are such expressions—and arguably there are many of them and every sentence contains at least one—we have to choose: either semantics is defined as

to confine semantics to the representational function of the linguistic expression is untenable. For one thing, it is too much in conflict with the common understanding of the word "meaning" to exclude the expressive and appeal functions of linguistic expressions from a study of meaning in language. For another, the pioneer of semantic studies, Michel Bréal, included these functions on equal terms with the representative function in his work *Essaie de sémantique*, a book that was written long before the attempts to distinguish semantics from pragmatics.[25] From Bréal and onward, the quest for conventional meanings has really been the gist of "semantic" studies, even in periods when they have been restricted to the representational function of the semantic unit. The birth of pragmatic theories like Austin's speech-act theory and Grice's theory of conversational implicature, came very much as reactions to the neglect of contextual factors in the linguistic study of meaning. Consequently, the opinion that semantics deals with conventional meaning is more to the point than the view that it is the study of representation in language. Thus, when I henceforth use the term "semantic meaning," it refers to what I have here called conventional meaning, whereas "pragmatic meaning" corresponds to situational meaning. However, I shall take the term "conventional" in a very restricted sense and include as semantic only those meanings that are most intrinsic to the form, as I will explain in the following subsection.

1.3.2. Criteria for Explanatory Semantics

Even if the distinction between semantic and pragmatic meaning is well motivated, it has to be admitted that an exact dividing line can be hard to draw. It is a well-known fact that semantic meanings develop from pragmatic meanings. What occasions this is probably that semantic units in given contexts can be ambiguous between a semantic meaning and a pragmatic meaning that is naturally inferred from it. If the inference is made often enough, it may happen that the unit starts to be used with its pragmatic meaning also in contexts where the same ambiguity with the semantic meaning does not exist. That is to say, the pragmatic meaning has become so intrinsic to the unit that it is no longer dependent on the original context. At that stage, the once pragmatic meaning has reached a status that is normally understood as semantic. An example of an English word that has gone through this development is *since*. Originally, it was an adverbial with the meaning "after that," but when it started to be used

---

the study of conventional meaning, or it is defined as the study of words-world relations. We can't have it both ways" (Recanati 2004, 445).

25. See Bréal's treatment of the "subjective element" in language (Bréal 1964, chapter 25). Note also that Bréal contrasted semantics not with pragmatics (or syntax) but with phonetics (Bréal 1964, chapter 1).

as a conjunction it often acquired a connotation of causality. This ultimately led to a semantic *reanalysis* whereby it became possible to express the causal meaning independently of the temporal meaning.[26] Three examples borrowed from Hopper and Traugott illustrate the development of the form in its function as a conjunction. In the first sentence, *since* has only temporal meaning, in the second sentence, it is ambiguous between a temporal and a causal meaning, and in the third, there is only a causal meaning:[27]

(1) a. I have done quite a bit of writing since we last got together.
    b. Since Susan left him, John has been very miserable.
    c. Since I have a final exam tomorrow, I won't be able to go out tonight.

Exactly when a reanalysis is accomplished is impossible to tell, since it always must happen in contexts where there is room for ambiguity. Moreover, the use of a semantic unit may vary across generations, social groups, and even within individuals. Consequently, the answer to the question whether a certain meaning is semantic or pragmatic depends on whom you ask. In fact, we should not think that semantic meanings exist apart from the language users. A meaning is semantic because it is *thought of* as inherent in the unit. However, since language is a common good, semantic meaning cannot be entirely subjective. It has to be communicable, hence more or less stable, hence also definable, although it is also negotiable to a certain degree. Ultimately, semantic meaning will always depend on actual language use. Under these conditions, a meaning can be said to be semantic with some degree of objectivity if it is regularly used in contexts where it is not ambiguous with some other semantic meaning—a criterion that is met in the case of the causal meaning of *since* in example (1). Conversely, a meaning that only occurs in contexts where it is ambiguous with a semantic meaning must be defined as pragmatic. This applies, for instance, to the request function of *can*, as in *Can you give me some water?* (see further discussion in subsection 5.2.3).

For the purposes of this study, it is necessary not only to distinguish between semantic and pragmatic meanings but also to find out what meanings are more *basic* than others. In the case of *since*, I consider the temporal meaning to be more basic than the causal, because the temporal meaning explains the causal meaning, but the reverse is not the case.

I shall use two heuristic criteria for establishing basic semantic meanings. The first of these is the criterion of invariance. Semantic invariance means that

---

26. *Webster's Encyclopedic Unabridged Dictionary of the English Language*, new rev. ed. (1994), s.v. "since."
27. Hopper and Traugott 2003, 80, 81.

the same meaning can be applied in different contexts and on different lexemes thanks to our ability for analogical reasoning. For instance, across contexts, the sense of an ongoing dynamic process in the English progressive form is present in both *I am running* and *I was running*, although in the former it is set in the present, and in the latter it is past. Similarly, across lexemes, a sense of dynamism is imparted to the predicate when the progressive is formed on an adjective (*You're being naughty*), even though the adjective, lexically speaking, has a stative quality.[28] Now, the criterion of invariance requires that the basic meaning of a linguistic form should be defined so as to accommodate the widest possible range of contexts and lexemes. Thus, in section 3.5 below, I show that my definition of "progressive aspect" applies to the English progressive forms not only in all contexts for which the conventional definition of "imperfective aspect" holds but also in contexts where the progressive forms have aorist meaning, which is incompatible with imperfective meaning. Hence, according to the criterion of invariance, my progressive meaning is more basic to the English progressive forms than imperfective meaning.

Second, following a criterion of cognitive precedence, I shall consider the basic meaning to be the one from which other meanings of the forms can be derived through reanalysis. Reanalysis, as described in the discussion of example (1) above, is a semantic "rule-change" that overturns the basic meaning and gives rise to a new semantic meaning in the form.[29] A common example of reanalysis of verbal forms is the future interpretation of the so-called prospective constructions, such as the English *to be about to*. Normally, this construction has present meaning, referring to the pre-stage of some event (*Right now, I'm about to take a nap*), but through reanalysis of the temporal structure of the phrase, it may be thought of as referring to the ensuing event, and the tense becomes future (*I'm about to take a nap in a few minutes*).[30]

It is necessary to bear in mind that different aspects of the meaning of a form can give rise to different forms of reanalysis, which means that a form can be invariant with regard to one of its meanings while it is reanalyzed with regard to another. For example, the English perfect is derived from a so-called resultative source by a reanalysis of diathesis from passive to active, but it is invariant in terms of its aspectual meaning (which motivates my use of the term "resultative" for perfects; see subsection 3.4.1). It may also be the case that more than one meaning is invariant across lexemes, as in the above-mentioned example *You're being naughty*, which expresses both the *Aktionsart* and the aspect of the

28. Even in adjectives, however, there are shades of dynamicity; see further section 3.2.
29. Hopper and Traugott 2003, 50, 63–64, 71.
30. This kind of reanalysis, which is treated under the heading "temporalization" in section 3.6 below, is more common with the construction *to be going* to, which is another English form often said to be prospective.

prototypical progressive. In this study, I am interested in the temporal semantics of the verbal forms; hence the term "invariance" generally refers only to aspectual invariance. Aspectual invariance is dealt with below in sections 3.4, 3.5, 4.1.1, 4.2.1, 4.3.1, and 4.4.1. Reanalysis is discussed in sections 3.6, 4.1.2, 4.2.2, 4.3.2, and 4.4.2.

The approach to verbal morphosemantics taken in this study resembles the "principled polysemy" proposed by Andrea Tyler and Vyvyan Evans in their study of the meaning of English prepositions.[31] Their aim is to define various "distinct senses" of the prespositions and to identify a "primary sense" (cf. my "basic meaning") from which the other distinct senses can be derived.[32] Against this approach, it has been argued that "it may not be the case that a particular lexical form has a single primary sense from which language users perceive all other senses being derived."[33] This criticism raises several issues at once. Firstly, there may not be any original basic meaning (or "primary sense") from which to derive others, because the basic meaning may have gone out of use. If two semantic meanings (or "distinct senses") in such a form have developed from one and the same now lost meaning through different ways of reanalysis, neither of them is the basic meaning. The form has become a so-called doughnut gram with a "hole" in the place of the central node of the semantic network, where the unifying basic meaning once existed.[34] Second, it may be impossible to say with any reasonable certainty which meaning derives from the other without historical evidence from written sources.[35] And, third, even if this could be achieved through rigorous reasoning and/or comparative evidence, actual language users may not perceive the different meanings as related in that way.

There are different ways of dealing with these problems depending on whether the object of study is prepositions or verbal forms or some other category. As far as verbal forms are concerned, they tend to conform to well-known crosslinguistic types (e.g., resultatives and progressives), which makes the question of the diachronic relation between existing meanings relatively unproblematic. For the same reason, it is often possible to identify verbal doughnut grams (although this is not pertinent to the forms under scrutiny in the present study). As to the question of how language users perceive the relation between basic

31. Tyler and Evans 2003, 37–38.
32. See Tyler and Evans 2003, 42 n. 5, according to which prepositions can acquire distinct senses by the change of the spatial configurations or by changing from spatial to altogether nonspatial meaning. On their view of the role of reanalysis in this process, see, e.g., 60–61, 79–106 in the same study.
33. Tyler and Evans 2003, 59.
34. On doughnut grams, see Dahl 2000b, 10. The term "gram" is a shorthand for "grammatical morpheme" (Bybee, Perkins, and Pagliuca 1994, 2).
35. Tyler and Evans 2003, 46–47.

and derived meanings, it must at the very least be considered probable that such meanings are felt to be somehow semantically related; that is, there is a polysemy of related meanings within one form rather than a homonymy of distinct forms with unrelated meanings. The relatedness of basic and derived meanings can be very obvious when forms within the same semantic domain are compared. Thus, it has been noted that the original deontic and volitive meanings of the English verbs *shall* and *will* restrict their use even as future auxiliaries.[36] By contrast, the future meaning of the phrase *be going to* tends to be associated with intentionality, just as the nonfuture meaning from which it derives.[37]

It is worth pointing out at this stage that the parameter of frequency does not play a role in the kind of semantics that I am proposing in this study. In this regard, I differ from Tyler and Evans, who count frequency ("predominance") among the criteria for determining primary senses of prepositions.[38] The same can be said with regard to a study by Alexander Andrason and Christo van der Merwe, who in a similar fashion combine the factors of frequency and diachronic precedence to establish the "prototypical" (cf. "basic") meaning of the Biblical Hebrew *qatal*.[39] I do not see how this is helpful, given the above-mentioned fact that the oldest meaning of a form does not have to be the most frequent one.

Andrason and van der Merwe actually promote frequency at the expense of diachrony in their semantic analysis, since they claim that frequency alone defines prototypicality. The most frequent sense, they write, constitutes the "conceptual nucleus of the map from which [most] other senses cognitively emerge."[40] If this is so, however, prototypicality must be a very complex concept; the implication of Andrason's and van der Merwe's statement is that, when a new sense becomes more frequent than the prototypical, older sense from which it emerged cognitively by analogy or reanalysis, suddenly the older sense somehow begins to emerge cognitively from the new sense, and the prototype becomes the derivative. Moreover, it is unclear exactly what cognitive processes are triggered in this way by frequency. While it seems plausible to assume that the most frequent meaning will be the one that people are most likely to think of when the form is mentioned in isolation, the question here is how, and indeed whether, the most frequent meaning affects how we interpret the form in various contexts of actual use. Whatever the answer to that question may be, it is

---

36. Bybee, Perkins, and Pagliuca 1994, 15–17. It may be debated whether *shall* and *will* still can express their original meanings apart from the derived future meanings, but that does not affect the argument.
37. Langacker 2011, 85–88.
38. Tyler and Evans 2003, 47.
39. Andrason and van der Merwe 2015, 87.
40. Andrason and van der Merwe 2015, 87.

highly implausible that an old meaning suddenly ceases to provide a cognitive basis for a new meaning only because it becomes a little less frequent. Consequently, the inferences whereby less frequent meanings "emerge" from frequent meanings, if they exist at all, must exist side by side with the inferences that work diachronically. This possibility should perhaps not be ruled out, but, in my opinion, the role of the most frequent meaning in the semantics of a form is still very hard to assess, and it is probably not quite as important as Andrason and Van der Merwe claim.

1.4. The Biblical Hebrew Verbal System

The verbal forms under consideration in this investigation are the active participle *qotel* in predicative position, the suffix conjugation *qatal*, and the prefix conjugation *yiqtol*. The *yiqtol* conjugation is further subdivided into a "long" and a "short" variant, the *yiqtol*-L and the *yiqtol*-S. These are the main forms used in declarative utterances in Biblical Hebrew, and each of them is associated with certain aspectual and temporal meanings. The following overview lists some particular TAM meanings that are especially characteristic of the form in question:

qotel: progressive meaning regardless of tense, instant future;[41]
yiqtol-L: generic/habitual meaning regardless of tense, future;
qatal: perfect meaning regardless of tense, nonnarrative past;
yiqtol-S: narrative past, volitive (jussive-prohibitive, cohortative).

The subdivision of *yiqtol* into *yiqtol*-L and *yiqtol*-S is to a large extent an artificial reconstruction based on two early West Semitic forms (*yaqtulu* and *yaqtul*), whose distinctive morphological features in Biblical Hebrew are reduced to mere vestiges in the shape of a group of "apocopated" forms in some third-person singular verbs.[42] However, by means of these apocopated forms and

---

41. "Progressive" will be used in a wider sense below and "instant future" will at least partly be covered by the term "preparative" (see subsections 3.4.2 and 3.4.3).

42. On the derivation of the Hebrew prefix-conjugation from the West Semitic *yaqtul* and *yaqtulu*, see Bergsträsser 1929; Müller 1988, 164–66; Waltke and O'Connor 1990, §29.4f–j; Tropper 1998, 161–64. On the derivation of the Hebrew prefix-conjugation from the West Semitic *yaqtul* and *yaqtulu*, see Bergsträsser 1929; Müller 1988, 164–66; Waltke and O'Connor 1990, §29.4f–j; Tropper 1998, 161–64. The long and short variants that have been identified in the Canaanite elements of the Amarna letters are the closest genetic relatives (Moran 2003, 41–49). The morphological evidence for the existence of the short form in this source material is not entirely conclusive but can be corroborated through syntactic analysis (Baranowski 2016). Ugaritic has also been pointed out as a relatively closely related language where the distinction is preserved, although it is visible only to

comparative data from other Semitic languages, the descendants of the original long and short forms can mostly be identified even in Biblical Hebrew.[43] Furthermore, thanks to an idiosyncratic Hebrew development, the narrative past variant of the *yiqtol*-S is, in the vast majority of cases, recognizable through a special form of the proclitic conjunction *wə-* ("and"). When appended to the narrative *yiqtol*-S, it has an *a*-vowel and normally causes gemination of the first consonant of the prefix, or, alternatively, when this is prohibited for phonological reasons, the *a* is lengthened to an *ā*.[44] This variant of the *yiqtol*-S is conventionally glossed as *wayyiqtol* and is commonly treated as a verbal form in its own right. The volitive variants of the *yiqtol*-S are referred to as "jussive" and "cohortative."[45] Thus, at a maximum, the *yiqtol* is divided into no fewer than four individual verbal forms: the *wayyiqtol*, the jussive, the cohortative, and the imperfect. The last corresponds to *yiqtol*-L in the above list and is often simply called *yiqtol*.

My main reasons for using the term *yiqtol*-S for all the three subclasses mentioned are the following:

First, the *wayyiqtol* is not the sole representative of the narrative past *yiqtol*-S. There are also a number of free-standing *yiqtol*-S in the biblical corpus, which can be identified through analysis of their textual function and/or because

---

a very limited degree in the consonantal script. The nature of the relationship between the Biblical Hebrew and the Ugaritic verbal systems depends very much on how the long and the short forms are used in past contexts in Ugaritic, which is a highly disputed question. An overview (in chronological order) of the various standpoints on the issue can be obtained from Gordon 1955, § 13:31–32; Greenstein 1988, 13–14; Smith 1994, 39–41; Tropper 2000, § 76.341–48; Greenstein 2006, 79–91; Bordreuil and Pardee 2009, 46; Tropper 2012, § 76.412; Hackett 2012.

43. See, however, the problem with the free-standing declarative *yiqtol*-S (4.4.3).

44. There have been various attempts to explain the *wa*C-(C)-pattern in the *wayyiqtol*. McFall (1982, 217–19) provides a list of fifteen different suggestions. A few scholars believe that the proclitic *wa*- has nothing to do with the conjunction *wə-*; some hold that it contains nothing but the conjunction and that the gemination/lengthening of the syllable arose due to stress patterns of the verb in a pre-Masoretic stage of the language (after McFall's work, this view has been proposed by, e.g., Blau 2010, 285–86); others suggest that it consists of the conjunction and some adverbial/particle or auxiliary (for a later proposal, see Testen 1998, 190, 195–97); some have argued that it is an artificial invention of the Masoretes (see Furuli 2006, 147–48; Van de Sande 2008, 226–32). Wikander (2010, 265) understands the *wa*- as an original conjunction that has developed into a kind of augment marking past tense.

45. The cohortative differs formally from the jussive by the ending *-â* (except in some weak verbs and in verbs with object suffixes), but comparative evidence shows that this ending is appended to the short variant of the prefix-conjugation (see Lipiński 1997, §§39.5–11). The forerunner of the Biblical Hebrew cohortative in Canaanite is for this reason called *erweiterte jussiv* by Tropper and Vita (2010, §4.2.4; cf. the *erweiterte Kurzform der Präfixkonjugation* in Ugaritic [Tropper 2012, §77.33]). See also Cook 2012, 238–41. Larcher (2012, §1.1.4) confirms the above-mentioned findings within the context of Arabic when he derives the so-called *énergique* (the Arabic morphological parallel to the Biblical Hebrew cohortative) from the *apocopé* (cf. *yiqtol*-S), but his classification of the *apocopé* as a variant of the *imparfait* (cf. *yiqtol*-L) is confusing.

they are apocopated (4.4.3). Most of them are found in poetic texts, but there are also a few cases in prose.

Second, the issue of this study is the semantics behind the temporal meanings of the Biblical Hebrew verbal forms. I preclude the possibility that the volitive meaning of the *yiqtol*-S lies behind its past meaning and the traces of perfect/resultative meaning that are found in the material. If there is a common origin (which is practically certain), the development must have gone in the opposite direction.[46]

The *qatal*, too, is often divided into two different forms. Besides the ordinary *qatal*, often called the "perfect," there is the so-called perfect consecutive, which consists of the *qatal* preceded by the proclitic *wə-* ("and") and is primarily used for representing future or past habitual sequential events or for sequential events in commands. It is glossed as either *weqatal* or *weqataltí* in the literature. The latter variant is intended to distinguish the perfect consecutive from the past nonhabitual and nonsequential syndetic perfect, which also consists of the *wə-* plus *qatal*.[47] The *-tí* ending in *weqataltí* indicates that the perfect consecutive has the stress on the ultima in the first-person singular, a feature that distinguishes it from the ordinary *qatal*, which has the stress on the penultima (*qatálti*). The same shift of stress occurs also in the second-person masculine singular, but it is not obligatory in either of them, and in certain weak forms of the verb it never occurs.[48] It cannot serve as evidence that *qatal* and *wəqataltí* are morphologically distinct in Biblical Hebrew, and there is no comparative evidence that such a distinction ever existed in earlier stages of the language. Neither does the proclitic *wə* serve as a distinctive feature, since *wə* + *qatal*, as already said, may be a past nonconsecutive perfect as well. Moreover, there are undeniable cases of "consecutive *qatal*" without proclitic *wə* in Biblical Hebrew.[49] As for future meaning, it is well known to be expressed not only by *weqataltí* but also by nonconsecutive *qatal* (4.3.1). Consequently, there is little reason to treat *qatal*

---

46. On the existence of typological evidence in favor of this interpretation, see 4.4.4. There are indeed also examples of developments from volitive to past meanings, viz. the narrative imperative, which is found in a number of Balkan languages (Friedman 2012, 417–22). For several reasons, however, this phenomenon cannot be considered as a parallel to the Biblical Hebrew *yiqtol*-S: (1) It is an areal, *Sprachbund*-phenomenon, rather than a widespread, universal phenomenon that can be expected to occur independently in different languages (Friedman 2012, 417, 421); (2) the imperative, although volitive, does not correspond typologically to the jussive/cohortative; (3) the narrative imperative is a stylistic device, not a default narrative form; (4) a volitive source for the Biblical Hebrew narrative *yiqtol*-S cannot account for the resultative/perfect meanings of the form.

47. On the nonsequential *weqatal*, see Driver 1892, §132–33; Waltke and O'Connor 1990, §32.3; Gibson and Davidson 1994, §84. Joüon and Muraoka (2009, §43) call these cases "anomalous," but they are too numerous to be treated as such.

48. Joüon and Muraoka 2009, §43.

49. This highly significant but surprisingly overlooked fact is further discussed in subsection 4.3.1 below.

and *weqatalti* as two different forms with different meanings. Rather, the *weqatalti* is a *qatal* in a specific type of interclausal connection. Its largely divergent temporal and modal meanings must be assumed to be pragmatically, and not semantically, determined. Thus, when I use the gloss *weqatalti* in this study, it signifies not a verbal form but the syndetic *qatal* with consecutive function.

Completely outside the temporal system is the *imperative*. However, it will be used for contrastive studies in chapter 5 to illustrate the semantic feature of reduced appeal, which crosscuts the whole verbal system and may be relevant for the temporal interpretation of the other forms.

1.5. Scope

In this section, I shall comment on certain factors having to do with the scope of the study: first, the body of data that will serve as witness to the language here called Biblical Hebrew, and, after that, the two factors within this body of data that often (though not in the present study) are allowed to delimit the scope of studies of the Biblical Hebrew verbal system—namely, the diachronic diversity of the corpus and the distinction between prose and poetry.

1.5.1. Source Material

The linguistic data for this investigation are taken from the Hebrew Bible as it is preserved in the Masoretic tradition. A more comprehensive investigation would broaden the scope and consider manuscripts of other textual traditions as well as inscriptions and ostraca belonging to the same linguistic stage as the preserved text of the Hebrew Bible. However, these witnesses have been omitted for practical reasons.

The investigation of the data from the Hebrew Bible is adapted to the purpose of the investigation. This is foremost a synthetic study, attempting to apply new theory to verbal usages that have been studied by generations of grammarians. For the selection of examples, I have consulted Driver 1892; Waltke and O'Connor 1990; Gibson and Davidson 1994; Joüon and Muraoka 2009; and Joosten 2012. I have also worked with samples of continuous texts where all the verbal forms under consideration have been checked for their tense and aspect meanings. The samples were chosen so as to reflect the diachronic diversity of Biblical Hebrew (Exod 15; Judg 5; Ps 18; Gen 26–29; Neh 3:33–9:37). In addition to that, I have used various computer software for searching specific uses. The way of working has been designed to find verbal uses with relevance to the problem of verbal semantics and temporality in Biblical Hebrew, as well as to check and complement the established knowledge in the field. Hopefully, the synthesis arrived at can provide a basis for more extensive corpus studies, but that lies outside the scope of the present investigation.

With regard to the linguistic quality of the Masoretic Text, it is relevant to know that the Masoretic punctuation system for indicating vowels and geminated consonants was developed many centuries after the consonantal text was recorded. It cannot be excluded that the pronunciation of certain words has been corrupted. As far as the verbal system is concerned, it has been claimed in (at least) two recent studies that the *wa*C-(C)-pronunciation in the "consecutive" imperfect, *wayyiqtol*, is a Masoretic innovation. Evidence for this is sought in the fact that this pronunciation is not reflected in the fragments of the Hebrew-Greek transliteration in the second column of Origen's *Hexapla*. Rolf Furuli hypothesizes that the pronunciation arose spontaneously in the synagogal reading of narrative prose texts.[50] The Masoretes associated the reading with past meaning and made an attempt to distinguish systematically between past *wayyiqtol* and nonpast *wə + yiqtol*. For consistency's sake, they carried out the distinction even in nonnarrative texts, although the synagogal reading tradition, according to Furuli, did not use the *wa*C-(C)-pronunciation there. Moreover, the Masoretes allegedly had problems with the temporal interpretation of the construction in the prophetic and poetic books, which explains the unexpected appearances of *wayyiqtol* forms in those texts.

Axel Van de Sande has another explanation.[51] He suggests that the *wa*C-(C)-pronunciation was deliberately invented by the Masoretes in order to make it similar to the *ha*C-(C)-pronunciation of the definite article. The argument is as follows: (1) Arab grammarians called the Arabic variant of the prefix conjugation *al-muḍârî* ("the one that is similar") because it has certain formal properties in common with the noun. (2) Past meaning is, according to Van de Sande, similar to the definite meaning of the noun, whereas future meaning is similar to the indefinite meaning. (3) Influenced by the Arabic grammatical tradition and its analogy between the prefix conjugation and the noun, the Masoretes created the *wa*C-(C)-pronunciation for the syndetic preterite *yiqtol*, as if it contained the definite article (*ha-*) of the noun, while keeping the *wə-*(C)-pronunciation for syndetic future *yiqtol* on analogy with the *wə-*(C)-pronunciation of the syndetic indefinite noun. Like Furuli, Van de Sande supposes that many *wayyiqtol*-forms in poetry result from the misinterpretation of the Masoretes.

The main argument against these hypotheses may simply be that the assumptions they make about the grammatical thinking of the Masoretes are too speculative. In addition to that, they presuppose the somewhat unlikely scenario that the *wa*C-(C)-pronunciation was so important for the Masoretes as to impel them

---

50. See Furuli 2006, 139–41, 147–48.
51. See Van de Sande 2008, 226–32.

to meddle with their sacred tradition.[52] The generally held opinion is that the Masoretes did not invent forms, even though some punctuations reflect pronunciations that may be late or dialectal.[53] An alternative and perhaps less farfetched explanation is that either Origen's source failed to reproduce the distinct pronunciation of *wayyiqtol*—a construction that had been out of use for a long time in non-Biblical Hebrew—or Origen himself did not recognize it.

Another possible source of error in the Masoretic Text is the indication of stress. Some of the apocopated variants of *yiqtol*-S have the stress on the prefix instead of on the stem, which is the rule in other *yiqtol*-forms. According to some scholars, this is a residue from an earlier stage when all *yiqtol*-S could be distinguished from *yiqtol*-L by the position of the stress in the word. Possibly, the distinction was still made in biblical times but was lost in the subsequent textual transmission.[54] This hypothesis is interesting but has no great consequences for the study of the verb in Biblical Hebrew as preserved in any of the extant sources. Even if there once was such a distinction, it is no longer available. Our only possible point of departure is the Masoretic Text.

1.5.2. Diachronic Diversity

The texts of the Hebrew Bible may originate from a period of many centuries. It is common to distinguish between three diachronic stages within Biblical Hebrew: Archaic Biblical Hebrew, Standard Biblical Hebrew, and Late Biblical Hebrew.[55] This provokes the question of whether we should not expect the verbal system to have changed so much over time as to justify a study of diachronically conditioned uses rather than one universal use.

Indeed, some differences do exist. Typical of Archaic Biblical Hebrew is, for example, a high number of free-standing *yiqtol* with the same function as the narrative *wayyiqtol*. *Qotel* in predicate position is also rare, especially with progressive meaning.[56] This could perhaps indicate that a significant change in the verbal system took place in the transition from Archaic to Standard Biblical Hebrew, but it may also be due to the limitations of the corpus.[57] Special fea-

---

52. Furuli (2006, 147–48) says that the Masoretes would not make deliberate changes in the texts. However, it is somewhat unclear from his account how that statement complies with the fact that *wayyiqtol* occurs in poetry, since Furuli assumes that the *wayyiqtol*-pronunciation belonged to prose.
53. Sáenz-Badillos 1996, 78–79; Tov 2001, 47–49. See also Blau 2010, §3.3.2.2.7.
54. So Zevit 1988, 28. See also Bloch 2009, 42 (citing Qimron), and Blau 2010, §3.5.12.14–15.
55. Kutscher 1982, §17; Sáenz-Badillos 1996, 52. There is also a bipartite division, expressed with different terminology, which draws the main line between Standard and Late Biblical Hebrew, thus conflating the earlier phases into one. For a brief overview, see Young 2003, 3–4.
56. Sáenz-Badillos 1996, 58; Notarius 2010, 245; Bergström 2016, 217–26.
57. See 4.1.1 n. 277.

tures in Late Biblical Hebrew are, inter alia, a decrease of *yiqtol* and the virtual disappearance of *weqatalti* for expressing habitual events in the past, and a corresponding increase of the periphrastic *hayah* (perfect of *hyh*, "to be") *qotel* in the same function. However, except for the case of the past habitual *weqatalti*, most of the differences between Late and Standard Biblical Hebrew may be only tendencies.[58] Even if they are likely to reflect a real development in the verbal usage, there is a fundamental continuity in central functions, such as the ones exemplified in section 1.4.[59] The shift to the more tense-oriented system found in Rabbinic Hebrew has not yet occurred.[60]

1.5.3. Prose and Poetry

Another argument against a comprehensive description of the Biblical Hebrew verbal usage is the differences between prose and poetry. No doubt, most of the difficult uses occur in the poetic texts. Scholars have often explained them as violations of grammar or instances of poetic license, or claimed that the grammar of poetry differs from that of prose.[61] Grammatical irregularities due to strict adherence to various poetic functions are found in all kinds of languages. Possible cases of poetic license having to do with verbal uses are found, for example, in Medieval Romance verse. Harald Weinrich holds that especially

---

58. See Eskhult 2000; Joosten 2006, 141; 2012, 407.

59. Free-standing *yiqtol* with narrative function occurs also in later poetic texts (see, e.g., Bloch 2009, 61–66 on Isa 41:1–5 and Ps 44) and is even found in the prose text of Daniel (Dan 8:12). *Hayah qotel* with habitual meaning is used also in Standard Biblical Hebrew (Ehrensvärd 2003, 171 n. 33). On past habitual *yiqtol* in Late Biblical Hebrew, see Eskhult 2000, 85; Bergström 2015. Some scholars even argue that there is an essential continuity in the verbal usage all the way up to Qumran Hebrew. Thus, Holst (2008, 140) finds that the usage of *yiqtol* and *weqatalti* in instructional and hortatory discourse is the same in Qumran Hebrew (represented by the War Scroll) as in Standard Biblical Hebrew. Furuli (2006, 85–88), who claims to have investigated all available data, concludes that there is no difference in the understanding of the conjugations in Qumran as compared to Biblical Hebrew. While this may be correct for the central functions of the forms, there are enough minor differences to distinguish between Standard Biblical Hebrew and the later linguistic stages on the basis of verb usage. For surveys of this issue, see Eskhult 2000; Joosten 2012, 377–409.

60. See Kutscher 1982, §218; Geiger 2012, 492–93.

61. Thus, for example, Bergsträsser (1929, §6.i.) complains that the verbal usage in Biblical Hebrew poetry has developed to "einer völligen Verwischung der Bedeutungsunterschiede der Tempora und einem Regellosen Promiscuegebrauch sämtlichen Tempusbezeichnungen." Nyberg (1952, §86mm–oo) hypothesizes that some "irregularities" in the verbal usages of the poetic texts may be due to the dogmatic preferences of the Masoretes. Hatav (1997, 24) leaves out the poetic material from her thesis with the motivation that "the verb forms function differently in prose as opposed to poetry." A similar expression is found in Fensham 1978, 10. Niccacci (1997, 77–78) counts "non-detectable versus detectable verbal system" among his "main characteristics of poetry versus prose" (in a more recent work, however, he has rejected this description; see Niccacci 2006, 247). The influence of poetic license on verbal usage is considered by, e.g., Michel (1960, 11–13); Gross (1976, 32 n. 50); Hatav (1997, 24); Joosten (2002, 52); and Joüon and Muraoka (2009, §11 a).

the common and sometimes very abrupt switches between the *passé simple* (a preterite aorist) and *présent* (present tense) in the narration of past events are more likely motivated by the poetic demand for rhyme or assonance than by the narrators' wish to switch temporal perspective.[62] Others believe that the irregularities are due to metrical constraints.[63]

Rhyme or meter, if not nonexistent, is certainly not sufficiently constitutive for Biblical Hebrew poetry to force verbal forms to behave irregularly. The most characteristic feature of Biblical Hebrew poetry is parallelism, a kind of repetition of semantic or grammatical patterns in two or more adjacent lines. Wilfred G.E. Watson, in his work on classical Hebrew poetry, describes one characteristic of parallelism that is pertinent to verbal usage. Having first surveyed a number of repetitive verse patterns found in the poetry, he concludes that "the poets were well able to exploit repetition," and continues: "Too much of the same word or phrase, though, can lead to monotony and therefore become boring."[64] To prevent this monotony, Watson explains, there were some manoeuvers to ensure variation. For instance, the poets could alternate between *yiqtol* and *qatal* when verbs from the same root are used in two parallel half-lines, as in Ps 38:12:

(2) 'ōhăḇay wəre'ay minnæḡæḏ niḡ'î ya'ămōḏû
ûqərôḇay merāḥōq 'āmāḏû
My friends and my companions stay (*yiqtol*) away from the presence of my sores,
and my neighbors stay (*qatal*) far away from me.

According to Adele Berlin, the tense-shift does not occur "for semantic reasons" but functions as "a kind of grammatical parallelism."[65] This phenomenon is, to my knowledge, the only possible case where it has been demonstrated how the choice of verbal forms in Biblical Hebrew verse may have something to do with a well-defined kind of poetical feature. Nevertheless, this does not entail that the verse-lines in question are "ungrammatical." Berlin does not say that Ps 38:12 is an example of poetic license, but even her claim that the semantics plays no part in the shift of tenses may be an overstatement. True, the shift of conjugations may appear to us as a kind of antithetical grammatical parallelism, but it may at the same time be an "antithetical *semantic* parallelism." For an adequate description of the grammar of poetry one has to carry

---

62. Weinrich 1977, 252. Weinrich also says that the opposite opinion is common.
63. For a survey of the research in the field, see Fleischman 1990, 67.
64. Watson 1994, 279.
65. See Berlin 1985, 36.

out poetical and grammatical analyses separately. In particular, one should be careful not to speak of poetic license or similar to describe phenomena that are just not sufficiently understood. This only perpetuates the idea that everything in poetry that does not conform to the standards of prose is aberrant or at least more artificial or archaic and less representative of "the grammar of Biblical Hebrew"—an attitude that overlooks that the language of literary prose is also to some degree artificial, or at least stylistically and grammatically restricted, and that some facts of the Biblical Hebrew grammar might be better attested in poetic texts. As far as verbal grammar is concerned, it is possible that a too rigid distinction between the grammars of poetry and prose has led to a slight underestimation of the role of free-standing past narrative *yiqtol*-S in the prose texts (see 4.4.3).

That being said, however, the prose texts constitute the natural starting point for a study of the Biblical Hebrew verbal system, since they generally have clearer contextual indications of the temporality of the clauses. Therefore, most of the conclusions drawn in this study will be based on prose texts.

1.6. Summary

The aim of the present study is to provide a semantic description of the Biblical Hebrew verbal forms that explains their temporal meanings. Section 1.1 gave a background to the problem by exemplifying the abundance of diverging suggestions of what grammatical terms to use for a specific form. As a major factor in the controversy, I pointed to the lack of a common theoretical basis, especially regarding the central notion of aspect. An important contribution toward a solution was found to be provided within the so-called grammaticalization approach, according to which it is possible to classify the Biblical Hebrew verbal forms into cross-linguistic verbal types and reconstruct how their various meanings have developed along two main diachronic pathways in accordance with universal principles. The two specific pathways that have been found to be relevant for Biblical Hebrew run from progressive to future and from resultative to past; that is, from what I called "aspectual" to temporal meanings. *Qotel* and *yiqtol*-L belong to the progressive pathway, whereas *qatal* and *yiqtol*-S belong to the resultative.

In section 1.2, I stated that the overarching aim of the study will be accomplished by several steps. First, I shall develop a theory of aspect and tense that explains how tense meanings can develop from the resultative and progressive aspects. I shall then apply the theory to the Hebrew data to see to what extent the various uses of the forms express or can be derived from an original progressive and resultative meaning. Finally, the semantic difference between the forms on the same pathway needs to be investigated.

In section 1.3, some fundamental theoretical issues concerning the study of meaning in language were treated. The first part of the section (1.3.1) defined the notions of semantics and pragmatics. The second part (1.3.2), discussed how to distinguish between pragmatic and semantic meanings as well as between basic and nonbasic meanings.

Section 1.4 described the Biblical Hebrew verbal forms of interest for this study.

Section 1.5 defined the scope of the investigation and reflected on some problems that arise due to the nature of the source material. These problems concerned the linguistic accuracy of the Masoretic Text, differences between prose and poetry, and diachronic development. The conclusion to be drawn is that, in spite of some factors of uncertainty, a comprehensive analysis of the meaning of the Biblical Hebrew verbal forms is possible.

CHAPTER 2

Comments on the State of Research

THIS CHAPTER IS INTENDED to evaluate the research on the Biblical Hebrew verbal system from the point of view of our main question: What are the basic semantics that explain the temporal meanings of the forms? To that end, we shall look at some main functions that are generally thought to be semantically encoded in verbal systems, including that of Biblical Hebrew. The categories that have received the most attention are tense, aspect, and modality, or TAM, as they are often acronymed. Opinions differ as to how the TAM-complex is encoded in the Biblical Hebrew verbal system. In this survey I present some proposals for what may be called the tense- (absolute or relative), aspect-, and modal- approaches. My main concern is the theoretical viability of each approach. As I suggested an aspectual basis for the Biblical Hebrew verbal forms already in section 1.1, most space is devoted to the problem of aspect. Apart from TAM (2.1–3), we shall also look at the concept of linguistic attitude (2.4), which has been presented as an alternative approach to the problem of tense in language. Finally, a section is devoted to some issues raised by proponents of the grammaticalization approach to verbal semantics (2.5).

The problem-oriented approach adopted in this survey limits its scope somewhat. In order to obtain a more comprehensive overview of the history of research on the Biblical Hebrew verb, the reader may consult Kustár 1972; McFall 1982 (early epochs); Waltke and O'Connor 1990; Endo 1996; Holst 2008; Van de Sande 2008; and Cook 2012.

2.1. Tense

Tense is often described as the localization of the event (or "the time of the event" or "event time," often given as "E") that is referred to by the clause relative to the time of speech. It has been pointed out by linguists that this description is not very exact. The fact is that neither past nor future tense necessarily means that the event represented by the predicate of the clause has to be located in the past or in the future *in its entirety*. To use two examples afforded by Wolfgang Klein, if someone asks *Do you know where John is?* and gets the answer *Well, he **was** in the garden*, the intended meaning of the answer is probably that John is still in the garden, and if the question *Will you be here at eight?* is met with the answer *Yes I will be here*, then the future event has evidently already begun.[1] Therefore, tense, according to Klein, does not locate the event as such but rather locates "some time for which the speaker wants to make an assertion." Klein calls this time "topic time" (or "assertion time").[2] Other scholars with tense definitions similar to Klein's use the term "reference time" in this sense.[3] In the present study, the concept will be referred to as *focused time* (3.3).

It follows from this definition that perfects, at least normally, have present tense value. The sentence *I have set the table* is in the present tense because it makes an assertion about the state of the table at the time of speech—even though the activity that leads to the table being set is in the past. In like manner, the prospective sentence *Bill is about to make a cake* is also present, insofar as it is more an assertion that Bill is at present preparing to make a cake than a claim that he actually *will* make a cake in the near future. Thus, the perfect and the prospective have the same tense. The difference lies in the aspect.

Tense always locates focused time relative to a vantage point, which can be either the time of speech or a secondary vantage point before or after the time of speech. For instance, in the sentence *Yesterday they told me about what had happened on that occasion*, the main clause locates focused time to a past relative to the time of speech, whereas the subordinate clause locates focused time to a "past in the past," that is, a past relative to the time marked by the main clause. In other words, the focused time of the main clause creates a secondary vantage point to which the focused time of the subordinate clause is related. In linguistics, such vantage points are called *deictic centers*, from the notion of *deixis* (Greek: "pointing"/"showing"). Deixis is the linguistic function whereby words like *yesterday, they, me,* and *told* receive their meaning in relation to certain preestablished spatio-temporal positions, the primary of which is that of the speaker.

Tense is thus a form of deixis that can be classified into two main types based on the two types of deictic centers found in the above sentence: *Absolute tense* locates focused time relative to the time of speech. *Relative tense*, by analogy, locates focused time relative to a secondary deictic center—or at least it should, for the sake of consistency. In actual fact, however, "tense" in relative tense theory is generally understood to concern the temporal localization of

---

1. Klein 1994; examples from pp. 22, 23. The same point is made by Declerck (1986, 313).
2. Klein 1994, 24.
3. The latter is a problematic term, for reasons that will be made clear below; see 2.2.3.

the lexically represented event—that is, what I call "event time." This means that it complies not with the notion of tense suggested by Klein and others but rather with the faulty understanding that he criticizes.[4] Let us take the following sentences as examples:

(1) a. I had set the table.
    b. Bill was about to make a cake.

According to standard relative tense theory, the above sentences are indiscriminately taken as examples of "past in the past" and "future in the past," respectively, although the same phrases with a present auxiliary (*I have set the table* / *Bill is about to make a cake*), as we saw, normally refer not to the past or the future but to the present. This is so because the focused time is simultaneous with the deictic center—that is, the time of speech. If we are to be consistent with our premises, the sentences (1a) and (1b) are not "past in the past" and "future in the past." Rather, they are two past forms with different aspects: one perfect and one prospective.[5] In terms of the relation between focused time and deictic center, both express simultaneity rather than anteriority or posteriority.

The importance of this conclusion becomes evident when we compare with sentences that really do express past in the past and future in the past. Consider the following pieces of discourse:

(2) a. By the time the dinner was ready, I had set the table.
    b. He told me about the events on the day before. He had arrived to the railway station just when the train was about to leave.
    c. Federer, who would later win the tournament, impressed in his first match.
    d. She recalled an incident on the first day of the trail. It had been storming and they had sought cover under a big tree.

In (2a) a secondary deictic center is set in the past by the first clause *By the time the dinner was ready*. The predicate of the main clause, had set has perfect meaning and describes a state that is simultaneous with the secondary deictic center. This means that the tense value of the pluperfect here is past, not past in the past.[6]

---

4. Unfortunately, even Klein himself fails to apply his tense definition consistently in the case of relative tenses, with the result that he ends up not distinguishing between relative past and past perfect meaning (Klein 1994, 131). For a criticism of Klein's position, see Bohnemeyer 2014.
5. See Maslov 1988, 69.
6. On this, see, e.g., Comrie 1976, 56; Declerck 2006, 444–45; and Bohnemeyer 2014, 918–19, 930–31.

The secondary deictic center in (2b) is set by the preterite *told*. The following pluperfect (*had arrived*) does not have perfect aspect. That is, it focuses not on a situation that is simultaneous with the deictic center but on one that preceded it. Accordingly, it is a true past in the past. From an aspectual point of view, it does not differ from an ordinary narrative preterite. Notice also the predicate *was about to leave*, which is a past prospective, to be contrasted with the past future *would . . . win* in (2c). The difference between the past prospective and the future in the past can be tested by putting simple past forms in their places: in the case of the prospective, a preterite changes the temporal relation between the events referred to by the clauses (cf. *just when the train left*), but that does not happen in the case of the future in the past (cf. *who later won the tournament*). In the final example, the pluperfect *had sought cover* is another example of a narrative past in the past. This one is preceded by a clause with a past perfect progressive (*had been storming*), which has the same relative past tense value but differs in terms of aspect.

These examples serve to illustrate the fact that relative tense and aspect are two entirely separate categories that are nonetheless easily confused unless proper attention is given to the distinction between deictic centers and focused time.

There is another way of describing relative tense—namely, to define it as the relative order of different events referred to in the discourse.[7] This understanding is reflected in the term "taxis" (Greek for "order"). Some scholars consider taxis and tense as overlapping but distinct concepts that should not be confused, even though, in practice, the terms are often used to describe the same linguistic phenomena.[8] However, a "taxis interpretation" of relative tense cannot account for the difference between the perfect and relative past meanings of pluperfects, since it only defines the relations between different event times while saying nothing about the relation between event time and focused time (the relation between the event times are the same in relative past and perfect past meaning). Neither can this model be used to define the present perfect, imperfective and prospective meanings, since it does not introduce the time of speech into the equation. It can only be used for analyzing interclausal relations.

---

7. See Binnick's (1991, 39–40) presentation of the early relative tense theorists Nebrija, Johnson, and Scaliger. According to Nebrija, the pluperfect is the tense in which "something had been done when something was done" (39). Similarly, Johnson describes it as the form referring to "a thing perfected before another" (40). The same notion of relative tense is expressed in Scaliger's understanding of the Latin past imperfective as "present" (i.e., simultaneous) with regard to the event expressed by a conjoined clause (Binnick cites his example *cum intravit* **caenabam**, which means "I **was having supper** when he entered"; 40).

8. The distinction between taxis and relative tense is maintained, e.g., by Jakobson (1971, 135) and Bondarko (1991, 116–18).

Bearing in mind this caveat as to the general understanding of relative tense, we now turn to the role of "tense" in Hebraistics.

The Biblical Hebrew verbal forms were first described as absolute tenses by the Jewish grammarians of the Middle Ages. According to them, the *qatal* was a past tense form and the *yiqtol* a future. The ubiquitous future use of *weqatalti* and past use of *wayyiqtol* was explained as due to the proclitic *waw*, which allegedly had the function of converting the tense of the form to its opposite—hence the term "*waw* conversive" (Hebrew: *waw-hahippuk*). The system was completed by featuring the participle *qotel* as a present tense.[9]

With the provision of the conversive *waw*-thesis, the grammarians managed to square the Biblical Hebrew verbal forms roughly with a classical tense system. Nevertheless, for a skeptic it was an easy task to find enough counterexamples to refute the alleged tense values of the forms. In particular, the very common use of *yiqtol* with present meaning speaks against its designation as a future.[10] New theories were bound to emerge.

N. W. Schroeder was the first to propose a solution based on relative tense. He claimed that there was no conversion of tenses involved in the case of the *waw*-prefixed conjugations but rather a transposition of perspectives. Thus, the future use of *weqatalti* meant that the speaker transposed himself mentally to a future vantage point and regarded the events as if they were already past, albeit still future in relation to the time of speech. Conversely, the speaker may also transpose himself to the past and predict an event by means of *wayyiqtol*. The predicted event thereby becomes future relative to what preceded it—hence the designation "futurum relativum."[11]

This, if anything, is mental acrobatics. Even if it is possible to think it, it is not likely that any language would develop such complicated strategies to express something as simple as past tense. It is also an exceptional understanding of relative tense. The hallmark of relative tense forms is that they are used to break the flow of events in discourse by nonsequential retrospection or anticipation, not to build up such a sequence, as the *wayyiqtol* and *weqatalti* do. Nevertheless, Schroeder's novel idea of secondary deictic centers before and after the time of speech paved the way for a less rigid way of thinking about how temporal relations could be expressed by Biblical Hebrew verbal forms. Moreover, since comparative Semitic studies made it possible to treat the *wa*-prefixed *yiqtol* as a preterite rather than a future, the approach has become much less far-fetched.

---

9. McFall 1982, 128.

10. McFall (1982, 20) summarizes his findings from the translation of *yiqtol* in various languages (including English, French and Latin): "There are over 700 examples of it translated by the Past tense; over 3,300 examples as a Present against 5,400 examples as a Future."

11. McFall 1982, 22.

Thus, whereas the advocates of absolute tense today are few and tend to be moderate as to what they claim, several ambitious relative tense-theories have emerged in recent studies.[12]

According to Rüdiger Bartelmus, the Biblical Hebrew verbal forms present a complete relative tense system. The function of the forms is to express *Vorzeit*, *Gleichzeit*, or *Nachzeit*, primarily in relation to speech time, secondarily in relation to a past or future point of reference. Interestingly, the place of the future in the past in his model is occupied by *wayyiqtol* and understood in terms of temporal succession, which creates basically the same problem as in Schroeder's model.[13]

Jerzy Kuryłowicz's system is simpler.[14] He holds that only two values are marked in the Biblical Hebrew verbal system—namely, *anteriority* and *simultaneity*—and that other functions pertaining to temporality, such as aspect, are context-conditioned. However, the basic problem inherent in all relative tense proposals for Biblical Hebrew is present also in Kuryłowicz's work: the role of focused time in tense is overlooked and hence also the distinction between past and perfect meanings. Furthermore, "anteriority" as a concept (like Bartelmus's *Vorzeit*) is hard to reconcile with the performative and future uses of *qatal*. As for aspect, Kuryłowicz shares the very common understanding that it consists of only two categories, the function of which is to give a perspective of the event either from within or from without. We shall return to this issue in section 2.2.

Some scholars prefer to treat tense in Biblical Hebrew as a discourse level function. Alviero Niccacci relates tense functions to the hierarchical structure of texts (mainline vs. off-line): "Verb forms have *fixed temporal reference* when they are verbal sentences [i.e., verb-initial] and/or indicate the mainline of communication. On the other hand they have a *relative temporal reference* when they are nominal clauses [i.e., verbless or noun-initial] and indicate a subsidiary line of communication."[15]

Niccacci's approach puts less weight on the semantics of the verbal forms as such but is not necessarily incompatible with a semantically oriented relative tense theory. Thus, Sven-Olof Dahlgren makes use of Niccacci's description to prove that the Hebrew verbal forms express relative tense.[16] Another attempt to integrate semantics with a discourse-oriented approach is made by Tal Goldfajn. Her thesis is that tense in Standard Biblical Hebrew prose is built up around two temporal "perspectives" (or "set-ups")—one default perspective in which

---

12. For a moderate proposal for absolute tense, see Blau 1976, §20.1, which describes *qatal* as "roughly corresponding to the 'past'" and *yiqtol* as "roughly corresponding to the 'future.'"
13. Bartelmus 1982, 71.
14. See Kuryłowicz 1972, 1973.
15. Niccacci 1994, 129.
16. Dahlgren 2008.

the "reference time" is simultaneous with speech time, and one contextually specified perspective with the "reference time" prior to speech time.[17] "Reference time" is here to be understood as the deictic center. Analyzing the functions of the forms within these set-ups, she concludes that they "do have temporal values."[18] Since these temporal values, according to Goldfajn's analysis, can be connected with different deictic centers, they are de facto relative tenses.

2.2. Aspect

This section is divided into four subsections. The first two contain an exposé of the history of the central aspectual categories from ancient to modern times. The purpose is to give a background to the divergent understandings of the concept of aspect that can be found in the literature. A synthesis of the previous discussion in the form of a possible taxonomy of aspectual categories is presented in 2.2.3. To define the aspectual categories, the concept of focused time, which was introduced in section 2.1 above, is used. The rest of subsection 2.2.3 explains how focused time is related to Reichenbach's notion of "reference point," which, in some form or another, is central in much modern research on both tense and aspect (the role of focused time in aspect and tense will be developed further in chapter 3). Lastly, subsection 2.2.4 surveys the aspectual approach within the study of Biblical Hebrew with special regard to the issues raised in the previous subsections.

2.2.1. Aspect in Classical Grammar

Historical accounts generally trace the roots of aspect to the ancient Greek grammarians, who distinguished between verbal forms that presented the event as *completed* (*syntelēs*/*syntelikos*) and *extended* or *continuing* (*paratatikos*).[19] As an alternative to *paratatikos*, the negative term *uncompleted* (*atelēs*) was also possible. The terms used for these concepts by Latin grammarians were *perfectum* for completed and the negative *infectum* (thus Varro), or *imperfectum* (Priscian) for the opposite, the uncompleted/extended.[20]

---

17. Goldfajn 1998, 114.
18. Goldfajn 1998, 142.
19. Apollonius Dyscolus (second century CE) 1997, 133 (*Peri syntaxeōs* 1.114–115), 240–41 (3.100–102). The terminology for the verbal forms varies somewhat between the Stoics and later grammarians; see, e.g., Lallot's commentary in Dionysios Thrax (second–first century BCE) 1989, 173.
20. Varro (first century BCE) 1938, 520 (*De lingua latina* 9.101) and elsewhere. Priscian (sixth century CE) 1855, 415 (*Institutionum grammaticarum* 8.54).

The verbal forms considered completed by the Greeks seem to have been the perfect (*enestōs syntelikos*), the pluperfect (*hypersyntelikos*), and, at least in many cases, the aorist (*aoristos*). The uncompleted forms were the present (*enestōs paratatikos*) and the imperfect (*parōchēmenos paratatikos*).[21] The distinction was also made within the nonindicative moods, as well as the nonfinite forms.[22] In some modern-day accounts of classical verbal grammar one is led to believe that the Greeks thought the aorist to be neutral with respect to completedness.[23] An argument for this would be the term *aoristos* itself, which literally means "undefined." This exegesis is often part of an attempt to reconstruct the theories of the Stoic grammarians, who were acknowledged by the ancients to be the originators of the completed/uncompleted-distinction. But whatever may have been the opinion of the Stoics, whose works are now lost, the few extant textual witnesses from ancient grammars that are explicit about the matter clearly associate the aorist with the completed category. The "undefined" quality of the aorist has to do with the idea of remoteness rather than completedness.[24] Thus, the grammarian Stephanos (seventh century CE) states that the perfect signifies an event that is recent in time and the pluperfect one that is remote, whereas the aorist, in contrast, can be either recent or remote.[25] The Latin writer Priscian in an elucidating passage describes the meaning of the aorist in a quite similar way, even though he does not positively claim to be explaining the term

---

21. This is the terminology coined by the Stoic philosophers. Later grammarians used other terminology but retained the idea of an opposition of completed and uncompleted (see Lallot in Dionysios Thrax 1989, 173).

22. Thus Apollonius Dyscolus (1997, 133) claims in the first book of his *Peri syntaxeōs*, paragraph 115, that the present imperative of the verb *skaptō* (dig, hoe) expresses the extension/continuance (*paratasis*) and the aorist imperative the completion (*synteleiōsis*) of the action. In book 3.100, he discusses the difference between present and aorist optatives (in the example, the present optative is *zōoimi* and the aorist optative is *porthēsaimi*):

> We must note that the thing requested by the optative is either something present which is to be extended so that it will keep on, as when one says *zōoimi ō theoi* ('O gods, may I live!') or else it is something not in existence, which is to be accomplished, as when Agamemnon prays *eithe ō theoi porthēsaimi tēn ilion* ('Grant me, O Gods, to sack Troy!'). Here the prayer looks to a time when the event [of sacking Troy] is past and finished. For he [Agamemnon] would consider prolongation [of the sack] as something not to be wished for. (Translation, glosses, and transliterations by Householder 1981, 191)

As for nonfinites, in book 3.56, Apollonius says that the present and aorist infinitives and participles express the same "time" (*chronos*) as their finite counterparts (Apollonius Dyscolus 1997, 113). Obviously, "time" cannot refer to tense here since we are dealing with nonfinite forms, but rather refers to what we would call aspect.

23. See, e.g., Pinborg 1975, 92; Lallot's commentary in Dionysios Thrax 1989, 174; Binnick 1991, 12; Robins 1990, 34.

24. By the same token, the Greek future is "undefined" as to the distinction between near or remote future. Compare with Priscian's comment (n. 91).

25. See Lallot's commentary in Dionysios Thrax 1989, 34.

TABLE 1. Completed and uncompleted in Greek and Latin

Completed		Uncompleted	
L: *scripsi* (PFCT) G: *gegrapha* (PFCT)	"I have written"	L: *scribo* (PRS) G: *graphō* (PRS)	"I am writing"
L: *scripsi* (PFCT) G: *egrapsa* (AOR)	"I wrote" (i.e., I completed my writing)	L: *scribebam* (IMPF) G: *egraphon* (IMPF)	"I was writing"
L: *scripseram* (PLUP) G: *egegraphein* (PLUP)	"I had written"		

"aorist" in doing this. Most interesting in Priscian's classification is that he acknowledges the fact that the Latin perfect corresponds to the Greek aorist as well as to the Greek perfect and that it designates completed events in either case: "It is to be known that the Romans use the perfect [*praeteritum perfectum*] not only for events that are recently completed, in which case it has the sense the Greeks call *parakeimenos* ['adjacent,' i.e., present perfect], which the Stoics named *teleion enestōta* ['completed present'], but it is also used for the *aoristou* [i.e., the aorist, here inflected in the genitive case], a tense that can signify an event completed recently as well as an event completed a long time ago."[26]

By way of example, the opposition of completed versus uncompleted with present and past reference according to this view can be put as in table 1.

An innovation made by Varro regarding the analysis of the Latin verbal system was the application of the completedness distinction even in the future sphere.[27] In Latin, the same verbal stems that are used for completed and uncompleted events in the present and the past also appear in the future tenses *futurum exactum* (***scrips****-ero*, "I shall have written") and *futurum simplex* (***scrib****-am*, "I shall write"). When Varro incorporated the completed and uncompleted categories in his Latin grammar, he assumed that these meanings follow the stems, and he classified *futurum exactum* as completed and *futurum simplex* as uncompleted. By doing this, he created a complete symmetric system with a completed and an uncompleted series crosscutting all temporal frames from past to future. Thus, we have the perfect series ***scrips****-eram*, ***scrips****-i*, ***scrips****-ero* and the imperfect ***scrib****-ebam*, ***scrib****-o*, ***scrib****-am*.

The weak point in the Varronian system, however, is the classification of the *futurum simplex* as uncompleted. Probably, Varro was led more by the

---

26. Priscian 1855, 415 (*Institutionum grammaticarum* 8.54; my translation). The Greek words in the quotation are written with Greek letters in the edition. The fact that the ancient grammarians connected the aorist with the completed category is acknowledged by Versteegh 1980, 350. See also D. Cohen 1989, 18.

27. Varro 1938, 516 (*De lingua latina* 9.96).

principle of formal symmetry than by semantic analysis in this regard. For example, the clause *litteram scribam* would naturally be taken to mean "I shall write a letter" with the implication that the letter will indeed be completed (contrast the imperfective *I shall be writing a letter*).

After having been implemented in Latin, the linguistic concepts of completedness and uncompletedness were not explored further for centuries, but they were preserved for posterity in the terms *perfectum* and *imperfectum*. It is to be noted, that no metaterm for this grammatical twin category has come down to us from antiquity. Apollonius seems to treat it as some kind of subcategory of the notion "time" (*chronos*), but this word, in Latin *tempus*, eventually came to be earmarked as a technical term for the notion of tense.[28] "Aspect," at any rate, came into use for it quite recently. The somewhat haphazard ways by which this happened are of some consequence for the modern treatment of the whole phenomenon.

2.2.2. Modern Times

"Aspect" occurs for the first time as a grammatical term for verbal categories in 1828 in the second edition of Karl Philipp Reiff's French translation of Nicolay Greč's grammar of the Russian language.[29] Etymologically at least, it is a rather apt translation of the Russian *vid*, since both words come from roots with the basic meaning "see"/"vision." The word "vid," which had long been in use among Russian grammarians, was in turn originally a translation of the Greek term "*eidos*," a word from the same Indo-European root as *vid*. In the ancient Greek grammar, *eidos* meant "sort," "kind." It was used as a general technical term for derived forms of words of all kinds: nouns, verbs, pronouns, etc. and had nothing to do with the completed/uncompleted-distinction.[30] For a long time, the same was true of the Russian *vid*. When the word began to be used for verbal categories in Russian, it did not refer to the semantic content of the forms in question but kept the general sense of "kind."[31]

Decisive steps toward a modern aspect theory were taken in the beginning of the nineteenth century. According to the historians, it started with the publication of Johann Severin Vater's Polish grammar in 1807, in which he revived the classical verbal analysis in the field of Slavic studies, suggesting the existence of

---

28. See n. 87 for an example of the use of *chronos* in Apollonius. Householder (Apollonios Dyskolos 1981, 162, 163, 176) in his English translation sometimes renders the word as "tense/aspect." Dionysios Thrax, however, uses it unambiguously for tense (1989, 56).

29. Greč 1828, §210. Sørensen (1943, 221) states that the word "aspect" occurs already in 1821, when the first edition of Reiff's translation appeared, but according to Regnéll (1944, 10), that edition employs another word for Russian *vid*, viz. *branche*. See also Binnick 1991, 140.

30. See Dionysios Thrax 1989, 48, 54, 60 (chapters 11, 12 and 13, 17, 19).

31. Regnéll 1944, 5; Dombrovszky 1961, 10, quoting Mazon.

TABLE 2. Imperfective and perfective aspect in Russian

Imperfective	Perfective
ja pisal "I was writing"	*ja napisal* "I wrote," "I have/had written"
ja pišu "I am writing"	
ja budu pisat' "I shall be writing"	*ja napišu* "I shall write," "I shall have written"

a completed and an uncompleted class in the Polish verbal system.[32] The innovation was taken up in Russian grammar. Greč, in the aforementioned work, identifies two *vidy* (plural of *vid*) that are rendered by Reiff as *parfait* (cf. *perfectum*) and *imparfait* (*imperfectum*)—but he also lists an iterative category and another with semelfactive meaning beside them.[33] At this stage, evidently, the completed and the uncompleted had not yet become the *vidy par preference*. Anyway, Reiff's choice to privilege the verbal *vidy* with the special term "aspect" seems to have given impetus to a reanalysis of the term itself: *Vid*/aspect now did not only mean "some formal category of the verb," but it began more specifically to refer to the meaning of those same categories. As the group of verbal *vidy*, with the increasing understanding of the nature of Russian word-formation, was eventually limited to the completed and uncompleted, or, as it was called, the *perfective* and the *imperfective*, the term *vid*/aspect had finally become exclusively associated with the grammatical concept of (un)completedness.

In Russian, the perfective/imperfective opposition is even more pervasive than it is in either Greek or Latin, as it is carried through also into the future temporal sphere. Just as in Greek, the distinction between completed and uncompleted events in Russian is marked in the nonfinite forms and the nonindicative moods as well. In the overview of the imperfective and perfective indicative forms in table 2, the English rendering is simplified in order to make the semantic contrast as clear as possible.

Now, useful though it may have been, "aspect" was at first no more than an empty label for the phenomenon of (un)completedness. There was no definition of this word that could be used to elucidate the meaning of its subcategories. This lack of a solid theoretical foundation of the concept left considerable room for interpretation. It is possible to point out two significant developments in the interpretation of aspect that must be considered as deviations vis-à-vis the classical Greek model as it has been outlined above.

---

32. Vater himself also wrote a Russian grammar but did not implement his system there, although he made some suggestions in favor of it in the foreword (see Regnell 1944, 10; Daiber 1992, 164).

33. Greč 1828, §212. The terms used by Reiff for the semelfactive and the iterative meanings are "uniple" and "multiple." On semelfactive meaning, see section 3.4 below.

One of the deviations happened when scholars within the field of comparative Indo-European linguistics became aware of the phenomenon of Slavic aspect and tried to apply the concept to Germanic languages. Already in 1824, Jacob Grimm noted the fact that perfective forms in Slavic were often marked by adding a prepositional/adverbial prefix to the imperfective form and suggested that German verbal prefixes like *ver-*, *be-*, *hin-*, *durch-* had a similar function.[34] It is somewhat unclear from Grimm's concise treatment of the matter how far he wanted to press his comparison—in effect he says no more than that there is a certain functional similarity between the systems in that the addition of prefixes to certain German verbs makes them inappropriate for present meaning, just as the perfectivizing prefixes of Slavic languages do. Later scholars of the Leipzig school, in any case, claimed that the German prefixes have exactly the same aspectual function as the Slavic—that is, making perfectives out of imperfectives.[35] That this is a false analogy is easily proven by the fact that the German prefixed verbs are not after all altogether incompatible with the present tense, even if they are rarer in that function than nonprefixed verbs. The question *What is that little rascal doing now?* could well in German receive an answer containing a prefixed verb, such as *Er zerstört das Service* (*He is destroying the tableware*). In Slavic languages such an answer would require an imperfective predicate. The function of the German prefix in cases like the above is actually to indicate not perfectivity but rather what we today would call *telicity*, which is to say that the verb denotes an event containing an inherent goal. The latter belongs to the lexical content of the verb, whereas perfectivity is a grammatical category.[36] Due to this transformation in the conceptualization of the perfective aspect, the meaning of the "imperfective" was also confused with the lexical meanings atelicity and durativity (see section 3.2). Along with the conflated telicity/perfectivity-category, the Leipzig school also introduced a whole array of other aspects, or *Aktionsarten*, as they called them, among which were the causative, the inchoative, and the iterative.

The mismatch between the *Aktionsarten* and Slavic aspects has been widely acknowledged ever since it was pointed out by Hermann Jakobsohn and other scholars in several studies published in the 1920s.[37] *Aktionsart* is generally no longer thought to have anything to do with perfectivity and imperfectivity, but it is still used for (a)telicity and other verb-semantic categories.

---

34. See Grimm's foreword in Karadžić 1824, LII.
35. Streitberg (1896) 1943, 279, §191; Brugmann and Delbrück 1913, 81, §47. On the Leipzig school, see Regnéll 1944, 13.
36. Telicity can also be encoded at phrase level (3.2).
37. Jacobsohn 1926, 379–81; Hermann 1927, 207–8; Porzig 1927, 152–53. Later, the Swedish Slavist Sigurd Agrell has become acknowledged as the first scholar to make the distinction (Regnéll 1944, 19; See Agrell 1908, esp. 1–2).

The other major deviation from the classical understanding of aspect concerns the interpretation of the meaning of the perfective aspect. Important for this development was Georg Curtius, a classical philologist with a great interest in comparative linguistics. Curtius suggested that, besides tense (which he called *Zeitstufe*), the function of which is to indicate different temporal relations between the event and the speaker, there was also a verbal category indicating temporal differences "within the event"—namely, *Zeitart* ("mode of time").[38] Curtius assigned one *Zeitart* each to the present, perfect, and aorist stems of the Greek verbal system. When developing his system of *Zeitarten*, he had the concept of aspect in mind, and he claimed that his *Zeitarten* corresponded to the meanings expressed by the Slavic aspectual forms. Curtius described the *Zeitart* expressed by the Greek present and perfect stems as the *dauernde* ("enduring") and the *vollendete* ("completed")—terms that fit well with the familiar descriptions of the classical aspectual opposition. The *Zeitart* of the aorist, Curtius labeled *eintretende* ("occurring").[39] His description of this *Zeitart* is complex and open to interpretation. The *eintretende Zeitart*, writes Curtius, represents the event as if at a distance, making it appear as a point rather than something extended, totally without regard to its duration or internal development. Curtius is not very clear as to how the "event" and the "point" in question are related. At first, he seems to mean that the point is the whole event represented by the verb, but then he goes on to speak of the points as the initial or final points of the event. The final point of the event is represented in the case of the so-called effective aorist.[40] To illustrate this meaning, Curtius borrows an example from Aristonicus, who contrasts the imperfect *exenarizen* ("s/he was despoiling") with the aorist of the same word, *exenarixen* ("s/he despoiled").[41] Curtius concurs with the ancient tradition stating that such an aorist belongs to the category *syntelikos*. In other words, it functions to assert the completion of events as opposed to the *paratatikos*. By contrast, the so-called ingressive aorist represents the initial point of the event denoted by the verb, as in *ērasthēn* ("I fell in love"). The imperfect of the same word, *ēramēn* ("I loved"), stresses the continuity of the same event.[42]

But Curtius also mentions a third possibility—namely, that a whole event, from beginning to end, is included in the point. This is at least what he seems to

38. Curtius, 1875, 181.
39. Curtius 1875, 182.
40. Curtius 1875, 186.
41. The translation of the imperfect given within brackets would be the typical meaning of the form. In the actual example, which is from the *Iliad* 11.368, the context implies a continuative nuance in the verb; see Murray's translation: "went on to strip his armour" (Homer 1924, 509).
42. Curtius 1875, 185. Curtius here implies that the ancients would not count the ingressive aorist as "completed."

hint when he writes that the aorist perspective makes the event appear as a point, without regard to its actual extension in time, just like a distant object appears as a point without regard to its actual extension in space.[43]

Curtius's theory developed the description of aspect in certain respects: it suggested a definition of the metaterm aspect, distinguished between perfect and aorist meaning, and pointed out the difference between ingressive and effective meaning of the aorist. However, as mentioned above, it also gave rise to a different understanding of the perfective aspect—a change that perhaps complicated matters more than it helped them. Not that this understanding can be read directly from the pages of his *Erläuterungen*, which on the contrary appears to be well rooted in the classical tradition. But the fact is that Curtius is somewhat vague about how he relates his *Zeitarten* to the classical aspectual pair completed and uncompleted and the Slavic aspects. Beyond doubt, the *vollendete Zeitart* conveyed by the Greek perfect seems to be a direct translation of the Greek/Latin *syntelikos/perfectum*. The *eintretende Zeitart*, in the shape of effective aorist, is also *syntelikos*, according to Curtius.

Furthermore, it is an undeniable fact that the term "perfective" used for one of the two Russian aspects is an adaptation of "perfectum," and also that the Russian perfective corresponds in meaning *both* to the Greek perfect *and* to the aorist. Hence, it would seem that Curtius is here indirectly giving us to understand that the perfective aspect, being a genuine *syntelikos*, corresponds both to the *vollendete* and to the *eintretende Zeitart*. However, when Curtius himself speaks about Slavic aspects he relates only the *eintretende Zeitart* to the perfective aspect. This connection somehow came to predominate in the description of aspect following Curtius's influential work, so that "perfective" is now most commonly earmarked for the *eintretende Zeitart* that we know from the Greek aorist.[44] Curtius's description of the aorist meaning by means of the point-metaphor has been restated or followed by others who, in a similar vein, define it as the aspect that views the event from beginning to end, as a total, nonanalyzable whole, from outside, etc.[45] Östen Dahl refers to this explanation as the "totality view of the perfective."[46] In accordance with this view, the imperfective is often described in opposite terms as viewing the event partially, analytically, from the inside, with reference to its internal constituency, etc. As a shorthand for this way of defining aspect I shall talk about the "external-vs.-internal" approach to aspect.

43. Curtius 1875, 184.
44. Binnick 1991, 161.
45. For a few examples, see Saussure 1987, 161–62; Hermann 1927, 213; Rundgren 1961, 57; Comrie 1976, 4; Thelin 1978, 31–32; Johnson 1981, 154; Borik 2006, 174.
46. Dahl 1985, 74; see Lindstedt 1985, 52–53 on the "totality-model."

The above-mentioned transformation of the perfective category has created some problems. One evident shortcoming is that the word "perfective" is used not only for the effective meaning of the aorist but also for the ingressive, which is a contradiction in terms, since the ingressive by definition means that the event is not brought to completion.[47]

Another effect of the external-vs.-internal description of aspect is that it presents aspect as a closed binary opposition of (aorist) perfective and imperfective, thus leaving the perfect outside the system without any evident theoretical foundation. This may explain why the perfect has such an unclear status in modern aspectology. Ever since Curtius, all kinds of solutions (not necessarily mutually exclusive) of how to deal with the perfect have been suggested: (1) Perfect and aorist meaning are variant meanings within the perfective aspect;[48] (2) perfect is an aspect of its own;[49] (3) perfect is a variant of imperfective aspect;[50] (4) perfect is an *Aktionsart*;[51] (5) perfect is a relative tense, or taxis;[52] (6) perfect combines features of imperfective and perfective;[53] (7) perfect combines features of aspect and tense;[54] (8) perfect combines features of aspect, tense, and *Aktionsart*.[55]

Yet another problem stemming from Curtius's treatment of the aorist is the above-mentioned fact that it is not clear what the "event" is in the definition of the *eintretende Zeitart*. In the other two *Zeitarten*, the "event" is the concept lexically represented by the verb, and it is this lexical event that is "enduring" (*dauernd*) and "completed" (*vollendet*). As for the eintretende *Zeitart*, Curtius says that it represents the event as a point. But that point does not have to contain the whole of the event—it can be the starting point or the endpoint of it. Thus, in the example *ērasthēn* ("I fell in love") cited above, the event that is likened to a point is the actual falling in love, not the whole of the event of loving. This means that the "event" in question is actually a subevent of the lexical event. The problem with this is that if the *eintretende Zeitart* pertains to subevents (that is, beginnings and endings) of the lexical events whereas the *dauernde* and the *vollendete* pertain to the lexical events themselves, then the *eintretende Zeitart* is strictly speaking not of the same order as the other *Zeitarten* but a distinct linguistic category. The inadequacy of the point-metaphor remains, of course, if we define the "point" as the lexical event as a whole, since the ingressive

---

47. I do not know whether the aspectual nature of ingressive aorists is treated by any ancient grammarian.
48. Forsyth 1970, 74; Rassudova 1984, 62.
49. Comrie 1976, 52; M. Johnson 1981, 154; Dik 1997, 221; Klein 1994, 108.
50. See below, n. 131.
51. Hermann 1927, 212.
52. Kuryłowicz 1972, 83–84; Thelin 1991.
53. Koschmieder 1971, 18;
54. Olsen 1997, 142; C.S. Smith 1997, 109.
55. Bache, 1994, 56–59.

aorist does not represent the whole of the event. For the ingressive meaning, using "perfective," "total," or any word that includes the endpoint of the event is a contradiction in terms. As for the effective aorist, on the other hand, it may represent the whole of the event, but it does not have to do so. For example, the natural interpretation of the clause *The student solved the problem* would be that the whole of the event from beginning to end falls within the scope of the assertion, an interpretation that may be reinforced by adding context (*The student opened the book, solved the problem, and went out*). In another context, however, the same verb would only assert the end of the event and not the beginning (*The student worked for a long time solving the problem, and finally she solved it*[56]). The event is brought to its completion in both cases, hence indeed "perfective," but only in the former case do we get a total view of it.

A way of avoiding this impasse is to define the aorist meaning solely with respect to what limit of the event it allows into the perspective. The ingressive meaning of the aorist can then be defined as the aspect that views the initial limit of the event, as opposed to the truly perfective aorist, which views the final limit. The imperfective meaning ("continuing") represents the stage in between. Within this theoretical framework, the perfect naturally fits in as the aspect that represents the stage after the final limit of the event. A consistent implementation of the approach will also lead to the detection of an aspect that does not belong to the classical inventory—namely, the aspect that represents the stage preceding the initial limit of the event. This is what we have in so-called *prospective* constructions, like the English auxiliary phrase "to be about to." Since the concept of the limits of the event can be used to define both "external" and "internal" (or "total" and "partial," etc.) aspect, as well as other aspectual distinctions, the limit-based approach seems to be more complete than the external-vs.-internal approach. However, for all its flexibility, a drawback with the limit-based model is that it becomes somewhat awkward with regard to the aorist aspect in so-called achievement verbs—that is, verbs denoting instantaneous events.[57] Is it at all possible to imagine "limits" to an instantaneous event, as in *Lucy found a twenty-pound note*? One could, of course, argue that both limits are viewed in the utterance but that it is impossible to distinguish them from what is in between, since the duration of the event is subliminal, or, alternatively, that even the event of finding contains some undefined process of perceptible duration, such as an act of searching or simply the process of turning one's eyes toward the object, pausing, and realizing the significance of what has

---

56. In Russian, this sentence would typically be rendered by putting the verb "to solve" in the imperfective in the first clause and in the perfective in the second clause: *Studentka dolgo rešala* (ipfv) *zadaču i nakonets rešila* (pfv) (see corresponding examples in Forsyth 1970, 71–71).

57. See chapter 3, example (18).

happened. Nevertheless, we may find it simpler in this case to say that the utterance gives a total view of the event. It is to be noted that in all other verbs except for achievement verbs, the totality view of the perfective is directly translatable to a strictly limit-based definition to the effect that "both limits of the event are viewed." As for the explanation of the imperfective as an "internal" view, it entails the idea of initial and final limits. Thus, we may understand a "limit-based approach" to aspect largely as a way of drawing out the implications of the external-vs.-internal approach.

Limit-based descriptions of aspect are not uncommon in modern linguistic research, although they may vary considerably as to what categories they count as aspects and how these categories are applied to the data. One proponent of the limit-based approach is Lars Johanson, whose aspectual subdivisions exactly correspond to Curtius's three *Zeitarten*.[58] The imperfective (or continuing) category is called "intraterminal" by Johanson with reference to the stage between the initial and final limit (Latin: *terminus*) of the event, the perfect corresponds to his "postterminal," and the aorist is labeled "adterminal." The term "adterminal," meaning "at a limit," covers both the ingressive and effective variant of the aorist meaning. Johanson does not treat these variants as different aspects, since he has no evidence that the meanings are marked by different forms in any of the languages that he is investigating. With regard to the postterminal aspect, too, the "terminus" in question, according to Johanson, may be the final *or* the initial limit of the event depending of which limit is "relevant."[59] In most cases, the postterminal aspect views the stage after the final limit of the event, but in the case of the so-called initiotransformative verbs, it views the stage after the initial limit. An example would be the English word "hide."[60] The perfect "has hidden" does not typically view a stage in which the hiding is ended; rather, it views it as a continuous event, just as the progressive "is hiding." Therefore, "postterminal" aspect with such verbs means after the *initial* limit of the event only.[61] Johanson's use of terminology here is ingenious but precarious, I believe. An aspect that represents the stage that is after the initial limit of an event and not after the final limit is logically equivalent to an intraterminal. It does not seem meaningful to use the word "postterminal" in that way. An alternative would be to count the so-called initiotransformatives as lexically polysemous. As Johanson notes, the initiotransformatives combine atelic and telic meaning in one and the same form.[62] Thus, "to hide" has both the telic meaning "go into hiding" and the atelic meaning "being hidden." The postterminal "has hidden"

---

58. Johanson 2000, 34–35. Johanson uses the term "viewpoint" instead of aspect.
59. Johanson 2000, 59.
60. Johanson 2001, 9.
61. Johanson 2000, 102; 2001, 7.
62. Johanson, 2000, 63.

is formed on the basis of the former meaning and, consequently, refers to the situation after the final limit of the event (cf. "has gone into hiding").

Wolfgang Klein's inventory of aspects includes the perfective, the imperfective, the perfect, and the prospective, the last of which is not treated by Johanson.[63] Limit-based descriptions are suggested for all aspects: The perfect, imperfective, and prospective are said to assert the time *after*, *within*, and *before* (the time of) the event represented by the verb, whereas the perfective aspect, according to Klein, asserts some time *at* the time of the event (cf. Johanson's *ad*terminal).[64] Klein's schematic illustration of the possible variants of perfective meaning predicts that the perspective may include the initial, the final, or both limits of the event—that is, all three possible variants of the aorist meaning mentioned above.[65]

In comparison, the limit-based model of aspect is more flexible than the external-vs.-internal model, although the latter deals more naturally at least with the aorist meaning of achievement verbs. A possible raison d'être for the poorer external-vs.-internal approach is that it focuses on the contrast between change and continuity in the predicated events, so that "perfective" (i.e., aorist) stands for change and imperfective for continuity. However, in this interpretation, not only the imperfective but also the perfect and the prospective belong to the category of predicates that expresses continuity—which means that the external-vs.-internal definition does not suffice anyway. Some scholars have indeed drawn this conclusion (at least as far as the perfect is concerned) and used the term "imperfective" for the perfect as well as for the "real" imperfective.[66] This step can be regarded as the final consequence of making perfective synonymous with aorist meaning. The fact that the terms "imperfective" and "perfective" are both thereby rendered meaningless only underscores that this shift in the way of describing aspect was a mistake from the beginning.

The limit-based approach is closer to the classical model in that it incorporates the perfect within the system. On the other hand, it distinguishes perfect and aorist meaning, whereas the ancient system treated both as one perfective category. One way to treat both perfect and aorist meaning as one perfective aspect within

---

63. Klein 1994, 108.

64. This is not exactly how Klein formulates it, but it can be read from his description of aspect as a relation between "topic time" and "situation time" (Klein 1994, chapter 6, 108). My term "event" corresponds to Klein's "situation."

65. Klein 1994, 103. Klein seems somewhat at a loss for good examples of perspectives including only the initial limit. However, I would suggest that sentences like *Suddenly, I knew* and *He opened his mouth and sang* fit his model very well.

66. DeCaen 1995, 205. Smith approaches this thought with her concept of "resultative imperfectives" (C.S. Smith 1997, 77). Resultatives have a temporal structure similar to that of perfects (see section 3.4.1 below). As for perfect meaning, however, Smith considers it to be a combination of tense and aspect (109).

a limit-based system could be to define aspect on the basis of the latest attained limit of the event. That is, the final limit of the event is attained in both perfect and aorist meaning; hence both are perfective. However, within such a system, ingressive and imperfective would be one and the same aspect, too, since the initial limit of the event is the latest-attained limit in both these meanings. This does not seem to comply with the classical understanding of the imperfective as the expression of *paratasis* ("continuity," "extension").

It turns out that it is impossible to make a consistent theory of aspect based on the "classical" approach, at least not as it has been presented here. Rather than adopting it wholesale with its contradictions, we are well advised to take some hints from it in order to work out some alternative theoretical framework, such as has been attempted within the external-vs.-internal and the limit-based approaches to aspect. The crucial question is, of course, which theory deals best with the semantics of verbal forms of the type that we find in classical Greek and other languages.

One phenomenon that neither the limit-based nor the external-vs.-internal approach can explain is the rather frequent occurrence of aorist meaning in forms that are defined as imperfective and perfect. To this group belong, for example, reportive and historical presents, as well as performative presents and perfects (of the type often called "resultative"). In section 3.5, I shall argue that such uses are better accommodated within a theory that defines aspects according to which *stage* of the event is in view, regardless of whether some limit of the event is also included or not. To give a preliminary idea, in the following two sentences, the same stage of the event is viewed, with the difference that the stage is viewed in the first example as continuous and in the second as emergent, with the first limit of the event being included in the view (ingressive meaning):

(3) a. The bird is flying.
 b. The young bird flaps its wings vigorously, and suddenly it is flying for the first time.

2.2.3. Reference Time, Focused Time, and Deictic Centers

So far in this exposition, the meaning of aspect has been explained rather informally in terms of different views, or perspectives, on events as they unfold in time. There is, however, a more analytical way of saying the same thing, and this is in fact adopted by most theorists today. Basically, the idea is that, if the aspects differ as to what view they offer of the event, then it follows that the view and the event have different times. Accordingly, aspect can be described as the temporal relation obtaining between the time of the view and the time of the event referred to by the verb. In section 2.1, we have already encountered the "time of the view" and "time of the event" in the shape of "focused time" and "event time." By way of summarizing the preceding discussion, these terms are here tentatively applied to the various aspectual categories that have been suggested. I use familiar terminology, avoiding only the problematic term "perfective." Thus:[67]

> Perfect: Focused time is after event time.
> Imperfective: Focused time is included in event time.
> Prospective: Focused time is before event time.
> Aorist: Focused time includes at least one limit of event time.
>   a. Completive: Focused time includes both limits of event time
>   b. Ingressive: Focused time includes only the beginning of event time.
>   c. Egressive: Focused time includes only the end of event time.

The external-vs.-internal approach to aspect would only include the aspects represented by aorist and imperfective in the above list, but it would state that in the aorist (i.e., the "perfective," as it is normally called), the focused time includes the whole of the event time.

Having come this far in our review of aspect, some further remarks concerning the term "focused time" and its relation to the more familiar "reference time" are called for, since the latter has been used in different ways in the literature.

The term "reference time" goes back to Hans Reichenbach's "point of reference." One of the purposes of the introduction of this concept was to account for the semantic difference between the English preterite and perfect. According to the standard tense logic of Reichenbach's day, there was no temporal difference between the sentences "I saw John" and "I have seen John"; both were said to indicate that the event occurred previous to the time of the utterance. Reichenbach solved the problem in the following way: He assumed that the event and the time of speech correspond to points on a time line and called them "the point of the event" (E) and "the point of speech" (S). He also assumed that each utterance contains a point of reference (R) that relates, on the one hand, to E and, on the other hand, to S. The difference between the English preterite and perfect,

---

67. This list is quite similar to the one in Klein 1994, 108, but Klein has "situation time" (TSit) for event time and "topic time" (TT) for focused time, and he has one common definition for ingressive and effective aorist, viz. that TT is situated *at* TSit (cf. Johanson's "adterminal"). Bohnemeyer has extended Klein's model so that it contains all the categories proposed here (with slightly different terminology). However, rather than defining the perfect and prospective aspects in terms of topic time (i.e., my focused time) "after" and "before" the event he prefers to say that these aspects put topic time inside the post- and pre-states of the event (Bohnemeyer 2014, 920; see further comments on Bohnemeyer in n. 263 below).

Reichenbach claimed, was that the former sets R in the past, contemporaneous with E, while the latter makes R co-occur with S. Thus, schematically,[68]

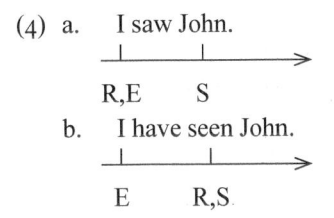

(4) a. I saw John.
       |⎯⎯⎯|⎯⎯⎯⎯→
       R,E   S
   b. I have seen John.
       |⎯⎯⎯|⎯⎯⎯⎯→
       E   R,S

Unfortunately, since Reichenbach did not define what a reference point is, the term has been used rather indiscriminately for things that are quite distinct. In one of his own examples the reference point stands for "the year 1678."[69] But it is evident that "the year 1678" cannot have the same function as the R in the above examples, since the verbal forms in the latter are able to set R without adverbial complements. The S-E-R relation is not affected by changing sentence (4a) to *I saw John in January in the year 1678*. Strictly speaking, R cannot *be* "the year 1678," but it can be *contained* in it. The year 1678 is thus more correctly called the temporal *frame* of R.[70]

Reichenbach's R-time also stands for two other opposing concepts in the temporal set-up of the utterance. On the one hand, it can be the time that the utterance refers to—that is, the focused time.[71] On the other hand, the R-time can be

---

68. This subsection discusses the examples and illustrations found in Reichenbach 1947, 288–92.
69. Reichenbach 1947, 289.
70. See Dahl (1985, 30) on "temporal frames" and Binnick (1991, 308) on "frame adverbials."
71. The problem with the dual nature of the notion of "reference time" has been clarified by Declerck. In his article "From Reichenbach to Comrie and Beyond," (1986) he distinguishes between the "time pointed to," or "time referred to" (TR; cf. my "focused time") and the "time pointed from," or "time of orientation / orientation time" (TO; cf. my "deictic center"). TR is changed to "situation time" (more fully, "the time of the predicated situation") in his monumental 2006 monograph on the English tense system ("situation time" is otherwise mostly used in the literature for Reichenbach's "event time"—which is called "time of the full situation" by Declerck; see Declerck 2006, 116). A similar distinction is expressed with Klein's "topic time" (TT; my "focused time") and "deictic relatum" (my "deictic center"; Klein 1994, 3, 67–70) and Smith's "reference time" (my "focused time") and "orientation point" (my "deictic center"; C.S. Smith 1997, 101). See also Bohnemeyer 2014, which builds on Klein. Declerck's theoretical system is particularly rich and useful, but his notion of situation time / TR is complicated by his definition of the present perfect, where the situation time, in his words, is located in "the pre-present zone of the present time-sphere," which appears to mean that the tense value is neither past nor fully present (212). Another difficulty in Declerck's analysis is his notion of "temporal focus," which means slightly different things depending on whether it is applied to relative or absolute tense. Thus, in the present perfect, which is an absolute tense form, temporal focus coincides with situation time, but not so in its relative tense counterpart, the pluperfect. In the latter, the temporal focus, according to Declerck, is what distinguishes the past perfect meaning from the relative past meaning, whereas the situation time remains the same in both meanings (573, 575).

the deictic center in relation to which the focused time is located. At least, this is how R-time has been interpreted after Reichenbach. In (5), focused time (F) and deictic center (D) are annotated separately. Comparing this with (4), we see that Reichenbach's R corresponds fully with our focused time, which is situated in the present in the perfect and the past in the preterite. The deictic center in both sentences coincides with S. To judge from these examples alone, Reichenbach's R seems to be identical with our F:

(5) a. I saw John.

F,E   S,D

b. I have seen John.

E   S,D,F

However, the question is whether F always coincides with D in the perfect, rather than with E. If it is the case in the present perfect, it surely is not in the pluperfect, and here is where Reichenbach's R does not really serve its purpose. Let us look again at a couple of the examples from section 2.1:

(6) a. [By the time the dinner was ready,] I had set the table.
    b. [He told me about the events on the day before.] He had arrived to the railway station just when the train was about to leave.

Reichenbach has only the following configuration for the English pluperfect:

(7)

E   R   S

This annotation of the pluperfect cannot account for the difference between the perfect-in-the-past in (6a) and the past-in-the-past in (6b). Splitting R into F (focused time) and D_2 (secondary deictic center), and identifying S as the location of D_1 (primary deictic center), however, makes the difference visible:

(8) a. [By the time the dinner was ready,] I had set the table.

E   F,D_2 S,D_1

Thus, Declerck's "temporal focus" corresponds quite closely with my "focused time," although my definition of the present perfect sets focused time in the present (speech time) rather than in the pre-present. Another difference between Declerck's "temporal focus" and my "focused time" is that Declerck does not use the concept for his definition of aspect (see Declerck 2006, 28–38).

b. [He told me about the events on the day before.] He had arrived to the railway station just when the train was about to leave ...

```
 |_____|_____|_>
 F,E    D₂    S,D₁
```

Later commentators who have read the concept of deictic center into Reichenbach's R have treated D1 in (8) as the "first" R.[72]

The germ of a definition of aspect in terms of R-E relations is present already in Reichenbach's theory. This becomes especially visible in his representations of the English progressive forms. The event is here symbolized as rectangles extending over the R-point, which suggests that R is included in E:

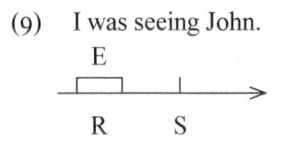

(9) I was seeing John.

```
       E
 __☐___|___>
   R   S
```

A modified version would look like (10), where the focused time is shown to be included in E, but preceding the deictic center:

(10) I was seeing John.

```
       E
 __☐___|___>
   F   S,D
```

2.2.4. Aspect in Hebraistic Studies

Aspect analysis of Biblical Hebrew began with the Austrian theologian and philologist Johann Jahn.[73] In his *Grammaticae linguae hebraicae* of 1809 he offered a purely Varronian analysis of the Biblical Hebrew verbal system. Like Varro, Jahn claimed that there is an opposition between *perfectum* (completed) and *infectum* (uncompleted) in all three tenses, but whereas Varro's system contains six forms, Jahn's has only two. According to Jahn, Biblical Hebrew *qatal* expresses a completed situation (*rem perfectam*) in all tenses and *yiqtol* an uncompleted one (*rem infectam*). His strictly symmetrical system contains the same weakness as Varro's in that it posits an imperfective future (2.2.1). The Hebrew *yiqtol* is very often used with perfective meaning, just like the Latin *futurum simplex* (see chapter 4, example [24]).

---

72. Prior 1967, 13
73. McFall 1982, 43.

Jahn's student Heinrich Ewald adopted his teacher's thoughts in modified form and applied them to both Biblical Hebrew and Arabic.[74] He called the *qatal* and *yiqtol* perfect and imperfect in line with Jahn's analysis, but in other respects he abandoned the Varronian symmetry in favor of an analysis that better suited his own understanding of the Semitic verb. Most significantly, he reinterpreted the meaning of the imperfective category. Drawing on a negative definition of the imperfective, he stated that it signifies events as "not yet completed," hence also "becoming."[75] According to Ewald, this includes events that are not yet begun. Since "not yet begun" with regard to the time of speech is tantamount to "being in the future," Ewald concluded that future meaning was part of the basic meaning of the imperfect.

Another approach to the problem was Samuel Driver's attempt to combine Ewald's perfect/imperfect-model of the Hebrew verbal system with Curtius's concept of the three *Zeitarten*, which in Driver's version became the three "kinds of time."[76] By counting the participle *qotel* as a third form alongside *qatal* and *yiqtol*, Driver got one form for each of his three kinds of time: *completed, continuing,* and *incipient,* or *nascent*.[77] It seems that these terms, in that order, correspond to Curtius's *vollendete, dauernde,* and *eintretende Zeitart*. If this is the case, however, the application of Curtius's concepts, with the exception of the continuing kind of time, is not very precise. In Driver's study *qatal* is the completed kind of time, *qotel* the continuing, and *yiqtol* the incipient. Given that the "incipient" kind of time of Driver corresponds to Curtius's *eintretende Zeitart*, it is remarkable that Driver assigns that meaning to *yiqtol*, since he obviously does not mean that the form corresponds in meaning with the Greek aorist, which represents the *eintretende Zeitart* according to Curtius.[78] On the contrary, as Driver himself notes, aorist meaning is often expressed by *qatal*, a form that Driver connects with Curtius's vollendete *Zeitart*—that is, perfect meaning.[79]

74. McFall 1982, 44.
75. Ewald 1870, 138.
76. Driver 1892, §2.
77. Driver 1892, §2.
78. In the case of *wayyiqtol*, which Driver classified as a variant of *yiqtol*, there is actually a considerable correspondence in meaning with the Greek aorist, but Driver's description of the aorist meaning differs radically from that of Curtius, since Driver based his explanation of *wayyiqtol* on the same semantic notion of incipiency that he also used to explain the uses of the ordinary "imperfect" (*yiqtol*-L) as well as the cohortative and jussive (i.e, the volitive variants of *yiqtol*-S). As Randall Garr writes in his preface to Driver's work, the problem with the incipient category is that it is defined very much as if it were a phasal aspect referring to the initial phase of the event (see 3.4.4 below on phasal aspect), whereas the usages to which it is applied are much more readily understood in terms of other semantic concepts, such as imperfectivity (Garr 1998, xlviii–li). It is not surprising that Driver's attempt to come up with an all-encompassing semantic category to account for all these heterogeneous usages failed to convince his contemporaries (Garr 1998, xlv–xlvii).
79. Driver 1892, §§3, 7.

Driver may have misunderstood Curtius's term *eintretende*, or he may deliberately have reinterpreted it to account for the many uses of *yiqtol*. In any case, his description of *yiqtol* as indicating "action as nascent, as evolving itself actively from its subject" is influenced more by William Turner than by Curtius, and in this regard it has even less in common with the classical understanding of imperfective than Ewald's description of the same form.[80] At the same time, as a form encoding a "kind of time" indicating both present and future time, Driver's version of the Hebrew imperfect is very reminiscent of Ewald's.

The Hebraic/Arabic branch of early modern aspectology from Jahn to Driver is interesting in that it appears to be fairly independent from the contemporary research about aspect within Slavist and Indo-Germanist circles (in spite of a certain superficial connection with Curtius in the case of Driver). Eventually, the branches merged, as evidenced by the use of the term "aspect" in the works of Paul Joüon and Marcel Cohen. In Joüon's Hebrew grammar of 1923, aspect is used in a sense much like the *Aktionsarten* of the Indogermanists.[81] Cohen, by contrast, in his *Le système verbal sémitique* (1924), works only with the notions of perfective and imperfective. He leaves the participle *qotel* aside, like Jahn and Ewald before him. In his work, there are still traces of the idea that future time reference is part of the meaning of the imperfective aspect.[82]

The next phase of the development of aspect studies within Semitic languages, inaugurated by the great showdown with the *Aktionsarten* in the second half of the 1920s (see 2.2.2), was initiated on the part of Biblical Hebrew already by Erwin Koschmieder in 1929 and given further impetus in an article by Carl Brockelmann in 1951.[83] From this time on, it has been a recurring theme also in Hebraistics that aspect consists of an opposition between aorist and imperfective meaning, or, if more aspectual categories are counted, that these aspects, rather than imperfective and perfect, for example, are the most basic categories within the system. This understanding is theoretically founded in an external-vs.-internal definition of the aorist and imperfective meanings and in the use of the term "perfective" for the former.[84] The trend has been reinforced strongly

---

80. Driver 1892, §21. See his comment on Turner's description of what he calls "egressive" meaning as a "manifestation of an energy residing in the subject" (II, §6 Obs. 2).

81. Joüon 1923, §111.c–d.

82. M. Cohen 1924, v, 208.

83. Koschmieder 1971 [1929], 58–71; Brockelmann 1951, 134.

84. See, e.g., Koschmieder 1971, 35; Kuryłowicz 1972, 79 (Kuryłowicz does not think that the Biblical Hebrew forms are marked for aspect); Waltke and O'Connor 1990, §29.6; Hendel 1996, 164; Hatav 1997, 6–7 (In Hatav's study perfective/external is seen as a component of "sequentiality" and is defined as the inclusion of the situation [= the event] in "reference time"; conversely, imperfective/internal is defined as the inclusion of the reference time in the situation and is called "progressive"); Gentry 1998, 14–15; Tropper 1998, 154; Rogland 2003, 7; Joosten 2012, 28.

by the linguist Bernard Comrie's version of this approach.[85] A variant of the approach involves the classification of perfect meaning as imperfective.[86]

Among more original contributions may be mentioned, for example, Frithiof Rundgren's theory of the hierarchically ordered opposition of aspects. According to this theory, the perfective and imperfective aspects (in his own terms, "konstativ" and "kursiv") belong to a superordinate aspectual category *fiens*, which in turn is opposed to the *stative*.[87] The difference between the latter terms is one of dynamicity: fiens represents dynamic events, whereas stative represents all kinds of states, ranging from properties such as being rich in *X is rich*, to habits/faculties such the ability to speak French in *X speaks French*.[88] In addition, Rundgren takes a limit-based approach and claims that the stative in Semitic is basically *extraterminal*.[89] This means that the phase that lies outside the limits of the event (*extra terminos*) is represented by means of the verbal form. Rundgren's attempt to explain the fiens-stative opposition in terms of terminality is fraught with some rather complex or even abstruse ideas, such as the statement that "*extra*terminal" with regard to stative verbs should be understood as "after the first limit" (*post terminum initialem*)—notwithstanding that "after the first limit," given that it does not also mean "after the second limit," is equivalent to being between the first and the second limit, hence "*intra*terminal."[90] Most scholars today would probably argue that the semantic distinction between fiens and stative lies in the *Aktionsart* of the verb rather than the aspect.[91]

Another suggested new aspect category is Hatav's *sequence* aspect. This aspect is used for the representation of courses of events. In Hatav's wording, the sequence aspect has the effect of moving the reference time forward in discourse. A condition for sequentiality is that the event (Hatav's "situation"; our "E") is temporally included in its R-time (our "focused time").[92] In other words, sequence aspect is identical with perfective aspect understood according to the totality view. As to the feature of R-time movement, it brings the relation between different R-times to bear on the definition. The question, however, is why R-R relations should be considered aspectual, especially since the inclusion of E in R does not entail R-time movement.

85. Comrie 1976, 4.
86. DeCaen 1995, 205 (see n. 66 above).
87. Rundgren 1961, 72.
88. Rundgren 1959, 38; cf. his fundamental opposition *Ruhe/Sein* vs. *Bewegung/Geschehen* (91).
89. The same terminology was later employed by Johanson, as we have seen above (2.2.2).
90. See Rundgren 1961, 62–66. Johanson has a similar argument with regard to the so-called initiotransformative verbs (2.2.2).
91. "Fiens" can be regarded as synonymous with dynamicity. See Waltke and O'Connor 1990, e.g., §§20.2h and 22.2.1. See 3.2 on dynamic and stative verbs.
92. Hatav 1997, 6.

2.3. Modality

The temporal implications of modality are often productive in the grammaticalization of various temporal functions. For example, future tense in English may be expressed by auxiliary verbs with a dynamic as well as a deontic modal meaning:[93]

(11) a. He will finish his dinner with a dessert.
b. He shall finish his dinner with a dessert.

Generalizing meanings, such as the habitual and generic meanings, are also commonly expressed by modal phrases in many languages, including English:

(12) a. He would finish his dinner with a dessert.
b. Wealthy people would finish their dinner with a dessert.

The parallel situation in German has led Beat Zuber to suggest that there is a modal function encoded in the Biblical Hebrew *yiqtol* (i.e., the *yiqtol*-L) and *weqatalti*, which puts them in contrast with the indicative forms *qatal* and *wayyiqtol*.[94] In later studies by Joosten and Hatav, the other finite forms plus the predicative participle have been included in the opposition, so that we get an indicative subsystem consisting of *qatal*, *wayyiqtol* and *qotel* versus a modal one, which, aside from *yiqtol*-L and *weqatalti*, also includes the imperative, the jussive, and the cohortative.[95]

Above (section 1.4), I have already given some reasons why I prefer not to count *weqatalti* as a separate verbal form. As for *yiqtol*-L, one argument against defining it as modal is that it is typologically an old progressive and that it still has in Biblical Hebrew some traces of prototypical progressive meaning.[96] Even if it has similar functions to modal constructions like the English ones in examples (11) and (12) above, it simply does not belong to that type. The only way to conclude that *yiqtol*-L is modal is to (a) dismiss all prototypically progressive uses of the form and (b) define the rest of the meanings that *yiqtol*-L is able to express as modal per se. Even if we rashly grant the former manoeuver on the grounds that the prototypically progressive *yiqtol*-L is disappearing in

---

93. "Dynamic" modality expresses the will and other subject-internal factors in an event, "deontic" modality stands for subject-external factors such as obligation or permission. On this terminology, see Palmer 2001, 9.
94. Zuber 1986, 7–15, 25.
95. Joosten 1997, 57–58; 2002, 67; 2012, 39–41; Hatav 1997, 118–62.
96. As for Andrason's suggested nonprogressive derivation of habitual meaning in *yiqtol*-L, see section 2.5.

Biblical Hebrew, it is not theoretically feasible to postulate the future and generalizing meanings of *yiqtol*-L as modal.

For an expression to be modal, the event that it refers to must, in the definition of Heiko Narrog, be "marked for being undetermined with respect to its factual status."[97] Put differently, a modal expression is primarily concerned not with the question of whether something really happens or not but rather with the conditions under which it happens. A consequence of this is that the truth or nontruth of a modal statement does not depend on the actual occurrence or nonoccurrence of the event represented by the (main) verb. For example, a statement like *She must have left already* can be falsified merely by demonstrating that it is not necessarily the case that the event took place—irrespective of whether it actually did. By contrast, a nonmodal statement like *She has left already* is false only if the event in fact has not occurred.

According to this definition of modality, generalizing meanings are not inherently modal, since they can often be falsified if the event referrred to does not occur on a sufficient number of occasions (*Swedes often take their bikes to work*, *Mats plays tennis on Saturdays*). The fact that certain generalizing meanings are factually undetermined (e.g., *This machine crushes oranges*; see 3.2) does not make the whole class of generalizing meanings modal. The common defining feature of all generalizing meanings is generality, not modality.[98]

These facts outweigh the argument of those linguists who claim that generalizing meanings are modal by force of a law-like character that makes them resemble epistemic *must*- or *may*-meanings.[99] Whatever "law" may be expressed by a truly habitual sentence like *Mats plays tennis on Saturdays* has to be empirically induced—that is, based on the factuality of the event—and not deduced or hypothesized, as in the case of epistemic modality (cf. *She must have left already*).

As for future meaning, it is every bit as factually determined as the present and the past. Thus, a statement like *It will rain tomorrow* can only be untrue if the event does not occur. It is true that the future can be felt to be more open than the present and the past, since there are no witnesses to it, but that does not determine the way we talk about it.[100] If we want to present it as fact, we do; if we want to modalize our statements, we can do that, too (*It will probably rain tomorrow*). In this respect, the future does not differ from the present or the past (*It is raining / It must be raining, It rained / It probably rained*). The idea that

---

97. Narrog, 2005, 679.
98. Carlson 2012, 829.
99. Dahl 1975, 105; Krifka et al. 1995, 49–57; Bertinetto and Lenci 2012, 870–71.
100. The openness of the future is the most important factor in Hatav's treatment of future statements as modal (Hatav 1997, 123–26).

future statements are always modal because the future is uncertain neglects the fundamental fact that linguistic meaning is primarily defined not by the world as such but by our conceptualization of it.

2.4. Linguistic Attitude (*Sprechhaltung*)

Harald Weinrich is a linguist whose influence within Hebraistics has been considerable. Significant for his theory of the verb is the refusal to credit any of the categories tense, aspect or modality as being primary functions of the verbal forms.[101] Their basic function, he claims, is rather to signal by which attitude (*Haltung*) the listener should receive the utterances in which they occur. The attitude can be either one of *tension* (*Gespanntheit*) or one of *relaxation* (*Entspanntheit*).[102] Weinrich links these attitudes to two basic modes of communication: relaxation characterizes all kinds of narration (*Erzählung*), whereas tension characterizes *discussion* (*Besprechen*). The latter is a wide concept that perhaps is most easily described simply as everything that is not narration. When counting the verbal forms that appear in narration and discussion in many languages, Weinrich finds that verbal forms tend to be used predominantly in either the one or the other text-type. Based on these distributional patterns, he divides verbal systems into two groups: *tense group one* for the forms belonging to discussion and *tense group two* for narrative forms.[103] The division of texts into these two fundamental types forms the basis for Weinrich's text linguistic method. When scholars such as Schneider, Talstra, Niccacci, and Baayen have applied Weinrich's text linguistics to Biblical Hebrew, they have embraced the theory of linguistic attitudes without modifications or critical discussion.[104]

In my opinion, the essential point in Weinrich's thesis is very plausible: Utterances are received with different degrees of tension or relaxation, and the verbal forms have something to do with it. Consider the following sentences:

(13) a. A wolf is coming.
 b. A wolf has come.
 c. A wolf came.
 d. A wolf was coming.

---

101. Weinrich develops ideas from, among others, Benveniste (1966b, 238), which he makes clear only in the first edition of his Tempus (1964, 40).
102. Weinrich 1977, 33.
103. Weinrich 1977, 18.
104. Schneider 2001; Niccacci 1990; Talstra 1997. Baayen (1997) elaborates on Weinrich's notion of linguistic attitude (Baayen's "focal referential concern"; see section 1.1) without applying other parts of Weinrich's text linguistic apparatus.

If the reader was asked to intuit a prototypical speech situation for these utterances, I assume that s/he would be most likely to associate (13a–b) with some kind of alarm situation in which the listener is called to action, whereas (13b–c) would be associated with a relaxed narrative setting. In Weinrich's terminology, the forms in (13a–b) can be ascribed to tense group one, indicating the tense attitude of communication, whereas sentences (13b–c) can be said to indicate a relaxed mode by means of tenses of the second group.

But what about the following?

(14) a. A wolf comes.
b. A wolf will come.

According to Weinrich, the English present and future belong to tense group one. But are these utterances likely to evoke the same alarm as (13a–b)? The most plausible interpretation of example (14a) is that it describes a nonspecific event (e.g., *A wolf comes every year*). Does it not rather align with sentences (13c–d), in that it allows the listener to remain quite relaxed? As for (14b), it might cause some unease if you are a shepherd, but in a more typical scenario, I would say, the most appropriate response would be to stay calm and enquire about the matter (e.g., "Why do you think so?"). In (13a–b), by contrast, if you ask anything at all, it would be while you are already in a rush to defend your sheep (e.g., "Where?!").

Here it is appropriate to point to some weaknesses in Weinrich's line of arguments. First of all, he supports the claim that verbal forms do not mark tense by referring to certain special verbal uses often employed in fiction. Thus, authors may narrate a futuristic science fiction story with the past tense forms, or tell about past events by means of present tense forms, and so on.[105] However, these phenomena are easily explained within ordinary tense theory as mental transpositions of the primary deictic center of the utterances. The temporal relations obtaining between the (imagined) events and the (imagined) point of reference remain the same as in the normal uses of the tenses.

Furthermore, Weinrich's theses about the linguistic attitudes are debatable, especially at two points. First, it seems questionable to found the claim that the verbal forms indicate linguistic attitude on mere statistics, and moreover, statistics that do not fully substantiate the claim. Second, the same statistics tell us that not only utterances with habitual meaning, like the one above, but also texts such as *das Wissenschaftliche Referat* and *der Philosophische Essay* are dominated by tense group one, which forces Weinrich to state that these genres evoke an attitude of tension in both listener and speaker. It is hard to see how

---

105. Weinrich 1977, 45–47.

these kinds of written utterances, being totally detached from the here and now of the speech situation, can fit the characterization of tense communication as Weinrich formulates it: "In Äußerungen dieser Art ist der Sprecher gespannt und seine Rede geschärft, weil es für ihn um Dinge geht, *die ihn unmittelbar betreffen und die daher auch der Hörer im Modus der Betroffenheit aufnehmen soll. Sprecher und Hörer sind engagiert; sie haben zu agieren und zu reagieren.*"[106]

Pace Weinrich, I would argue that there is no significant correlation between his tense groups and the linguistic attitudes of tension and relaxation. Even though there is a connection between tense group two and the relaxed attitude, the same goes for some forms belonging to tense group one, such as the English *present tense*. The pragmatic conditions of the here and now of the speech situation and the semantics of the verbal forms seem more pertinent to defining the phenomenon than the text-types of narration and discussion as defined by Weinrich. However, this does not invalidate the hypothesis that linguistic attitudes can be indicated by verbal forms. An alternative way of looking at this problem is presented in my discussion of communicative appeal in chapter 5.

2.5. The Grammaticalization Approach

The so-called grammaticalization approach, represented within biblical studies most notably by David Andersen, John Cook, and Alexander Andrason, has cast new light on the Biblical Hebrew verbal system with its combination of typological and diachronic perspectives. It was stated above that a reliable result of these studies is that the semantic evolution of the Biblical Hebrew verbal forms starts from two main nontensed source domains that gradually develop tense meanings. One of these lines of development, or "pathways," is traveled by *qotel* and *yiqtol*-L and runs from progressive, via imperfective, to future; the other, to which *qatal* and *yiqtol*-S belong, runs from resultative, via perfect and eventually to past. There are some diverging opinions among these authors concerning the details of the diachronic reconstruction as well as the overall synchronic description of the meanings of the verbal forms. There is also no total agreement about the semantic range of all forms in the diachronic stage represented by Biblical Hebrew. In my own assessment, both *qatal* and *yiqtol*-S range from "resultative/perfect" to past meaning, and *qotel* and *yiqtol*-L are "progressive/imperfective" as well as future. This statement has to be qualified

---

106. Weinrich 1977, 36; emphasis added. My translation: "In utterances of this kind, the speaker is eager and his speech intense, since he is talking about things that concern him directly—things that the listener therefore also should receive with an attitude of concern. Speaker and listener are highly involved; they have to act and react."

by my definitions of the terms resultative and progressive, which will be given in section 3.4.1 and 3.4.2. The main point at this stage is not exactly what the terms mean but that the range covers both aspectual and temporal uses. In this section, I shall clarify my position with regard to certain claims made by the aforementioned authors.

Andersen suggests that *qatal* at an early stage underwent a semantic split, where it developed progressive meaning alongside its earlier resultative meaning, due to reanalysis of the latter.[107] The progressive meaning, he argues, lies behind the future and habitual uses of *weqatalti*, whereas the resultative meaning has given rise to the perfect and perfective meanings of the free-standing *qatal*. This might seem plausible in view of the fact that progressives tend to develop both future and habitual meanings, but an even more pertinent argument *against* such a conclusion is that the *weqatalti* never has a prototypically progressive meaning in Biblical Hebrew, and neither do the cognate forms in other Semitic languages that Andersen cites as evidence.[108] Andersen also presents typological parallels in the shape of verbal constructions with double resultative/progressive meaning in Japanese and Dravidian languages.[109] However, as he points out, the lexical meaning of the verb (the *Aktionsart*; see section 3.2) in these constructions decides whether it has resultative or progressive meaning. Biblical Hebrew *weqatalti*, on the other hand, has future and habitual meaning regardless of the lexical class of the verb.

Karen Ebert, who has studied the phenomenon of resultative-progressive ambiguity in several languages, confirms the principle that the *Aktionsart* of the verb decides whether it gets resultative or progressive meaning.[110] Less often, the derived progressive meaning of the resultative form generalizes to all lexical verbal types, but, according to Ebert's reconstruction of the development, this happens only if the ordinary progressive becomes a general present.[111] If we were to reconcile this scenario with Andersen's hypothesis of the progressive *qatal*, we would have to imagine that an originally resultative *qatal* eventually turned progressive and supplanted the former progressive (*yiqtol*-L) before being replaced itself by *qotel*. This is very unlikely, especially considering that *yiqtol*-L in Biblical Hebrew, in contrast to *weqatalti*, have some prototypically progressive uses (4.2.1).

---

107. Andersen 2000, 41–42, 45–46.
108. Andersen 2000, 36–39. Andersen (p. 54) also offers three examples of free-standing *qatal* in Biblical Hebrew, where he considers that the old progressive meaning has been preserved (2 Kgs 5:6 [*šālaḥtî*]; Jer 3:22 [*'ātānû*]; Judg 20:40 [*'ālâ*]). However, although it is possible to translate with the English progressive form in these cases, as Andersen does, the perfect (2 Kgs 5:6; Jer 3:22) or the pluperfect (Judg 20:40) serves just as well.
109. Andersen 2000, 40–41.
110. Ebert 1995, 186–91.
111. Ebert 1995, 199–200.

```
                  ↗ frequentative → habitual ---- ┐-------------→ modal → (modal future)
        iterative                                  ├ imperfective
                  ↘ continuative  → progressive - ┘-------------→ present-future
```

FIGURE 1. Andrason's diachronic pathways of *yiqtol*-L (adapted from Andrason 2012b).

Another split pathway is proposed for *yiqtol*-L by Andrason (not to be confused with Andersen!) in order to account for what he refers to as the "indicative" and the "modal" uses of *yiqtol*-L.[112] Andrason suggests that the various modal nuances that can be expressed by the form can be derived from its habitual meaning. The habitual meaning, in turn, is supposed to be based not on the progressive but on a frequentative meaning, which goes back to an original iterative meaning.[113] According to Andrason, a parallel pathway from the same iterative starting point leads via continuative meaning to progressive, the latter of which coalesces with the habitual meaning, forming a general indicative/imperfective stage on the pathway (see figure 1).[114] There are some debatable points in Andrason's reconstruction of the *yiqtol*-L pathway. I shall focus on the portion of the inferential chain that, in my opinion, is the weakest—namely, the habitual-modal link.

First, the alleged connection between the habitual and the modal meanings of the *yiqtol*-L consists in the fact that verbal forms used for the expression of habituality are sometimes ambiguous between a habitual reading and an ability-reading. By means of an illustrative example, Andrason explains that "the sentence *He speaks Spanish* may mean that the person does it repeatedly: *He speaks Spanish every day at school* or that he knows how to and thus can speak this language: *He will help you with this translation; he speaks Spanish*."[115] Thus, it is clear that habituality functionally overlaps the modality of ability. Now, the modality of ability, in turn, is known to have its own diachronic pathway. It starts with the basic meaning of denoting mental or physical abilities in animate subjects (*I can read*) and continues gradually by analogical extension to develop a general meaning of possibility, "root possibility" (*This dam can burst*).[116] Other

---

112. Andrason 2010b, 30, 35.
113. Andrason 2010b, 25; see also Andrason 2012a, 17. "Iterative" meaning indicates that "the action is repeated on one occasion" (Bybee, Perkins, and Pagliuca 1994, 317). Example: *The child was coughing when I first met her.* "Frequentative" means that "the action occurs frequently, not necessarily habitually, nor necessarily on one occasion, as the iterative" (Bybee, Perkins, and Pagliuca 1994, 317). Example: *Last year I visited my parents several times.*
114. "Continuative" meaning is to "keep on doing what is being done" (Bybee, Perkins, and Pagliuca 1994, 317), as in *I tried to soothe him but he **kept crying**.*
115. Andrason 2012a, 17–18.
116. For the evolution of *can*, see 1994, 192.

modal meanings are also inferred, such as epistemic (*They can[= may] win, but I'm not sure*), intentional (*I can get that door for you*), permissive (*You can take another sandwich if you like*), and prohibitive (*. . . —no, sorry, on closer thought, you can't*).[117] In some languages, future meaning can develop, but this is not common within this type of modality.[118] Thanks to the overlap between habituality and ability, Andrason's argument goes, it is possible to establish a pathway from habitual meaning to the various kinds of modality that can be inferred from ability.

However, there are good reasons to doubt that habituality gave rise to the modal meanings of *yiqtol*-L. The link from habituality to ability in the first place and from ability to general modality in the second is too weak. As for the habituality-ability link, one problem is that the habitual function is by definition generalizing and accordingly can only be used to imply *general* abilities, not specific abilities, as in the examples within brackets above. By contrast, *yiqtol*-L, as well as auxiliaries like *can*, often expresses *situation-specific* possibility (4.2.2). To get an idea of just how unrelated habituality is to situation-specific ability, one can insert real habitual constructions in the place of "can" in the examples within brackets above (*This dam usually bursts*; *They usually win but I'm not sure*; *I usually get that door for you*, etc.).

As for the link between ability and modality, ability is an unlikely source for several kinds of modal functions that *yiqtol*-L can have. The idea of ability is connected with *allowance* and is too inherently passive to be used for commands (*Speak thus to my Lord Esau* / cf. *You can/may speak thus*) or expressions of strong obligation or necessity (*Our livestock must go with us* / cf. *can/may go with us*).[119] A future construction in the same context works better (*You are going to speak thus*). Below (4.2.2), I argue that these and other modalities can be inferred naturally from the prospective/future meaning that is a secondary function of the progressive (imperfective/present) verbal type in many languages.[120]

The second tenuous connection in Andrason's semantic reconstruction of *yiqtol*-L is the iterative-frequentative-habitual chain. It is based entirely on the idea that *yiqtol*-L originates from a verbal form that was morphologically marked by reduplication and denoted iterative action, which cannot be said to be sufficiently proven.[121] The main arguments against an iterative-frequentative-habituality path in *yiqtol*-L, however, are typological and semantic, for, although

---

117. See Bybee, Perkins, and Pagliuca 1994, 192, 197–99, 240, 266; Andrason 2010b, 35–36.
118. Bybee, Perkins, and Pagliuca 1994, 266.
119. Gen 32:5; Exod 10:26.
120. "Prospective" can be replaced by "preparative." For the distinction between these terms, see subsection 3.4.3.
121. Andrason (2010b, 41–42) traces *yiqtol*-L from an original *yaqattal*, cognate with the Akkadian *iparras*.

TABLE 3. Evidence for an iterative-continuative-progressive-habitual pathway in verbal forms (based on Bybee et al. 1994, 160–74; the asterisk indicates reduplicated forms)

Iterative	Continuative	Progressive	Habitual	Language
X	X	X	X	Gugu-Yalanji*
X	X		X	Atchin
X		X	X	Rukai*
		X	X	Nakanai*
X		X		Karok
X	X			Baluchi, Tok Pisin*, Yessan-Mayo*

the description of the diachronic pathways of reduplicated verbal forms from iterative to imperfective as described by Andrason and sketched in figure 1 above follows the model outlined by Bybee, Perkins, and Pagliuca, the fact is that the data adduced by Bybee, Perkins, and Pagliuca themselves provide a stronger case for an iterative-(continuative-)progressive-habitual path in reduplicated verbs (notwithstanding that they do not recognize this possibility themselves).[122] Thus, a closer look at the evidence shows that coexistence of progressive and habitual meaning in a reduplicated form occurs in three languages, which is to be compared with one single case of a frequentative-habitual coexistence.[123] Furthermore, the cases of reduplicated habituals compiled by Bybee, Perkins, and Pagliuca are morphologically closer to the reduplicated progressives than to the reduplicated frequentatives, which might also be an indication that the progressive-habitual connection is more probable.[124] This probability is strengthened by the fact that the tendency of progressives to develop habitual meaning is proven to be universal in other morphological types. By contrast, Bybee, Perkins, and Pagliuca present only one example of a nonreduplicated frequentative-habitual that is not also progressive.[125]

Bybee, Perkins, and Pagliuca base their hypothetical iterative-frequentative-habitual diachronic path on a sample of verbal forms that have iterative, continuative, or frequentative meaning and/or are reduplicated. However, that same sample contains a much higher number of forms that would fit into the

---

122. See the model in Bybee, Perkins, and Pagliuca 1994, 172.
123. Progressive-habitual coexistence in reduplicated forms is found in Gugu-Yalanju, Nakanai and Rukai (Bybee, Perkins, and Pagliuca 1994, 168, table 5.10); frequentative-habitual coexistence is found in Maung (ibid.).
124. See Bybee, Perkins, and Pagliuca 1994, 170, table 5.11. The table shows that habituals and progressives are relatively more common with partial reduplication than frequentatives are.
125. Bybee, Perkins, and Pagliuca 1994, 141; 165, table 5.9 (Slave, form 38).

TABLE 4. Evidence for an iterative-frequentative-habitual pathway in verbal forms (based on Bybee et al. 1994, 160–74; the asterisk indicates reduplicated forms)

Iterative	Frequentative	Habitual	Language
X	X		Bongu, Temne
	X	X	Maung*

iterative-continuative-progressive-habitual path that I suggested above. Table 3 shows the evidence for such a path, according to my reconstruction of the data from Bybee, Perkins, and Pagliuca; table 4 shows the evidence for the iterative-frequentative-habitual path.[126]

This counter-evidence aside, Andrason's thesis that the habitual and the progressive meanings of *yiqtol*-L belong to two distinct diachronic pathways that converge in an imperfective stage makes best sense if the form is a fusion of two originally independent forms, and this we have no reason to believe. The alternative explanation—that the two semantic paths somehow developed in parallel in the same form—is complicated and calls for some justification. Failing that, it is simpler to assume that all the meanings of the form are interrelated and belong to the same path. Above I have already mentioned the abundant evidence for progressives developing habitual meaning. As for frequentative meaning, if it has to be assigned a special place in the semantic evolution of *yiqtol*-L, it could well be thought of as an intermediate station between the progressive and the habitual.

Andrason's approach also differs from mine when it comes to more fundamental questions concerning semantic inquiry in general. To begin with, Andrason is very skeptical toward synchronic approaches to semantics. Claiming that the different meanings expressed by verbal forms must appear as heterogeneous and chaotic from a synchronic perspective, he proposes a "panchronic" method that explains synchronic facts as the result of diachronic processes.[127] In this perspective, the meaning of a form cannot be expected to be reducible to one underlying semantic category such as tense or aspect.[128] Rather, it is an "amalgamation" of the meanings of the form, the "sum of all of its uses in all possible

---

126. See especially tables 5.7 (p. 162), 5.9 (p. 165), 5.10 (p. 168). "Karok" in my table 3 refers to Karok verbal form no. 19 in Bybee, Perkins, and Pagliuca 1994, table 5.7 (p. 162). Instead of "progressive," Bybee, Perkins, and Pagliuca gloss it as "continuous," which is a more general kind of progressive (see definition, Bybee, Perkins, and Pagliuca 1994, 127, 317). "Bongu" in my table 4 refers to Bongu verbal form no. 5 in Bybee, Perkins, and Pagliuca 1994, table 5.9 (p. 165).

127. For a presentation of the panchronic method, see, e.g., Andrason 2010b, 18–22; 2011a, 31–34.

128. Andrason 2010b, 19; 2011b, 3.

environments."[129] This complex situation makes it impossible to maintain a distinction between "inherent" and "contextual" (i.e., semantic and pragmatic) meanings.[130] Another consequence is that semantic distinctions between individual forms "can never be simplified to a single opposition between two domains" (such as imperfective-perfective).[131]

In short, Andrason's method leaves little or no room for some ideas that are important in my own semantic analysis: first, that it is possible to distinguish between semantic and pragmatic meaning; second, that many of the so-called heterogeneous meanings of a form can be reduced to a single underlying meaning through analogic reasoning; third, that it is helpful as far as possible to reduce the semantic difference between two forms to an opposition of two semantic domains, such as the resultative and the progressive, even though each form will be likely to display a certain degree of semantic heterogeneity as a result of having gone through a process of reanalysis.

Yet, I believe that Andrason's borderless "panchronic" method is more a matter of not focusing on dichotomies than escaping them, for he does at times presuppose them himself. Thus, whereas Andrason claims that the different meanings developed over time by verbal forms are heterogeneous and not reducible to single overarching meaning-labels that distinguish them from other forms, he also argues that each form *originates* in only one single homogeneous input meaning. Moreover, this input is supposed to be "semantically transparent and cognitively plausible" at every stage of its evolution, which is to say that "any value of the formation [i.e., a verbal form] should be *easily* derivable from the initial expression."[132] This seems to contradict the earlier claim that the various meanings of forms are heterogeneous.

Regardless of whether or not these seemingly contradictory claims can somehow be reconciled within Andrason's theory, his quest for a "cognitively plausible" verbal semantics is very much in line with the aim of finding basic semantic meanings by means of the criteria of invariance and cognitive precedence described in subsection 1.3.2 above. One difference is that I do not consider original meanings as basic if they are no longer in use. Another difference that makes it difficult to compare our methods is that Andrason does not pay much attention to the definitions of either the input values of the verbal forms, or of the taxis-, aspect-, tense-, or modal values they are said to subsequently acquire.[133] A third difference is the factor of frequency, which, in the final analysis, appears to eclipse all other factors in Andrason's semantic approach. Thus, on the one

---

129. Andrason 2011b, 18; see also 2012d, 10.
130. Andrason 2011b, 18.
131. See Andrason 2011a, 29.
132. Andrason 2010b, 3, 28; italics original.
133. See, e.g., Andrason 2011b, 12, 13–14, 17. For the concept of taxis, see section 2.1.

hand, the input value is described as the "prototypical" or "core" meanings that cognitively motivate all the other uses.[134] On the other hand, exactly the same qualities, prototypicality and core-ness, are ascribed to those meanings that are most *frequent* in each form, which is something completely different.[135]

Another inconsistency in Andrason's semantics is that he makes a sharp distinction between those developments that are based on the "virtues" intrinsic to the form itself and those that are induced from the contexts in which the forms appear.[136] This is an approval of the distinction between semantics and pragmatics, which he elsewhere claims to be untenable.

For these reasons, I do not find that Andrason's radical panchrony offers a viable alternative to the approach chosen in this study. However, his method of letting diachronic and typological facts inform the synchronic understanding of the Biblical Hebrew verbal system is very rewarding and has inspired my own approach, especially with regard to *qatal* and *wayyiqtol* (4.3, 4.4).

John Cook's semantic analysis is based on the recognition of the need of a synchronic perspective, in which semantic meanings are identified with due consideration to the interplay of the forms within the system as a whole.[137] His definitions of tense and aspect are basically similar to the definitions used in the present study. Thus, he defines the categories by drawing on Declerck's factors of reference time (my "focused time") and orientation time (my "deictic center").[138] He uses a kind of limit-based aspect definition, where the perfect is counted as an aspect and the aorist aspect ("perfective") is understood in terms of the inclusion of reference time in event time (the totality view of perfective aspect).[139] A difference between Cook's approach and my own is that I do not consider that the limit-based system is the best way of describing the aspectual character of the Biblical Hebrew verbal system.

Another issue is Cook's principle of associating each form with one single TAM-meaning as a defining, or "general," meaning that explains all the specific meanings that the form is able to express in the texts.[140] While I concur with Cook's call for an explanatory semantics based on clearly defined and discrete conceptual categories, I do not find that his principles for assigning the general meaning features to the forms are entirely clear. Cook considers the

---

134. Andrason 2010b, 3, 28; 2012a, 9.
135. Andrason 2011b, 18: "In between the two edges of a path, the prototypical and most frequent meanings of the formation are located." Cf. p. 49, where statistical analysis is pointed out as the proper method for establishing "coreness and periphericity" in the semantics of the verbal forms. See also the discussion in subsection 1.3.2 above.
136. Andrason 2010b, 36; 2012b, 317–20; 2013b, 19.
137. Cook 2012, 178, 191.
138. Cook 2012, 69.
139. Cook 2012, 67. Cook uses the terms "reference frame" and "event frame."
140. Cook 2012, 184–85, 190.

whole verbal system to be centered around a perfective-imperfective opposition, in which the main perfective proponent is *qatal* and the main imperfective is *yiqtol*-L (Cook's *yiqtol*). This requires that the perfect meaning of *qatal* is considered as a secondary, "persistent meaning," (i.e., a remnant from an earlier stage) despite the fact that perfect meaning in Biblical Hebrew, according to Cook, is expressed only by *qatal*.[141] In *yiqtol*, on the other hand, imperfective aspect is not considered as a persistent meaning even though the form has largely lost the central imperfective function of expressing progressive meaning to *qotel*, while itself developing into the main form for aspect-neutral future reference. The *wayyiqtol*, finally, is called a past tense, although it no doubt has perfective meaning more often than *qatal*. This creates the paradox that the central perfective-imperfective opposition is ascribed to the two forms within the system (*qatal* and *yiqtol*, respectively) that are least restricted to these meanings and most specialized for meanings that are rare in the other two forms. In sum, there is no obvious principle behind the identification of the general meanings of the forms, whether in terms of diachronic precedence or frequency.

More than anything else, Cook's semantic classifications are intended to fit the typology used by Bybee, Perkins, and Pagliuca, with the exception that the *qatal* is called a perfective, rather than an "old anterior."[142] Within this framework, Cook convincingly argues for the centrality of aspect in the semantics of the Biblical Hebrew verbal system.[143] However, since the typology is not designed to say anything about the basic meanings of the forms, I find it less suitable for the purposes of the present study.

As regards the description of the various uses of the Biblical Hebrew forms, Cook holds that the perfect meaning sometimes expressed by the *wayyiqtol* is altogether pragmatic ("contextual"), since it "does not apply in enough cases to explain it as a persistence of the form's presumably earlier perfect meaning."[144] This is a difficult question, but my own assessment is that the perfect uses of *wayyiqtol* are too atypical for an ordinary past tense form (4.4.1).[145]

2.6. Summary

In my comments on the state of research, I have engaged critically with the main approaches to explaining the temporal meanings of the Biblical Hebrew verbal system. Starting with theories that consider some kind of tense meanings

---

141. Cook 2012, 207; see p. 264 on the lack of perfect meaning in *wayyiqtol*.
142. Cook, 2012, 207.
143. Cook 2012, esp. 270. For a brief and comprehensive statement, see also Cook 2006.
144. Cook 2012, 264.
145. On this issue, see Andrason's conclusion, 2011b, 48.

as semantically marked by the forms (2.1), I argued that both absolute and relative tense fail to account for a very large portion of the usages of the forms. While this is probably a widely accepted claim as far as absolute tense is concerned, the reason why it is also valid for relative tense is that the concept of relative tense is understood in a way that confuses aspect and tense. The most common fault resulting from this is that perfect meaning (present or past) is not distinguished from true past and relative past meaning. In technical terms, the root of the problem is that relative tense is defined in terms of the relation between a deictic center and event time, instead of the relation between a deictic center and focused time, as it should.

Section 2.2 described how the concept of aspect has developed from ancient to modern times. It was shown that a decisive shift in the understanding of the completed category took place after the work of Curtius, leading to the split between the aorist/perfective and the perfect category that is so common today. Several theoretical contradictions in the most common definitions of the perfective category were pointed out, but it was also shown that the ancient conception of the completed and uncompleted categories are contradicted by some usages of forms ascribed to those categories. In conclusion, the most important definitions of aspect, which I call the classical, the internal-vs.internal, and the limit-based, are more descriptive than explanatory. Inasmuch as these definitions dominate also in Biblical Hebrew scholarship, they limit the explanatory power of the aspectual approach. The addition of other aspect categories has not resolved the fundamental theoretical problem. Consequently, if aspect is going to be our basic semantic category for the Biblical Hebrew verbal forms, we need to modify the existing definitions.

Although modality (2.3) can be expressed with Biblical Hebrew verbal forms, I found little support for the idea that an inherent modality explains the future and generalizing meaning of certain forms. From a typological perspective, it can be stated beyond doubt that the Hebrew forms do not stem from modal sources. As for the theory that future and generalizing meanings are modal per se, it neglects the role of factuality in the definition of modality. As a result, the fundamental difference between future and generalizing meanings, on the one hand, and modal meanings, on the other, is overlooked. The same is true for the similarity of future and generalizing meanings with other declarative meanings.

The somewhat nebuluous semantic category of linguistic attitude, which distinguishes between verbal forms that mark relaxed speech and those that mark tense speech, was found to be partly useful (2.4). However, the grounds upon which scholars within this approach ascribe verbal forms to either tense or relaxed speech are obscure. The main problem is that tense speech includes generalizing and future meanings—something that seems blatantly counter-intuitive. Based on comparisons between different kinds of declarative sentences, it seems better to posit that the proximity of the represented event is a precondition for tense speech. In this way, an analysis of linguistic attitude, which was once introduced as an alternative to a tense-oriented approach to verbal systems, could be relevant for the study of tense meanings as well as for the semantic distinctions between the Biblical Hebrew verbal forms.

The purpose of the final section (2.5) of this chapter was to motivate my take on the semantic evolution of the Biblical Hebrew verbal system by explaining in what respects it differs from the approaches of some of the pioneer studies within the grammaticalization approach—studies to which the present work is much indebted. Thus, in contrast to David T. Andersen, I do not think that any of the uses of *qatal* are progressive or developed along a progressive diachronic path. As for Alexander Andrason, I do not follow his reconstruction of an iterative-frequentative-habitual-modal pathway in *yiqtol*-L. I am also more optimistic than Andrason when it comes to the possibility of distinguishing between pragmatic and semantic meaning. Finally, although John Cook's analysis of aspect and tense have much in common with my own, I differ from Cook with regard to his use of limit-based aspect for defining the meaning of the forms and his identification of *qatal* and *yiqtol* as the two main proponents of a fundamental opposition between perfective and imperfective aspect within the Biblical Hebrew verbal system.

CHAPTER 3

A Theory of Aspect and Tense

AGAINST THE BACKDROP of the complex of problems concerning tense and aspect described in the previous chapter, I shall now deal with the first two tasks that were set up in relation to the aim of this study—namely, to define aspect and the possible aspectual categories and to account for how tense meanings are derived from aspectual meanings.

Section 3.1 in the present chapter introduces various contextual factors that contribute to the interpretation of tense independently of the semantics of the verbal form. As a background for the discussion about aspect, section 3.2 describes the phenomenon of the *Aktionsarten*, which are lexical categories of the verb intersecting in different ways with the aspects. Section 3.3 discusses in some detail the concept of focused time, which is a central factor in the definition of both tense and aspect. In section (3.4), I introduce the category of "stage-based aspect," and in the following section (3.5), I explain why this aspectual category defines the semantic character of the forms of the universal progressive and resultative pathways better than the limit-based aspect presented in section 2.2. Finally, section 3.6 describes how tense meanings may develop through reanalysis of the stage-based aspects.

To illustrate the theory, English language examples are used throughout, apart from a few German ones, which are used where English forms do not serve to illustrate a certain point. The application to Biblical Hebrew will follow in chapter 4.

3.1. Introductory Note: Nonsemantic Factors Indicating Tense

In many languages, tense is indicated by the semantics of the verbal forms. The English simple past is one example of a form that directly marks past time reference (*Dad came*). Other forms do not mark tense as unambiguously, although at the same time it is clear that their range of possible temporal interpretations is semantically restricted. A typical such restricted range is the one found in the German perfect, which is used with either present or past meaning. Thus:

(1) a. Vati ist gekommen! Er sitzt in der Küche.
    Dad has come. He is sitting in the kitchen.
  b. Gestern ist Vati gekommen.
    Yesterday, dad came.

Even though the past interpretation of the perfect here is contextually indicated by the adverb *gestern*, the tense also has something to do with the semantics of the perfect form. This is proven by the fact that the perfect does not combine as easily with future adverbials, such as *morgen* ("tomorrow"). By contrast, the German present tense form, which shares with the perfect the property of referring to present situations, is not good with past adverbials and could not be exchanged with the perfect in (1b). Historically, the perfect meaning of the German perfect is older than the past meaning, and we are safe to conclude that the latter developed as an inference of the former. Even more accurate, as I shall continue to argue further below, would be to posit a *resultative* meaning of the form as the rational basis for the inference.

There are also nonfinite verbal forms whose temporal meaning depends completely on the context. Thus, the English perfect and progressive participles always share the tense value of the main verb:

(2) a. Having mended the car, he informed / will inform the owner.
  b. I had / will have my breakfast sitting on a cosy balcony.

The possibility of using syntactically dependent, nonfinite forms that borrow their tense from a finite verb is exploited to the full in clause-chaining languages, where lengthy sequences of speech and even entire narratives may consist of a series of nonfinite verbs syntactically dependent on only one main verb. The textual context can, of course, indicate tense even with finite verbs, and sometimes—for example, with historic presents—it can be necessary for a correct interpretation of tense:

(3) Yesterday, I was walking on the street when up comes this man.

If examples (2) and (3) illustrate the function of the spoken (or written) context in the interpretation of tense, another context with bearing on tense is the purely situational one—that is, various kinds of extratextual knowledge. That this factor alone often gives sufficient information for temporal interpretation is evident in the following examples where explicit tense markers are absent:

(4) a. Napoleon MARCH to Moscow.
    b. I BE BORN here and I DIE here.
    c. Guess who I MEET tonight.

The tense of sentence (4a) would in our post-Napoleon era be taken as past. In (4b) the first verb is naturally interpreted as past and the second as future, since birth to a living and speaking person is always a past occurrence and death a future one. Sentence (4c) uttered by a person returning home late at night has probably in more than nine cases out of ten a past meaning, whereas a future meaning is the most likely option if said by a person who is preparing to go out.

The possibility of anchoring the tense of an utterance by means of temporal adverbs as well as interclausal and situational context makes the obligatory marking of tense and/or aspect that we see in the majority of finite verbs across languages almost superfluous. However, while a few languages do lack tense, and a very small minority are radical enough to dispose of tense and aspect altogether, the normal state of affairs in language is to allow a redundancy of tense-determining components.[1] It is important to be aware of this complex interplay of factors when trying to determine the function of verbal semantics in the representation of tense in Biblical Hebrew (see, e.g., the various verb-external factors in the temporal interpretation of invariant resultative *qatal* in subsection 4.3.1).

3.2. *Aktionsart*

Tense and aspect are meaning categories that define the events that we speak about with regard to time. An event is here understood in the broadest possible way as any phenomenon that is considered with regard to its extension in time. In this view, everything that is represented by the predicate of a clause is an event. Some linguists prefer the term "situation" for this concept.[2] In that case, the term "event" is often understood in a narrower sense as denoting a subclass of situations. Carlota Smith, for instance, counts events as the major subclass of situations together with states.[3] The main difference between events and states according to this definition is that events are dynamic and states are static.[4] The

---

1. On tenseless languages, see Comrie 1985, 50–53, Binnick 1991; 444–47; C.S. Smith 2008, 234–40. On languages without both aspect and tense, see Dahl 2001.
2. E.g., Klein, 1994; C.S. Smith 1997, 17.
3. C.S. Smith 1997, 35.
4. C.S. Smith 1997, 35–36. Smith characterizes events as discrete, bounded entities and says that this feature can be derived from the dynamism of the event. Binnick (1991, 188; referring to Dowty) writes that "events are properties of intervals of time, but only those at which something

broader understanding of "event" as a term for both dynamic and static situations is not only inherent in Reichenbach's theory (see 2.2.3 above) but also found in more recent studies.[5]

In the present study, dynamism is thus not taken to be the defining property of events. However, the dynamic event is understood as prototypical for the class of events as such. Furthermore, the verb is taken as the primary linguistic category for representing events. Accordingly, prototypical verbs are marked for dynamism. This semantic property is here called *dynamicity* (adjective: *dynamic*).

As opposed to the dynamic verbs, *stative* verbs denote phenomena without any necessarily perceptible manifestations of dynamism. To this group belong postural verbs (*stand, sit, lie*), verbs of knowing (*know, remember*), emotion/attitude (*love, hate*), ownership (*have, own*), verbs of habitation (*live, dwell*), and verbs of inert perception (*see, hear, feel*).

Dynamic events bring about change, whereas states, being nondynamic in themselves, do not change except by the intrusion of some dynamic event. The notion of change is lexically encoded in the so-called *telic* verbs (noun: *telicity*), which denote events with specific inherent results. Verbs unmarked for telicity—that is, atelic verbs—may convey a telic meaning by the addition of qualifying adverbs or objects. Thus, the verb *to run* as in *Ingrid is running* is atelic, but by adding the phrase *to the station*, the result brought about by the event (being at the station) is indicated and the meaning of the whole verbal phrase is telic.

The *duration* of events is also dependent on dynamism, in that dynamic events are maintained by dynamism, whereas states are interrupted by dynamism. The duration of the event, and the lack thereof, is reflected in the semantic features of *durativity* and *punctuality*. The importance of durativity as a factor in the classification of events stems from the fact that prototypical events are transitory, rather than permanent, phenomena.

A common term for the semantic properties connected with the concepts mentioned here is *Aktionsart*. Although the *Aktionsarten* are properly understood as the properties of the linguistic units and not of the events themselves, I will occasionally speak of "telic/atelic events" as shorthand for events that are signified by telic/atelic verbs.

It is to be noted that the polarization between stative and dynamic meanings is present also within the nonverbal classes. An adjective like *rude* has dynamic connotations entirely lacking in *blue*, for example, and embedded in a progressive construction it is practically equivalent to a dynamic verb:[6]

---

enters into a new state." See also Binnick 2006, 245: "States are properties of times, whereas events and processes occur at times."

5. See, e.g., Stutterheim, Caroll, and Klein 2009, 195.
6. See Comrie 1976, 36.

(5) Oh sorry, am I being rude? (= am I behaving improperly?)

The existence of both dynamicity and stativity in verbs as well as adjectives attests to the fact that word classes are defined not solely by semantic content but also formally in terms of morphological and syntactic properties. In the case of the English examples above, as in many languages, the formal factors alone are sufficient to recognize a verb. In Biblical Hebrew, as well as other Semitic languages, a formal distinction between verbs and the nominal word-classes is not always made.[7]

Just as language provides means for dynamicization of stative lexemes, so there is also a corresponding phenomenon of stativization of dynamic verbs in the shape of various kinds of generalizing meanings.[8] Consider, for example, the following sentences:

(6) a. Henry drinks two cups of coffee every morning.
 b. Ella speaks French.
 c. Deer shed their antlers.

Sentence (6a), besides referring nonspecifically to several occasions of coffee drinking, makes specific reference to a state—namely, Henry's *habit* of coffee drinking. Sentence (6b), presumably, speaks first and foremost of about Ella's *ability* to speak French. In (6c), we are informed about a normal physical *disposition* of a certain species of animal. The latter sentence is special for having *generic* meaning, which means that the stativized predicate characterizes kinds rather than individuals.[9]

In stativized sentences, there is thus a kind of double exposure between the underlying state, which is the habit, ability, disposition, etc. that is implied by the predicate, and its actualization, which is the dynamic event that is lexically encoded by the verb. Typically, stativized predicates are associated with repetition of the dynamic event, or *pluractionality*. Pluractionality can be analyzed with regard to either the *macroevent*, which is the plurality of events seen as a whole, or with regard to the *microevents*—that is, the individual instantiations of the macroevent. Pluractionality is not obligatory in stativized predicates, however. The next example, taken from the New Testament story of Jesus calming

---

7. See the adjectival *qatal* in Biblical Hebrew (4.3.3). The corresponding conjugation in Akkadian, (*parVs*), is very frequent with adjectives as well as with verbs, and the inflection is used also for the predication of nouns (Huehnergard 1997, 25–26, 219–23).

8. On generalizing meanings as stative, see C.S. Smith 1997, 33–34; Bertinetto and Lenci 2012, 861; Carlson 2012, 829.

9. C.S. Smith 1997, 33; Carlson 2012, 830–31.

the storm, illustrates the fact that it is possible to make a generalizing statement based on one single event:

(7) Who is he? He commands even the winds and the water, and they obey him.[10]

The event may even be wholly potential. For example, the following utterance may be true regardless of whether the machine ever crushes an orange or not:

(8) This machine crushes oranges.[11]

All the predicates in (6)–(8) have a generalizing function and refer to more or less permanent states. They do have aspectual properties (see 3.4.2) but are less illustrative in that regard than predicates referring to prototypical events.

Aktionsart is distinct from aspect, but there is doubtlessly a genetic relation in language between atelicity and progressive aspect as well as between telicity and resultative aspect (3.4.1–2), and *Aktionsart* also plays a role in the development of tense from aspect (3.6).

3.3. Focused Time and the Definition of Tense and Aspect

Whereas *Aktionsart* is lexically encoded by the verb, tense and aspect are considered as more peripheral, grammatical categories.[12]

Tense and aspect can be defined in terms of different constellations of certain factors in the speech situation. In line with much modern linguistic research, I assume that the factor variously called "reference time" (in the sense of "time pointed to"), "topic time" or similar is central for both tense and aspect (see above, 2.1, 2.2.3). Since this is a more abstract and nebulous concept than "speech time" and "event time," and even "deictic center," we shall now try to pinpoint more exactly what it stands for by means of an example. Consider the sentence:

(9) The baby is crawling toward the stairs.

10. From the Gospel according to Luke 8:25 (NIV).
11. The example is borrowed from Bertinetto and Lenci 2012, 869.
12. Some linguists use the term "lexical aspect" for what is here called *Aktionsart*, whereas "grammatical aspect" often stands for aspect (Olsen 1997). Other terms used for *Aktionsart* include: "situation aspect" (C.S. Smith 1997), "action" (Bache 1997), "actionality" (Bertinetto and Delfitto 2000). Aspect is also called "viewpoint aspect" (C.S. Smith 1997).

The goal of the speaker and a cooperative listener in this utterance is to arrive at a mutual focus of attention on the same event. In the typical case, this means a sensory perception of a real event. In reality, however, there does not have to be any sensory perception because the listener can "get the message" before seeing what is going on, thanks to the human capacity for mental representation. In fact, the event referred to does not even have to be real. The interpretative process will be similar with an imaginary event, as indeed the above example illustrates. The important thing for successful communication is that speaker and listener know that they are both aware of the same thing, real or imagined, as a consequence of the speech act. Also important to note is that the mutual focus of attention does not span the whole of the event referred to. It starts after the actual event has begun and may well end before it—for instance, with the listener responding something like *Oh, thanks! Just mind your cooking, I'll attend to her*. Thus, we have to distinguish between the *focused content* of the event and the *whole* event. The latter term is the equivalent of the "event-time" or "situation time" in modern tense theory, whereas the time span of the focused content of the event is the interval known as "reference time," taken in the sense of Declerck's "reference time pointed to" or Klein's "topic time," etc. (as opposed to "reference time pointed from," "deictic center," etc; see section 2.1, 2.2.3). When the time interval of the focused content of the event is referred to in this study, it is called "focused time," whereas "event time" is used for the time of the whole event.[13] The relation between the focused time and the event time in example (9) is marked by the act of speech itself. In other words, the act of speech functions as a contrasting event against which a particular part of the event is brought into focus. I shall call this kind of contrasting event a *focalizing* event.[14] The speech act in (9) also has the function of marking the temporal anchor point, or *deictic center*, of the utterance.

With the factors that have been isolated in this example, both tense and aspect can be defined. The function of tense is to describe the temporal location of the mutual focus of attention—or focused time—in relation to the deictic center. Aspect locates the focused time relative to the event; in other words, it defines which part of the event is in focus. This "part of the event," however,

---

13. "Focused time" combines the functions of Declerck's "temporal focus" and "vantage time." The former is decisive for the tense value of the sentence, according to Declerck, whereas the latter defines aspect. See n. 136. A close parallel to focused time is Bohnemeyer's "perspective time," which defines both tense and aspect (Bohnemeyer 2014, 951).

14. Cf. "focalization point" in Bertinetto, Ebert, and deGroot 2000, 527. On a clarifying note, the term "focus" in the linguistic literature often has to do with the information structure of the sentence and then means something other than it does here. In terms of information structure, the "focus" is the part of an utterance that conveys new information—that is, it is a focus of cognitive effort serving to update the working memory rather than a focus of attention to a particular part in the structure of the event (see, e.g., Lambrecht 1994, 213). The two types of focus are not mutually exclusive.

be described in different ways. Above, I have defined aspect in terms of the relation between the focused content of the event and the *limits* of the event. In the next section, I shall describe it in a way that I think is better adapted to the basic semantics of many verbal systems. In this model, the event is viewed as a complex entity consisting of subsequent stages, and the limits of the event play no part in the definition of the basic aspectual categories. Thus, we turn from a limit-based to a stage-based description of aspect.

3.4. Stage-Based Aspect

Telic verbs and phrases denote events that contain a connection between two causally related stages: a preceding, dynamic event and an ensuing, normally stative, event, which is the outcome, or *telos*, of the first one.[15] Without any clear indication as to which of these stages obtains at a given time, such units could easily invite different interpretations. Thus, consider

(10) The gates CLOSE.

By marking the verb of this sentence for focus on either the second stage of the complex event (*are closed*) or the first (*are closing*), the ambiguity as to whether the gates are still open or not is definitely resolved. The particular stage in focus defines the stage-based aspect, according to the definition of aspect as the relation between focused time and the whole event (see the previous section).

3.4.1. Resultative

The *telos*, thus, is the goal or, with a synonymous term, the result of an event. Although the above-mentioned semantic opposition between the resultative and the progressive (*are closed* / *are closing*) in all likelihood stems from the need to distinguish between the result and the preresult stage of the event in connection with telic verbs, it can also be transferred to atelic verbs, mostly with the perfect fulfilling the aspectual function of the resultative. What happens when an atelic verb is conjugated as a perfect is that the general idea of result is attached to it by means of morphology originally designed for telic verbs. In this case, the result is not an inherent *telos* but anything that can be imagined to ensue from the event and is pragmatically relevant—that is, a kind of indirect result. For example:

(11) I have been working hard (result: I am tired, the room is tidy, etc.).

---

15. Predicates with nonstative *telos* would be *to light a fire, burst out in laughter*, etc.

The transfer of the idea of a result to a dynamic verb like *to work* is natural, considering the fact that dynamicity always leads to some change of states. But the idea can spread even to stative verbs:[16]

(12) I have been standing up all day (result: I am tired, my feet are numb, etc.).

Obviously, the event of standing is not totally devoid of dynamism, in spite of being a state, since it causes changes in the states of the participants in the clause. With the perfect morphology, grammar has provided a means to highlight this fact.

For the sake of transparent terminology, I shall call all forms that set the focus of attention on the result stage of an event *resultative*, regardless of whether the verb is telic or atelic. "Resultative" is already an established term in linguistic nomenclature, but my use of the term differs somewhat from the conventional one, according to which resultatives are distinguished from perfects. Vladimir P. Nedjalkov and Sergej J. Jaxontov (1988) have presented several criteria for making the distinction, the first two being the following:

1. The after-effects of the actions expressed by the perfect are nonspecific, and they are not attributed to any particular participant of the situation.
2. The perfect form, unlike the resultative, can be derived from any verb, either transitive, or intransitive, either terminative or durative, including those verbs that denote situations which do not change the state of any participant.[17]

Perfects, according to these criteria, include constructions like *to have worked*, *to have sung*, *to have laughed*, and also the perfect progressive *to have been working*. The resultative category contains verbs for events that change the state of a participant.[18] Some examples would be *to be fallen*, *to be gone*, or the above *to be closed*.

Looking closer at the criteria of Nedjalkov and Jaxontov, we observe that in a resultative sentence, such as *The gates are closed*, the verb refers specifically to the state of the subject referent, whereas in the sentence with an atelic perfect

---

16. Alternatively, perfect morphology applied to stative lexemes may imply inchoative meaning, thus adding a notion of telicity to the stative lexeme. So, for instance, the Nigerian language Engenni has an adjective meaning "sweet," which acquires the meaning "to have become sweet" when it occurs in a certain resultative construction. This and other examples are cited in Bybee, Perkins, and Pagliuca 1994, 75 (N.B., they use the term "anterior" instead of "perfect").
17. Nedjalkov and Jaxontov 1988, 15.
18. Nedjalkov and Jaxontov 1988, 5.

predicate, such as *I have been working hard*, the result is nonspecific and has to be inferred from the context. As we can see, however, Nedjalkov and Jaxontov prefer to speak of "after-effect" instead of "result" in relation to perfects. It is not altogether clear in what way "after-effect" means something other than "result." In a sentence with a perfect, telic predicate, like *I have set the table*, the most obvious after-effect of the event of setting would be that *the table is set*. In what way, then, does the "result" referred to by the resultative sentence *The table is set* differ from the "after-effect" expressed by *I have set the table*?[19]

Nedjalkov and Jaxontov also state that the perfect expresses the "continuing relevance" of the event referred to. This term—with some variations—is common in the literature. Jouko Lindstedt calls it "current relevance" and states that it distinguishes the perfect from the resultative: "Semantically, the change from resultative into perfect means the generalization of meaning from 'current result' to 'current relevance.' Lexically, this is reflected in the spread of the gram from telic to atelic verbs."[20]

I am not convinced that Lindstedt's distinction between current result and current relevance adequately expresses the difference between prototypical resultatives and perfects. The two concepts are not mutually exclusive, since "relevance" pertains to the evaluation of knowledge, whereas "result" pertains to the objects of knowledge. If anything, the continuing relevance of a past event would seem to consist entirely in the fact that there is some result from it. Thus, I submit that both prototypical resultatives and perfects are characterized by setting the focus on results, the difference being that, in the former, the result is always a *telos*, whereas in the latter it can be anything that ensues from an event. For this common semantic function, a common term is needed, and "resultative" seems most fitting for the purpose. This choice is all the more justified considering that a morphological distinction between prototypical resultatives and perfects is more or less deficient in many languages, for example, Biblical Hebrew, which has no special resultative form for intransitive telic verbs.[21] Rather than a change from resultative meaning to something else, then, the step from the prototypical resultative to the perfect represents a spread of the aspectual meaning of the form in which the idea of result is applied to new lexemes and in new contexts.

In the shape of the perfect, the resultative category undergoes a further development, which has been described as a "gradual relaxation of the requirements on current relevance."[22] In this development, two distinct processes can

---

19. The term "resultative perfect" has been used with reference to this overlap between the perfect and the resultative (Dahl and Hedin 2000, 390).
20. Lindstedt 2000, 368.
21. The only possible candidate for a real, prototypical resultative in Biblical Hebrew would be the passive participle, *qatul*, but this form occurs mainly with transitive verbs (Blau 2010, 226).
22. Dahl and Hedin 2000, 391.

be discerned. The first consists of a continued generalization of the concept of result.[23] Thus, the intended result may be indirect instead of direct also with telic verbs (13a), it may be a lasting experience or merit stemming from past events (13b, c),[24] or an interval in space or in time (13d, e):

(13) a. I have done my homework. (Intended indirect result: I am allowed to watch TV).
b. I have made my mistakes.
c. She has received the Pulitzer Prize.
d. The athletes have now run thirty kilometers.
e. I have run this business for many years.

The utterances in (13d–e) illustrate a use of the perfect that is often called "the perfect of persistent situation."[25] It might at first seem odd to interpret them as resultative, since the lexically denoted events are going on at the time of speech. However, this is a natural inference of the atelicity of the verb. It is only with telic predicates that resultative meaning implies completion. Telic events have an incremental structure with a climax occurring at the point of transition into the lexically denoted *telos*, and the resultative aspect always projects the limit between the preresult and the result stage onto that transition point. We can be sure that the incremental phase of the event does not continue beyond it. Atelic events, like living, or walking, on the other hand, have an even structure without any *telos*. This means that a shorter interval of such an event is as "complete" as a longer one.[26] Since there is no *telos*, the resultative aspect can project the limit between the preresult and the result stage at any moment of the lexically denoted event, without necessarily implying that it has ended. Accordingly, a person uttering the statement in (14) as a comment on his/her sunburn may or may not still "be doing" what s/he says that s/he "has been doing." The focus, in either case, is on the result:

(14) You see, I have been walking around in the city without sunscreen.

Besides the generalization of the notion of result, the other process connected with the decrease of current relevance in the perfect is one of *temporalization*.

23. See Declerck (2006, 302) on the distinction between indirect and direct results of the perfect. Declerck, however, considers the notion of result to be only a pragmatic inference, and not the semantic meaning of the perfect.
24. See Detges 2006, 55–56, 65–66.
25. Following Comrie 1976, 60.
26. See Garey 1957, 106: "Atelic verbs are those which do not have to wait for a goal for their realization, but are realized as soon as they begin."

The process can be described as a relaxation of the requirement that the focus of attention be set on the aspectually marked stage of the event. This means that the resultative aspect is overturned and the temporal meaning is changed from present resultative/perfect to simple past meaning (see [1b] above). But as long as the perfect keeps the more prototypical resultative functions as well, the basic meaning of the form remains the same. Temporalization is dealt with further in section 3.6.

The perfect verbal type has one particular characteristic that may appear to prove that it has drifted away from a genuine resultative meaning and acquired a meaning that is more preterite-like—namely, the fact that perfects cannot be modified with the adverbial *still* in the same way as prototypical resultatives can. Compare, for example, the following sentences:

(15) a. The table is still set.
     b. I have still set the table.

Only in sentence (15a) does the adverbial indicate that the result state ensuing from the event of setting the table still exists. Sentence (15b) cannot be read that way. It makes sense only if "still" is understood as a modifier of the whole clause, roughly synonymous with "nevertheless." According to Bybee, Perkins, and Pagliuca, this is because only the resultative refers to the result of the event. The perfect, they say, "points to the action itself."[27] However, the difference probably has more to do with the syntactic properties of the verbal forms than with their semantics. Thus, the more plausible explanation, in my opinion, is that the resultative marker has wider scope in perfects than in prototypical resultatives—that is, it includes both the verb and its modifier.[28] This is what we see in examples (13b–c); the resultative meaning applies not solely to the verb *to run* but to the whole phrases *run thirty kilometers* and *run this business for many years*. In other words, the result is not just some indirect consequence of having run; it is rather a certain distance and a certain amount of time that has been run, as specified by the adverbial modifiers. The hierarchical composition can be given as below:

(16) [[[to run] thirty kilometers/alt. for many years]RES]

Now, the meaning of the adverbial "still" is that an event persists at the time of a deictic center, such as speech time. But, since the perfect form requires that the resultative marker has scope over the adverbial, the combination with *still*

---

27. Bybee, Perkins, and Pagliuca 1996, 65.
28. On this, see Katz 2003, 207.

in (15b) absurdly entails that the clause refers to the result of "still setting the table" (cf. [[[to set the table] still]RES]). Of course, there can be no result of "still setting the table," since that would imply that the adverb "still" does not refer to the time of the deictic center. Consequently, the combination is avoided, not because the perfect is not resultative but because it prevents the adverb from performing its normal semantic function.

With prototypical resultatives, this semantic conflict does not arise. Adverbials like *still* here refer to the result stage of the event and not the precedent part of the event. Accordingly, in (15a) it is the state of being set that persists at the time of speech.[29] This gives the following composition:

(17) [[[to set]RES] still]

There is some evidence that the structures (16) and (17) can occur in one and the same form in Biblical Hebrew (see 3.4.1).

3.4.2. Progressive

As for the aspectual category that focuses the preresult stage, it will be called *progressive*. The prototypical progressive form is constructed on a verb with dynamic and durative *Aktionsart*, representing a dynamic event as ongoing at the focused time.[30] However, in a way that mirrors the expansion of the resultative stage-aspect to atelic verbs, the progressive meaning can migrate beyond its prototypical lexical domain and become attached also to nondurative telic verbs, thereby grammatically adding the idea of a preceding dynamic stage to lexemes that do not denote this notion by themselves. Example:

(18) Carl is winning the race.

Another kind of nonprototypical use of the progressive occurs when the event itself is not actually happening at the time of speech, but the preconditions for the actualization of the event are somehow deemed sufficient to consider it as ongoing. Thus, sentence (19a) below can be uttered by a person who has just jumped out of the bathtub to answer the phone. Sentences (19b–c) are also typically uttered by someone who is actually not performing the action described at the time of speech:

---

29. This criterion for distinguishing between prototypical resultatives and perfects is proposed by Nedjalkov and Jaxontov 1988, 15–16.

30. See the description in Bybee, Perkins, and Pagliuca 1994, 137.

(19) a. May I call you back? I am bathing.
   b. We are building a new house.
   c. I'm taking medicine to get better.

In sentence (19c), the verb has pluractional function. It is not generalizing in the sense that it implies the existence of a habit, predisposition, or similar; it is just an accidental activity that occupies the subject referent for a limited period of time. In other contexts, pluractional progressives may have stronger implication of habituality or other stative conditions, without, however, losing the sense that they refer to something temporary. Comrie gives a couple of examples:[31]

(20) a. We're going to the opera a lot these days.
   b. At that time I was working the night shift.

In comparison, habituals with the English present tense (6a) imply a more static condition.[32] The relative lack of dynamicity in the form is a main reason why it is not, according to the established understanding, counted as a progressive.[33] However, the present does nevertheless resemble the progressive in some ways. In the words of Anna Granville Hatcher, "the progressive, the invader construction, has not yet driven out the simple form from every predication of an activity obviously in progress."[34] The most prototypically progressive use of the simple present that Hatcher mentions involves unequivocally dynamic verbs:

(21) You walk as if your feet hurt.[35]

Another case in point is a class of predications designating events of "nonovert activity." Hatcher's examples include the following:

(22) My back (head, stomach) aches. My nose itches. I see it. I hear it.[36]

One may of course object that the events referred to in these clauses should be called states rather than activities, but Hatcher's description—"activity in progress"—captures well the element of transitoriness that these states have in common with dynamic events. Moreover, the question is whether "state" is

---

31. Comrie 1976, 37.
32. See Comrie, 1976, 37.
33. Bybee, Perkins, and Pagliuca 1994, 141.
34. Hatcher 1951, 261.
35. Hatcher 1951, 274. See further discussion on this example in section 5.3.
36. Hatcher 1951, 266.

really an adequate term for perceptions, since they normally expose the perceiver to impressions that are anything but stative. For this reason, Smith says that a perception verb like *to see* "is not a simple stative when it has an Activity complement," as in

(23) a. I saw him run.
b. I saw him running.[37]

Perception verbs are naturally associated with the idea of a result and, consequently, are very susceptible to stage-aspectual morphology. The present tense here takes the same paradigmatic slot as the progressive (*I'm about to see* [3.4.3], *I see, I have seen*).

Furthermore, from an aspectual point of view, the present tense resembles the progressive even when it comes to its generalizing meanings. Generalizing meaning occurs when a form typically used to refer to dynamic events is understood as referring to a state, in the shape of a habit or similar. It overturns the dynamic character of the progressive, but not the aspectual meaning. Thus, a present tense with habitual meaning, for example, sets focused time on the atelic habitual state, just as the progressive form sets focused time on the atelic activity in dynamic atelic events:

(24) Lucy plays the piano (cf. Lucy is playing the piano).

Just like any progressive, the generalizing present contrasts aspectually with a resultative, which puts focus on some implied result following the state (*Lucy has played the piano* [possible result: she has strong fingers]).

Accordingly, since it is very hard to make a semantic distinction between the English present and progressive constructions, and since they have the same stage-aspectual properties, they can both be considered as members of the progressive family. However, since the English present tense does not normally stand in for the most prototypical progressive functions, it can be called a progressive form only with some qualification. From the diachronic perspective, it might, of course, be termed an "old progressive," since it was formerly used with prototypically progressive meaning. The question is whether it is possible to find a qualification that works on the synchronic level. In chapter 5, I shall suggest that the English present tense belongs to a type of progressive with "reduced appeal." For now, we shall only keep in mind that, when I occasionally use the English present tense as an example of a progressive form, it is not a prototypical progressive.

37. C.S. Smith 1997, 57.

3.4.3. Preparative

Alongside the progressive and the resultative, there is yet another stage in a complex event structure that can be focused by grammatical means. In the so-called *prospective* forms, the focus is on the preparatory stage of the event. Here, I shall refer to this meaning as *preparative*. Preparative forms are often constructed periphrastically, like the English phrase *to be about to*. They may also contain a semantically bleached auxiliary with the basic meaning of motion toward a goal. The English *be going to* can be used in this way, although it also functions as future tense:

(25) Look, he is about to / going to jump!

In this example, the part of the event that is represented lexically lies in the future, but attention is directed toward what is going on at present. The truth of the utterance is not affected if the jumping does not occur, because what is asserted is not the jumping but the preparations for it.[38] Therefore, the tense is present and the stage-based aspect is preparative. Typically, preparative meaning refers to some perceptible process, but underlying that, there is always an idea of a present intention or necessity, which sometimes becomes the main event in focus.[39] Thus, while the intention of the subject referent may be a rather dominant notion behind (25), this is even more exclusively the case in the following example:

(26) I think I am going to quit my job.

In (27), the driving force is a necessity conditioned by physical factors:

(27) That rack is about to tip over.

The preparative is the reverse of the resultative in the sense that it always sets the focus on the first stage of a complex event, whereas the resultative sets the focus on the last stage. On the other hand, it resembles the progressive in that the progressive, too, in the case of telic verbs like *to close*, sets the focus

---

38. See Comrie 1974, 64–65 on the truth conditions of the prospective aspect.
39. In the nongrammaticalized usage of *the be going to*-construction, where the verb refers to a spatial movement (*See you in a minute, I am going to buy some fruit in the market*), there is a strong implication of intentionality (see Bybee, Perkins, and Pagliuca 1994, 270; Langacker 2011, 85, 86). However, in more developed stages, this element is not necessarily present. Langacker (2011, 88) writes that the preparative *be going to* construction implies that there is an underlying "impetus," or "force" behind the coming event, and he points out that this can be an external circumstance as well as an intent. See Fleischman 1982, 96.

on a stage that can be considered as preparatory in relation to the *telos* of the event. An interesting consequence of this is that, when progressive meaning is generalized to encompass punctual, telic verbs (achievements), like *to win*, it becomes indistinguishable from preparative meaning, because in this kind of event there is no visible progressive stage to be distinguished from a preparatory stage; only a preparatory stage that instantaneously turns into a result. With such verbs, progressives and preparatives become more or less synonymous:

(28) a. Carl is winning the race
b. Carl is going to win the race.

Both sentences can be said to be equally valid from the moment when Carl takes a firm grip on the lead until the moment when he crosses the finishing line.[40]

Thus, although preparative and progressive are two distinct meanings that are often morphologically separable, their close intertwinement is seen in the case of achievement verbs, where both constructions set the focus of attention on a stage that is preparatory with regard to the actual achievement. Further, it seems that preparative interpretation of progressives is possible also with durative lexemes in contexts where prototypical progressive meaning is not an option. For instance, the persons B in the next couple of examples are obviously referring to the preparative stage of the respective event:

(29) a. A: What are you doing? B (putting on his shoes): I'm going out.
b. A: I'm hungry. B (already on his way to the kitchen): No problem, I'm making lunch.

Presumably, the preparative meaning of the progressive spreads to the durative verbs on analogy with the progressive/preparative-conflation in punctual verbs.

Östen Dahl treats the preparative use of progressives in terms of "'preparatory' use" of presents and progressives, citing motion verbs as the typical case.[41] Dahl's category is narrower than my own "preparative," since he restricts it to events that involve an element of intentional preparation, or planning, but he is also aware that there is a more general notion behind it, stating that there is a "clear analogy" between the "preparatory use" of the progressives (see [29a–b] above) and their use with achievement verbs (see [28a] above). However, Dahl

---

40. Vlach (1981, 279) proposes a similar interpretation of the progressive with the verb *to win*. See C.S. Smith (1997, 75), who says that the focus in cases like (29) is on the "preliminary stages" of the situation (on Smith's view, see further n. 263), and Cook (2012, 73), who makes a similar analysis using the term "preparatory interval" (alt. "period"). None of these authors notes the parallel with the preparative construction, however.

41. Dahl 2000a, 312.

treats this function as a subclass of future meaning, whereas I consider the preparative as an aspect that has present tense value when the deictic center coincides with the time of speech.[42]

In Marion R. Johnson's model of the aspectual system, the "imperfective" aspect includes both preparative and progressive meaning. She regards the preparative and progressive stages as one single "developmental phase" ending with the event denoted by the verbal lexeme, and she defines the imperfective aspect as a perspective on the developmental phase anywhere prior to its final point.[43] In this way, her theory can account for the preparative/progressive conflation in progressive forms, such as the Kikuyu imperfect, but she does not acknowledge that preparative is also a separate aspect.

Biblical Hebrew has no separate grammaticalized preparative construction but uses the same form for progressive and preparative meaning, like Kikuyo. For this reason, one could indeed talk about a "preparative/progressive" verbal form (*qotel*; see section 4.1). However, I shall mainly use the designation progressive, since the progressive meaning is more basic.

3.4.4. Stage-Based Aspect and Aktionsart: *An Overview*

Above, we observed that stage-based aspects have different effects depending on whether the predicates are telic and/or durative. So far, we have considered predicates denoting activities (dynamic, durative, and atelic events like *to run*), accomplishments (dynamic, durative, and telic verbs like *to tie*), and achievements (dynamic, telic, and punctual verbs like *to win*). Before summing up on the issue of the intersection between stage-based aspect and *Aktionsart*, I shall complete the picture by commenting briefly on the semelfactive category, which is also often considered as a separate *Aktionsart*.

Semelfactives are punctual verbs that are generally classified as atelic, because they signify events that just come and go without bringing about any specific change in the prevailing state of affairs. As progressives, they imply the repetition of the event:[44]

(30) She is hiccuping.

This sentence represents a subtype of the pluractional meaning that has been called "event-internal." In event-internal pluractionals, the whole macroevent

42. Cf. Soga's "futurate progressive" (Soga 1983, 29).
43. M. Johnson 1981, 154–56.
44. C.S. Smith 1997, 30, 46. The class of semelfactives includes verbs like *hit*, *knock*, *tap*, *flash*, *blink*, *sneeze*, *jump*, *flap*. Whether or not atelicity is really an adequate defining feature for the whole class is an issue I will not discuss here.

is counted as one occasion. By contrast, pluractional meaning of the type found, for example, in habituals is "event-external," which means that the event repeats itself at different occasions.[45] It is to be noted that progressives can imply event-internal pluractionality not only in combination with semelfactive verbs, even if it is typical for that particular verbal type; it may also occur with undisputably telic verbs of limited duration:

(31) He is perforating the leather with a stitching awl.

The combination of the stage-based aspects with various *Aktionsarten* involves the bringing together of two different event models. If stage-based aspect operates with the idea of an *extended event* consisting of causally related stages, *Aktionsart* pertains to what I shall call the *nuclear* event. The metaphor of the "nucleus" of the event is used for different things in the literature.[46] In this work, the nucleus is understood as the most conceptually coherent segment within the continuous flow of events that is referred to by the predicate. It is denoted by the verbal lexeme, sometimes in combination with adverbial qualifiers (3.2). It is "nuclear" with regard to the extended event, in which it can be embedded. The extended event, in turn, is denoted by the verbal lexeme in combination with the stage-aspectual markers (resultative, progressive, and preparative).

In telic events, the nuclear event minimally contains the moments on each side of the climactic, subliminal point of transition from the dynamic source into the *telos*. To locate the *telos* outside the nucleus, as some scholars do, I find somewhat counter-intuitive.[47] If the defining property of a telic event is the transition from a source to a *telos*—a transformation of some situation—then source and *telos* are equally important parts of the event. In this regard, neither is more "nuclear" than the other. There is even experimental evidence to buttress this; it has been shown that human observers of behavior streams identify *telos*-like boundaries of action units ("breakpoints") as the defining part of the units.[48] Thus, cognitively, the *telos* is actually the more important part of the event.

However, the nucleus does not contain the whole result stage, only the first moment of the *telos*, by which the event reaches closure and coherence

---

45. Bertinetto and Lenci 2012, 852.
46. For Moens and Steedman, *nucleus* is specifically associated with telic event structure, i.e., events with some kind of "culmination." ("A nucleus is defined as a structure comprising a culmination, an associated preparatory process, and a consequent state"; Moens and Steedman 1988, 18). Freed (1979, 30–37; followed by Binnick 1991, 195 and Olsen 1997, 52) understands nucleus as that part of the denoted event that is not a *telos* (which in Freed's terminology belongs to the *coda*). Cook (2012, 63) integrates this variant of the nucleus in an extended event model (instead of the "stages" of the event he speaks of "phases"; see the comment on phasal aspect last in this section).
47. See the previous note.
48. See Newtson et al. 1977, 849.

a. Atelic durative (*to run*, *to stand*)

prepatory	progressive	resultant
0 0 0 0 0 0	1 1 1 1 1 1	0 0 0 0 0 0

b. Telic punctual (*to win*)

prepatory/progressive	resultant
0 0 0 0 0 0 0 0 0	1 1 1 1 1 1 1 1 1

c. Telic durative (*to tie*)

prepatory	progressive	resultant
0 0 0 0 0 0	1 1 1 1 1 1	2 2 2 2 2 2

d. Atelic punctual (*to hiccup*) or durative (*to take* as in (19c)) pluractional

prepatory	progressive	resultant
0 0 0 0 0 0	1 1 1 1 1 1	0 0 0 0 0 0

FIGURE 2. The nuclear event in the framework of the extended event model.

is established. In this respect, telic events differ from atelic events, in which coherence is established by the principle of continuity.

Figure 2 shows schematically how the various kinds of nuclear events fit into the framework of the extended event. The figure includes the pluralizing realizations of progressive forms (d and e), as exemplified above.[49] In this figure, the event is broken down into a string of numbers, symbolizing single moments of time. The nuclear event is marked in gray. If the event is atelic, the gray marking contains only one number, so as to indicate that the event consists of one uniform phase; if the event is telic, the gray marking contains two different numbers, so as to indicate that the event combines two distinct phases. Numbers above zero indicate lexically denoted phases. Accordingly, the nuclear event of an activity (*to run*) or a state (*to stand*) is marked by the number one, indicating that it consists of one lexically denoted phase. An achievement (*to win*) is marked with the numbers zero and one, indicating that it consists of two distinct phases, of which the first is not lexically denoted. An accomplishment (*to tie*) is marked by the numbers one and two, indicating that it consists of two lexically marked phases.

---

49. The phrase *to take medicine* is atelic in that it signifies the consumption of an unspecified amount of something, like *to eat bread* or to *drink water*. Telic versions of the same predicates would be *to take the medicine*, *to eat the bread*, and *to drink the water*.

The stages of the extended event are symbolized by the rectangles that contain the strings of numbers. The boundaries between the rectangles represent the transitional points between the stages. In order to illustrate that transitional points are inherent parts of telic events, their gray marking crosses the boundaries between the progressive and resultant stages. In cases where the gray marking does not reach the boundaries, it is to indicate that transitional points are not inherent in the nuclear event as such but only created secondarily when the event is framed within an extended event model. This also illustrates the fact that the extended event is conceptualized relatively independently from the nuclear event, despite the common transitional point in telic verbs. Another illustration of this is the multiplication of nuclear events within the progressive stage in connection with pluractionality.

What I here call the "stages" of the event is otherwise also known as "phases."[50] Thus, instead of "stage-based" aspect, one could as well speak of "phase-based" aspect. The main reason for choosing the term "stage" is that "phase" is also used in another sense—namely, "to refer to a situation at any given point of time in its duration."[51] From this comes the notion of "phasal aspect," which includes a wide spectrum of categories built on verbal auxiliaries like *begin*, *stop*, *finish*, *resume*, *keep on*, and so forth.[52]

3.5. Stage-Based Versus Limit-Based Analysis of Aspect

Returning now to the definitions of the limit-based aspectual categories in subsection 2.2.2 above, we can see that they are based on a nuclear event model. That is, when the perfect aspect is claimed to set the focused time "after event time," it is the event time of the nucleus that is intended. This is the normal way of treating event-time in the analysis of aspect and tense. Within the framework of the extended event model, we could say instead that focused time is set on the result stage of the event. It works in like manner with the prospective: focused time "before" the time of the nuclear event, means focused time on the preparatory stage of the event.

The above observations on the intersection between the aspects and the *Aktionsarten* suggest that the extended event-model is the more appropriate point of departure for the semantic analysis of progressive(/imperfective) forms and hence also that the semantic opponents of such forms are resultative(/perfect)

---

50. See Binnick 1991, 297.
51. Comrie 1976, 48.
52. Binnick 1991, 195–207. I am aware of one author that uses the term "stage" synonymously with phase in this sense (Soga 1983, 28–29).

a. I am running/I am standing.

prepatory	progressive	resultant
0 0 0 0 0 0	1 1 [1 1 1] 1 1	0 0 0 0 0 0

b. I am tying my shoelace.

prepatory	progressive	resultant
0 0 0 0 0 0	1 1 [1 1 1] 1 1	2 2 2 2 2 2

c. I am winning the race.

prepatory/progressive	resultant
0 0 0 [0 0 0] 0 0 0	1 1 1 1 1 1 1 1 1 1

d. I am hiccuping.

prepatory	progressive	resultant
0 0 0 0 0 0	1 1 [1 1 1] 1 1	0 0 0 0 0 0

e. I am taking medicine.

prepatory	progressive	resultant
0 0 0 0 0 0	1 1 1 [ ] 1 1 1	0 0 0 0 0 0

FIGURE 3. Typical positions of focused time in relation to the extended and the nuclear event.

and preparative forms rather than aorist (or "perfective") forms. This becomes even clearer when we take the role of the focused time into consideration.

Thus, if we understand the aspectual value of the progressive as imperfective in a limit-based sense, focused time should be included in event time. In the more prototypical cases where the progressive is formed on durative verbs, this means that the focused time is included in the time of the nuclear event (fig. 3a–b below). However, in the case of achievements, focused time actually falls before the time of the nuclear event, contrary to the definition (fig. 3c; see also example [28]). With an extended event model, on the other hand, focused time falls on the conflated progressive/preparatory stage, in compliance with the definition of stage-based aspect. As for semelfactives, the focused time includes several nuclear events (fig. 3d), instead of being included in the time of one nuclear event, as it were to be expected if the nuclear event had been essential for the definition of progressive aspect. The problem disappears in the extended event model, however, where the series of nuclear events as a whole makes up the progressive stage on which the focus falls, quite according to the definition. Finally, in the event-external pluractionals, the focused time typically comes *in between* the nuclear events (fig. 3e), rather than *within* one of them. But the stage-based definition of the progressive still holds, since the extended event model again allows that the progressive stage consists of the whole series of nuclear events.

But would it not be possible to retain a limit-based way of defining aspect while exchanging the nuclear event model for the extended event model? If so, progressive meaning could be defined as the aspect where focused time is included in the time of the progressive stage of the event, and resultative meaning as the aspect where focused time is included in the time of the result stage of the event.[53] True, these definitions would accommodate all the examples in figure 3 above, but I would nonetheless like to submit that they do not adequately describe the semantics of the forms involved. This will become clear below, as we consider some examples where progressive and resultative forms have aorist meanings. These uses indicate that the aspectual meanings of the forms are best explained by means of definitions that do not take the limits of the event into account.

Looking at the examples of progressive aspect cited in the previous section (*The gates are closing*, etc.), we can see that they are all best understood as imperfective in terms of limit-based aspect (not considering the secondary

---

53. This way of defining aspect comes close to the system proposed by Bohnemeyer (2014, 949), who works with a kind of extended event model in which the extended event is described in terms of a "causal chain" consisting of a "central part" (cf. the progressive stage) and its pre- and post-states (cf. the preparative and resultant stages). Alternatively, the central part is simply called the "event" (Bohnemeyer 2014, 920). Within this model, the aspects are defined with respect to limits, so that "imperfective" (cf. progressive) is said to put "topic time" (my focused time) *inside* (and not at the boundaries of) the central part of the event, whereas "perfect" (cf. resultative) puts topic time inside the post-state of the causal chain (Bohnemeyer 2014, 920, 949). An important difference between Bohnemeyer's concept of the extended event and mine is that Bohnemeyer does not work with a concept of a nuclear event that is distinct from, and embedded in, the extended event. This means that his model cannot account for the instances when the nucleus does not coincide with the progressive stages, as in the examples in figure 3 above. Another scholar who includes all the three stages in the description of the event is C.S. Smith (1997, 13), who says that an event (her "situation") can have "preliminary stages, internal stages, and resultant stages." However, the external (i.e., preliminary and resultant) stages are not relevant for aspect, according to Smith, who states that aspect has to do with whether there is focus on the internal stages of the event or its endpoints (C.S. Smith 1997, 3, 62). Curiously, though, she also says that the focus can sometimes be on the external stages, e.g., in progressive forms with achievement verbs (see example [28a], "Carl is winning the race"), where it falls on the "preliminary" stage (C.S. Smith 1997, 75). On the face of it, it would appear that such a meaning does not comply with her definition of "imperfective" aspect, which supposedly means that the focus falls on the *internal* stage of the event. Moreover, the fact that a similar meaning is regularly expressed by means of preparative constructions such as the verbal phrase with *to be about to* would seem to suggest that preparative is an aspectual category of its own. But Smith, adhering to a strict principle of semantic invariance, classifies even the preparative progressive as "imperfective," and she does not discuss the possibility that constructions like *to be about to* may indicate a separate aspectual meaning. As for the perfect, she analyzes it as a variant of the perfective aspect (my "completive aorist," C.S. Smith 1997, 107).

preparative function), whereas the resultatives (*The gates are closed*, etc.) are perfect. In terms of stage-based aspect, we may say that the respective stage is viewed as *continuous*, or unlimited.

The view of the stage as continuous is the default interpretation when the forms appear in isolation. In certain contexts, and with certain types of verbs, however, the stage is viewed as *delimited*, in that we observe its beginning and end, or just the beginning or just the end. In order to view a stage as continuous, the focused time has to be included within the time frame of that stage. For this to happen, the focused time must be tied to a contrasting event that is of shorter duration than the stage as a whole—a focalizing event (see ex. [9], section 3.3 above). The focalizing event then fixes the focused time for the mutual perception of the stage. Such a focalizing event is the event of speech in present time settings. In nonpresent settings, the focalizing event can be another event that is mentioned in the context, like John's entering in the ubiquitous example:

(32) John was reading when I entered.

In performative utterances, the focused time is construed differently. For an example, consider the following sentences with the two progressive English forms:

(33) a. I hereby declare you husband and wife.
     b. I am declaring you the winner of this competition.

Performatives are similar to imperfective progressives in that the event of speech marks the focused time. The difference is that speech time is not *included* within the marked stage of the event; it completely *coincides* with that stage, because it is the speech act as such that creates the event. By means of the progressive form (*declare, am declaring*), the act of uttering the sentence itself comes to mark the whole time-span of the progressive stage of the event; that is, when the utterance starts, the progressive stage starts, and when it ends, the progressive stage ends, only to be immediately followed by the result stage. The focus of attention is drawn to the climactic point of transition into the result stage, which is the most salient part of the marked stage. In terms of limit-based aspect, the sentence has completive meaning, since the focused time includes both the beginning and the end of the (nuclear) event.[54] In terms of stage-based aspect, the verbal forms here represent the progressive stage of the event as *transient*, reaching its goal.

---

54. It is a common view that performatives have aorist meaning (whatever term is used for it). See, e.g., Dahl 1985, 81; Thelin 1978, 34; C.S. Smith 1997, 111; Johanson 2000, 138.

Resultative forms, too, can be used in performative utterances (*You are excused, Case dismissed*, etc.).[55] In this case the implication is that the result stage of the event starts with the utterance. There is no implication that the result stage also ends with the utterance, however. The salient part of the result stage here is the initial moment, which is connected to the climactic transitional point in the nuclear event. Accordingly, the marked stage is here represented as *emergent*. Biblical Hebrew differs from English in that the resultative form is employed in performative utterances not only with passive (or de-transitive) but also with active, transitive meanings (4.3.1). In conclusion, the speech act does not have the same focalizing function in the aorist performatives as it has in present imperfective utterances. In performatives, the speech act functions as a *frame* for the salient *telos* of the event, rather than as a focalizer in itself.

The same aspectual relation as in the performatives also obtains in the so-called reportive present, with the difference that the acts of speech themselves do not constitute the events; they refer to the event as they unfold in front of the observer.[56] A typical case is the sports commentary:

(34) Ibrahimović picks up the ball, plays it to Beckham, Beckham lifts it over the defense ...

Comrie points out that the present tense is the most expected choice for a simultaneous report of a rapid series of events, but he also states that the prototypical progressive is acceptable as well, offering the following example of a "film commentary":

(35) Now the villain is seizing the heroine, now they're driving off toward the railway track, now he's forcing her out of the car, now he's tying her to the track, while all the time the train is getting nearer.[57]

I am not aware of any obvious example of reportive presents in Biblical Hebrew. Possibly, resultative forms could be used in this function, as well as in the performative, but I shall leave this issue outside the present investigation.[58]

---

55. On performative usages with resultative forms, see Kozinceva 1988, 465; Nedjalkov 1988, 415; Volodin 1988, 473. See also Andrason 2012d, 19.
56. "Reportive present" is used, e.g., in Dahl 1985, 81.
57. Comrie 1976, 77: Comrie describes such usages as aorist ("complete actions"). The predicate of the last clause (*is getting nearer*), however, is imperfective.
58. Some passages in descriptions of theophanies may be candidates for reportive speech (see esp. Ps 50:3–6, but also, e.g., Hab 3:3–16; Ps 29:3–9), but the cases are mostly rather uncertain. Cook mentions the possibility of reportive *qatal* in such contexts in his 2002 dissertation (Cook 2002, 219 n. 38) but seems to have dropped the issue in the second edition of the book (Cook 2012).

Inserted in sequences describing nonpresent courses of events, the English progressive and perfect constructions may also appear with aorist meaning together with other verbal forms:

(36) a. The young bird flaps its wings vigorously, and suddenly it is flying for the first time.
b. Sell this estate and you have made a fortune.

The progressive here has an ingressive aorist meaning. The perfect, which expresses punctual simultaneity with the second clause in the sequence, is completive. Neither of the uses requires any reanalysis of the semantic meanings of the form. Within their respective contexts, they simply present the progressive and the result stages of the event as emergent, rather than continuous.[59]

In Biblical Hebrew, the perfect consecutive *weqataltí* is regularly used for emergent resultative meaning (4.3.1). There are also examples of both emergent and transient progressives (4.1.1).

3.6. Temporalization

The development of past meaning from resultative forms and future meaning from preparatives is well attested in many languages. It is assumed here that this development arises because of the temporal implications of the internal structure of the events. Past meaning of the resultative is the consequence when contextual factors indicate that the result stage of the event is not important to communicate at the time of speech. The mutual focus of attention is then allowed to turn from the grammatically marked result stage that obtains around speech time (or a secondary deictic center) to the preceding nuclear event that is lexically denoted by the verb. In other words, the focused content of the event falls entirely within the time span previous to the deictic center, which means that the tense value is no longer present but past. The reanalysis of preparative into future meaning works the same way but in the opposite direction: the shift of focus goes from the extended preparative stage to the ensuing nuclear event. The process of inferring these particular tense meanings from the internal causal structure of resultative and preparative constructions will be referred to as *temporalization*.[60]

---

59. Even preparatives may perhaps have emergent meaning (*We start to discuss the matter and suddenly I'm about to lose my temper*), but this issue will not be investigated in the present study.

60. See Fleischman (1982, 104–5) who uses the term to describe the development of future meaning from various sources in Romance languages.

The complex temporal structures of resultative and preparative constructions are, of course, well known. It is also common that the past and future meanings that these verbal forms tend to develop are seen as the result of reanalysis of the semantic meanings of the forms, by which the focus shifts from a present subevent to a previous or ensuing one.[61] As for the development of futures from progressives, the connection with the semantics of the forms is less acknowledged. Bybee, Perkins, and Pagliuca go as far as to state that the future meaning of progressives is altogether "contextually determined."[62] If this is so, however, it is remarkable that it is such a widespread phenomenon cross-linguistically and that the construction does not combine with past time adverbials as naturally as it does with future adverbials in many (most?) languages (cf. *We are leaving tomorrow* / **We are leaving yesterday*).

61. My description of temporalization is particularly reminiscent of Hengenveld's account of the development from resultative to past and from prospective to future in three steps (from "resultative" to "anterior" to "past," and from "prospective" to "posterior" to "future"; see Hengenveld 2011, 590–91). He sees the process as an interaction of four factors: speech-time (S), event-time (E), reference-time (R), and a "focal point of information." The last term means, very roughly speaking, "the important part of the information in the linguistic unit," (see Hengenveld 2011, 590 n. 7; see also Harder and Boye 2011, 60–62 [same volume]). My main disagreement with Hengenveld concerns his account of the shift from resultative to anterior (perfect), which is illustrated by comparing the Spanish *Tengo preparada una cena* ("I have a meal prepared"—resultative) and *Había preparado una cena* ("I have prepared a meal"—perfect). According to Hengenveld, the focal point of information in the resultative sentence is a state of affairs at S that results from E, and in the perfect sentence it is "the previous state of affairs (E) itself, seen from the perspective of the reference time (R)." *Pace* Hengenveld, I would describe the difference between the resultative and the perfect not as a shift in temporal focus but as a shift of diathesis from passive to active. The shift from present to past meaning, i.e., temporalization, comes only in the third step, where the perfect construction takes on simple past meaning. Hengenveld's description of the temporal difference between resultative and perfect constructions echoes earlier explanations. Thus, Maslov says that the resultative (or "statal perfect," as he also calls it) denotes events "whose meanings, to one degree or another, include two temporal planes: that of precedence and that of sequence" (Maslov 1988, 64). When resultatives turn into perfects, he argues, "it is the temporal plane of precedence that assumes greater prominence," so that the perfect comes to refer to the "pre-present." Long before Maslov, Whitney (1875, 91) described the resultative-perfect reanalysis in similar terms: "the phrase shifts its centre of gravity from the expressed condition to the implied antecedent act." Andrason (2010a, 331) has applied Maslov's explanation in his account of the development of the resultative in Semitic (Akkadian). From a synchronic perspective, Musan has noted the shift between the temporalized and nontemporalized meaning of German perfects in her description of how the *tense time* (corresponding to my focused time; see Musan 2002, 5; see example [49]) vacillates between the present state and the previous event. She does not, however, give priority to the resultative meaning as the basic meaning of the form. As for the temporalization of preparatives, see, e.g., Fleischman (1982, 97–99), who describes the development of future tense meaning from so-called go-futures (English *be going to do*; French *aller faire*) in terms of a loss of "present relevance" and an "inversion of the tense / aspect ratio." Fleischman considers that this transformation mirrors the development of past meaning out of perfects (97–99).

62. See Bybee, Perkins, and Pagliuca 1994, 275, on what they call "imperfectives" and "present imperfectives." Such forms typically develop from prototypical progressives, and according to the inclusive definition suggested above (3.3.) they all count as progressives.

An alternative explanation for the future use of the progressives might be that it is based on an inference from a preparative reading of the form, which in turn originates in the preparative/progressive fusion in connection with achievement verbs (3.4.3). To repeat, in the next example, the progressive and the preparatives within brackets are synonymous as far as their preparative meaning is concerned:

(37) I'm starting the race (I'm going to start the race / I'm about to start the race).

By adding some context, the difference between a preparative (38a) and a future (38b) reading stands out more clearly:

(38) a. A: What are you doing right now? B: I'm starting the race (I'm going to start the race / I'm about to start the race).
  b. A: I'm starting the race (I'm going to start the race / I'm about to start the race). B: Right now? A: No, in about thirty seconds.

In dialogue (38a), the focus is fixed on the preparative stage. In dialogue (38b), the preparative reading is still in default in the first sentence due to lack of contextual indications to the contrary, but in the following two sentences there is a switch to an (immediate) future reading. The adverbial expressions (*now*, *in thirty seconds*) refer not to the preparative stage but to what ensues—namely, the instantaneous achievement of the event lexically denoted by the verb. The next step toward a grammaticalized temporalization is to integrate the adverbial in the predication, as in (39):

(39) I'm starting the race in thirty seconds (I'm going to start the race in thirty seconds / I'm about to start the race in thirty seconds).

That the preparative meaning of achievement verbs in the prototypical progressive construction is the default interpretation and not contextually determined is evident in speech situations where the listener has neither any prior knowledge nor contextual indications about whether the event is yet achieved or not. For example, let us imagine that the knowledge shared between speaker and listener prior to this speech act is that their father is in the same town:

(40) A: Daddy's leaving town.

The most plausible interpretation of (40) is that daddy *is going to leave* town—that is, a preparative interpretation. If the speaker chooses to temporalize the utterance, the only sensible option is to localize the achievement in the future (B: *When will he do that?* A: *Tomorrow*). A past localization simply makes no sense after the progressive (*A: *Daddy's leaving town.* B: *When did he do that?* A: *Yesterday*). With the perfect, the conditions are reversed; only a past temporalization makes any sense:

(41) A: Daddy has left town. B: When did he do that? A: Yesterday.
(cf. *B: When will he do that? A: Tomorrow.)

We may conclude that prototypical progressives with achievement verbs are just as prone to temporalization as preparatives and resultatives. I find it reasonable to assume that the preparative meaning as well as the accompanying possibility for temporalized future interpretation spreads from the punctual achievement verbs to durative verbs, probably in the first place to telic verbs (accomplishments), since preparative/future use of atelic verbs is not as common.[63] Since durative events have a progressive stage, the preparative interpretation requires that the listener be sure that the progressive stage is not ongoing. To illustrate, we return again to an example from section 3.4.2. In isolation, the sentence *I'm making lunch* stands in for progressive meaning, but in this context, the semantics of the form invites a preparative reading:

(42) A: Are you hungry? I'm making lunch. B: Yes, please do!

In analogy with the achievement verbs, temporalization of accomplishments can be carried out by means of adverbials (*Are you hungry? I'm making lunch in a few minutes*). The corresponding manoeuver in resultative forms is not possible with the English perfect, but the German counterpart allows it:

(43) Frau Merkel hat gestern die Stadt verlassen.
Mrs. Merkel left the town yesterday.

The difference between the basic, aspectual meaning and the temporalized meaning can be described as one of degree. There is often room for a certain amount of ambiguity. Thus, in the following example with the *be going to* construction, sentence (44a) invites us to pay full attention to the event at speech

---

63. The fact that atelic, and in particular stative, forms are more resilient to taking on preparative/future meaning is noted by Haspelmath (1998, 50). In contrast to me, Haspelmath believes that the development of future meaning of progressive forms begins with durative, rather than punctual, telic verbs. He does not ground this assumption in a theory of how the semantics of telic duratives favors future interpretation but thinks that this is a probable consequence of the fact that progressives in general are more common with durative verbs than with punctual verbs.

time; sentence (44b) less so, even if it clearly hints at a present intention by the speaker; sentence (44c) lacks any indication whatsoever that there is anything going on at speech time that will result in the envisioned future event:[64]

(44) a. Watch out, you're going to hit your head!
b. Now, we are going to show you the results.
c. I hope the sun is going to shine tomorrow.

Similar effects arise in connection with the temporalization of resultatives. We turn again to the German perfect for an example:

(45) a. Ich habe den Tisch gedeckt.
I have set the table.
b. Er schämt sich für das was er getan hat.
He is ashamed of what he has done/did.
c. Julius Caesar hat im Jahr 49 v. Chr. den Fluss Rubikon überquert.
Julius Caesar crossed the river Rubicon in the year 49 BC.

In (45a) the perfect has a default resultative meaning with full focus on the present state of affairs; sentence (45b) allows the focus to be set either on the present result stage or on the past nuclear event; sentence (45c), on the other hand, is purely historical.

The temporalization of stage-aspectual forms as described in this section shows that the localization of the temporal focus of attention in connection with complex event structures is negotiable. In some contexts, the exact temporal meaning is rather unclear, or not even necessary to settle. Examples of this in Biblical Hebrew will be dealt with in subsections 4.1.2 and 4.3.2.

Before closing this section, we shall look into the question of what happens to the limit-aspectual meaning of the verb in the process of temporalization. In brief, as the focus of attention in temporalization gravitates from the peripheries of the event toward the nucleus, perfect and prospective limit-aspects are no longer possible. The temporalized predicate becomes aorist or imperfective depending on factors like the *Aktionsart* of the event, the representation of focalizing events by surrounding clauses, the possible contextual indications of temporal succession, and the paradigmatic constraints set by the rest of the verbal system (the "division of labor" between the forms). A typical example of paradigmatic constraint is when there is a past progressive form in the system, which will be the primary choice for imperfective meaning. This probably

---

64. See Langacker 2011, 85–88 for a detailed description of the successive steps toward a "true future tense"-meaning of the English *be going to*-construction.

explains the specialization on past aorist meaning in, for example, the French passé simple and the classical Greek aorist. The German perfect, by contrast, which has no past progressive competitor, is regularly used with past imperfective meaning as well as aorist.[65] The following example, which is borrowed from Renate Musan, shows two perfect forms with either meaning in one and the same sentence:

(46) Hans hat im Garten gearbeitet [imperfective] und das Telefon nicht gehört [aorist].
Hans was working in the garden and did not hear the telephone.[66]

In sum, temporalization causes changes with regard to both the temporal and the limit-aspectual meaning of the verbal form.

3.7. Summary

In this chapter, the meanings of the progressive and the resultative verbal types have been defined with regard to their aspectual properties, and their tendency to take on temporal meanings has been explained as an inference of tense from aspect (cf. 1.2). The purpose of the chapter has been to develop a general theoretical framework with applicability to the Biblical Hebrew verbal system.

Aspect was defined as the focused content of the event that is represented by the verb, or, in time relational terms, the relation between focused time and event time (3.3).

The aspectual relation can be described in different ways depending on whether the event is envisaged in the shape of its bare nucleus or as an extended event (the nuclear and the extended event model). In the nuclear event model, aspect is often defined with respect to the limits of the nuclear events—what I call the "limit-based aspect." Categories like imperfective, aorist (perfective), and perfect are often defined in this way. In the extended event model, three different stages of the event can be identified: the preparatory, the progressive, and the resultant stage (3.4.1–3). The function of "stage-based aspect" is to set the focus on any of these stages, thus creating preparative, progressive, and resultative meaning. Preparative meaning, represented by the so-called prospective forms, partly overlaps with the progressive meaning and collapses with it in connection with achievement verbs (3.4.3).

---

65. See Bybee, Perkins, and Pagliuca 1994, 85.
66. Musan 2002, 93.

According to the proposed analysis, progressive meaning is expressed not only by the forms normally classified as "progressives" but also by presents and imperfectives. Likewise, resultative meaning has a wide application, including both resultatives proper and perfects. Both progressive and resultative aspect can thus be combined with all verbs regardless of diathesis and *Aktionsart*, and regardless of whether the verb has a specific or a generalizing meaning (like habitual or generic). In terms of limit-based aspect, the stage-aspectual forms normally represent the focused stage as continuous, whereby progressive forms get imperfective meaning, and resultative forms get perfect meaning. In certain uses, however, such as narrative, reportive, or performative, the progressive and resultative forms represent their marked stages as in change, which means that the limit-based aspect is aorist. Thus, the stage-based aspect of the form may be invariant while the limit-based aspect changes (3.5).

Whereas all aspectual distinctions can be defined in terms of how the focused part of the event relates to the whole event referred to by the predicate, tense was defined as the temporal relation obtaining between the focused part of the event and a deictic center, which can be either the time of speech or some other time before or after it (3.3; see also 2.1).

The resultative and the preparative aspects create complex event structures, in which the focus of attention is directed to the pre- and poststages of the lexically denoted, nuclear event. However, by using the resultative or preparative verbal form in nonprototypical situations, it is possible to pragmatically steer the focus of attention away from the aspectually marked stage to the nuclear event. This means a movement of the focus of attention toward the past in resultatives and toward the future in preparatives. The shift in the focus of attention overturns the stage-aspectual meaning and changes the temporal meaning of the clause. The process is here called temporalization (3.6).

Due to the overlapping semantics of progressives and preparatives, it was argued, progressives may undergo the same kind of temporalization as preparatives. This could explain the tendency of progressives to develop future meaning.

CHAPTER 4

Progressive and Resultative Verbs in Biblical Hebrew

IN THE INTRODUCTION to this study, it was assumed that the Biblical Hebrew verbal forms, in terms of their origin, belong to either of two cross-linguistic verbal types, the progressive and the resultative, but that, in terms of their synchronic status, they have developed from that origin to a higher or lesser degree. In the previous chapter, the meanings of the original verbal types were described as "stage-based" rather than limit-based aspects and labeled "progressive" and "resultative" aspect, respectively. It was argued that the stage-based aspectual meanings are invariant in several functions that are generally considered to belong not to the prototypically progressive or resultative verbal types but rather to more developed forms, such as imperfectives, presents, and perfects. Various ways in which progressives and resultatives take on different limit-based meanings were described, and finally, it was shown how progressive and resultative meaning can be reanalyzed as future and past tense meaning. The hypothesis emerging from all this is that the Biblical Hebrew verbal forms are progressive and resultative in the stage-aspectual sense described above and that this explains their temporal meanings. In the present chapter, we turn to the facts of the Biblical Hebrew verbal system in order to see whether they bear out the hypothesis.

The organization of the chapter is as follows. For each of the forms investigated there is a subsection devoted to verbal uses where the assumed basic aspectual meaning of the form is invariant and has not been overturned due to reanalysis (4.1.1, 4.2.1, 4.3.1, 4.4.1). First in these subsections, we consider the maximally unambiguous examples—that is, where resultative forms have perfect meaning and where progressive forms have imperfective meaning. Here, I include also the generalizing progressive uses, since they have the same aspectual meaning as the dynamic progressives. Then follow cases that are invariant, but less conclusive, because they have aorist meaning. In the case of the progressive forms, these subsections also contain examples of preparative uses. Preparative meaning is treated along with the basic progressive meaning, since these two meanings overlap, and since Biblical Hebrew seems to lack a separate preparative construction.

After the subsection on the invariant basic meanings, there follows another subsection containing verbal uses that can be argued to have resulted from temporalization—that is, a reanalysis of the basic semantic meaning (4.1.2, 4.2.2, 4.3.2, 4.4.2).

Finally, for all forms except *yiqtol*-L, there are one or more subsections dealing with special uses of various kinds (4.1.3, 4.3.3, 4.4.3–4).

Throughout, attention is paid to the limit-based aspectual analysis of various verbal uses. This is an aid in the identification of the basic stage-aspectual meanings (given the typical correspondence between imperfective and progressive and between perfect and resultative), but it also serves the important secondary purpose of showing the complexity that an "aspectual approach" to the Biblical Hebrew verbal system has to deal with.

The investigation in this chapter is largely an attempt at a synthesis of the established knowledge of the verbal uses in Biblical Hebrew as it emerges from the standard grammars, including the groundbreaking verbal grammars of Driver (1892) and Joosten (2012) (see further 1.5.1). Of course, it is neither possible nor desirable in this kind of work to present a comprehensive taxonomy of the Biblical Hebrew verbal usage, since much of the variation attested in the grammars is not semantic but pragmatic. The interest is centered on the basic semantic factors expressed within the system and how they can be related to the expression of temporality. In addition, certain modal meanings will be considered in order to give an idea of how the factors within the TAM-complex can be envisaged in terms of their relative basicness within the system. The verbal system is described as a synchronic phenomenon, but if there are noteworthy diachronic differences concerning a certain use, this will be mentioned.

When reference is made to the grammars, it is to indicate where examples of the particular phenomenon under consideration can be found. It does not mean that I agree on every interpretation they present, nor that the grammarians themselves agree with one another. Although there is often a general consensus, especially on how to translate various uses, no one who carefully compares the explanations they offer will fail to note the differences, or to recognize the importance of the theoretical outlook for the arrangement of the data. The contribution of the present chapter is not to provide ample documentation; rather, it is to demonstrate how the data can be arranged on the basis of the theory presented in this work. Documentation will be provided only in the case of some rare or less well-described verbal uses. Hopefully, however, the synthesis can serve as a basis for more comprehensive studies.

Besides the grammars, this synthesis is also based on the analysis of the verbs in text samples from the three main diachronic stages represented in the Hebrew Bible (see further 1.5.1). All the verbs were analyzed with regard to the factors of interest for this study—that is, first and foremost tense and aspect, but also, connected to that, (a)telicity, pluractionality, and stativization. Many of the examples in this chapter are chosen from these texts. The main reason for studying them was to have a fairly sizeable and representative body of "raw" data that had not been selected, classified, and arranged in advance by another scholar in accordance with certain theoretical outlook. This body of data contains many but not all of the verbal uses that are attested within the grammars. My investigation of the textual samples also provides an empirical basis for some statements about frequency of tense, aspect, and *Aktionsart* meanings, which are made in this chapter.

Database queries have been a valuable complement to the above-mentioned sources, especially in the case of rare or less well-described phenomena. This being said, I do not claim that the documentation is exhaustive in the cases where it has been provided.

4.1. *Qotel*

Qotel stands for the active participle. In this category are not counted the passive participle of the simple stem formation *qal*, the participle of the passive stem formations *pual* and *hofal* and the participle of the medio-passive stem formation *nifal*. Only *qotel* in predicate position is marked for stage-based aspect.

4.1.1. Invariant Progressive qotel

The active participle, also referred to as *qotel*, has progressive meaning when it occurs as the predicate of a clause. The limit-aspect is imperfective when the focused time is fixed by the speech act (1a) or another focalizing event in the past or the future (*wayyar'* and *upāğaʿtā* in [1b, c]). Typically, the progressive *qotel* has dynamic meaning:[1]

(1) a. hinneʰ   ʿām   **yôreḏ**   merāʾšê
       behold   people   go.down.QOT.M.SG   from=tops.of

---

1. Driver 1892, §135 (1)–(2); Waltke and O'Connor 1990, §37.6d–f; Gibson 1994, §113b–c, f; Joüon and Muraoka 2009, §121c, d, f; Joosten 2012, 134–37, 239–41. The dynamic continuous progressive *qotel* in predicative position is almost absent in Archaic Biblical Hebrew. Notarius (2010, 248, 262; also 2013, 298) notes one single occurrence (*'ōśæʰ* in Num 24:18) in her corpus consisting of Gen 49:2–27; Num 23:7–10, 18–24; 24:3–9, 15–19; Deut 32:1–43; Deut 33:2–29; Exod 15:1–18; Judg 5:2–30; 2 Sam 2:2–51 (= Ps 18); 1 Sam 2:1–10. My own investigation of this corpus has not yielded any additional findings. However, there is also no solid evidence that *yiqtol*-L functions as a prototypical progressive at this stage. Consequently, due to the absence of relevant data, I refrain from drawing any conclusions about the existence of a progressive predicative *qotel* in the oldest stage of the Archaic Biblical Hebrew verbal system. For a detailed discussion of the problem, see Bergström 2016, 211–18.

hæhārîm
the=mountains
Look, people **are coming down** from the mountain tops. (Judg 9:36)

b. wayyašqēp̄   'ăḇîmælæḵ   mælæḵ   pəlištîm
   and=lean.YQTL-S.3M Abimelek   king.of Philistines
   bə'aḏ   hahallôn   wayyar'
   through   the=window   and=see.YQTL-S.3M.SG
   wəhinneʰ   yiṣḥāq   **məṣaḥeq**   'eṯ   riḇqâ
   and=behold Isaac   play.QOT.M.SG   with   Rebekah
   'ištô
   wife=his
   Abimelech, king of the Philistines, looked out at a window and saw that Isaac **was caressing** Rebekah his wife. (Gen 26:8)

c. wîhî   kəḇō'ăḵâ   šām
   and=be.YQTL-S.3M.SG   as=enter.INFC=your   there
   hā'îr   upāḡa'tā   ḥæḇæl   nəḇî'îm
   the=town   and=meet.QTAL.2M.SG   company.of   prophets
   [...]   wəhemmâ   **miṯnabbə'îm**
   [...]   and=they   prophesy.QOT.M.PL
   It will happen that, when you enter the town you will meet a company of prophets [...] and they **will be prophesying**. (1 Sam 10:5)

Sometimes *qotel* has a stativized, generalizing meaning.[2] This is normally a function that belongs to *yiqtol*-L, except in Late Biblical Hebrew, where habitual *qotel* becomes more common.[3] In the typical case of stativized *qotel*, the state is seen as continuous around a focalizing event—that is, the speech act, as in (2a), or another event mentioned in the context, as in (2b) (*wayyar'*, "saw"), which means that the limit-aspect is imperfective. In (2a), the *qotel* form is juxtaposed with a habitual *yiqtol*-L (see 4.2.1):

(2) a. wayhî   kî   hiqšâ
       and=be.YQTL-S.3M.SG   when   be.stubborn.QTAL.3M.SG
       p̄ar'oʰ   ləšalləḥenû   wayyaḥărōḡ
       pharaoh   to=send.INFC=us   and=kill.YQTL(S).3M.SG

---

2. See especially Joüon and Muraoka 2009, §121d, f; Joosten 2012, 247. The others do not treat this usage separately from the previous, but some examples occur in their material. See Driver 1892, §135.1 2; Waltke and O'Connor 1990 §37.6d–e; Gibson 1994, §113b.

3. Joosten 2012, 395–96; Bergström 2015, 623.

100 Aspect, Communicative Appeal, and Temporal Meaning

YHWH   kol   bəḵôr   bə'æræṣ   miṣrayim   [...]
YHWH   every   firstborn   in=land=of   Egypt   [...]
'al   ken   'ănî   **zōḇeaḥ**   laYHWH
because.of thus I   sacrifice.QOT.M.SG   for=YHWH
kol   pæṭær   ræḥæm   hazzəḵārîm   wəḵol
every   firstborn.of womb   the=male   and=every
bəḵôr   bānay   'æp̄dæʰ
firstborn.of sons=my redeem.YQTL-L.1SG

When Pharaoh was too stubborn to let us go, the Lord killed all the firstborn in the land of Egypt [...] Because of this, I **sacrifice** to the Lord every male firstborn from the womb, and every firstborn of my sons I redeem. (Exod 13:15)

b. wayyar'   'ăḏōnāʸw   kî   YHWH
    and=see.YQTL-S.3M.SG   master=his   that   YHWH
    'ittô   wəḵōl   'ăšær   hû'   'ōśæʰ   YHWH
    with=him   and=all   that   he   do.QOT.M.SG   YHWH
    maṣlîaḥ   bəyāḏô
    let.prosper.QOT.M.SG   in=hand=his

And his master saw that the Lord was with him and that the Lord **made** everything he did **go well**. (Gen 39:3)

Exceptionally, in past time settings, *qotel* is integrated into the narrative mainline. In such contexts the event is framed within a course of events, and a focalizing event is lacking. As a result, the attention span overlaps one or both limits of the event, and the limit-aspect is aorist. The preferred scenario for this use seems to be when the event referred to stands out in the context by being markedly durative. The choice of *qotel* is wholly optional even then, however, as we see in the next example, in which events of equal duration are encoded both with *wayyiqtol* (*wayyiqrə'û*) and with *qotel* (*miṯwaddîm, mištaḥăwîm*). Here, the events are temporally bounded by adverbials. The limit-aspectual meaning is completive.

(3) wayyāqûmû   'al   'omḏām
     and=arise.YQTL(S).3M.PL   on   stand.INFC=their
     wayyiqrə'û   bəsēp̄ær   tôraṯ   YHWH
     and=read.YQTL(S).3M.PL   in=book.of law.of   YHWH
     'ĕlōhêhæm   rəḇi'îṯ   hayyôm   ûrəḇi'îṯ   **miṯwaddîm**
     god=their   fourth.of the=day   and=fourth   praise.QOT.M.PL
     ûmištaḥăwîm   laYHWH   'ĕlōhêhæm
     and=adore.QOT.M.PL   for=YHWH   god=their

They rose to their feet and read in the book of the law of the Lord, their God, for a fourth of the day, and for a fourth of the day they **praised** and **worshipped** the Lord, their God. (Neh 9:3)

The use of free-standing "aorist *qotel* of duration," as we may call it, appears to be a late phenomenon.[4] There is also a periphrastic variant with the copula verb *hāyâ* ("to be") in the *wayyiqtol*—a use found also in Standard Biblical Hebrew.[5] The durative nature of the event expressed by this construction often takes the shape of event-external pluractionality (3.4.4), and, more often than with the free-standing aorist *qotel*, there is an implication of ingressivity.[6] Sometimes, these predicates have generalizing meaning, as in the following example:

(4) wayyaʾasrûhû   banhûštayim
and=bind.YQTL(S).3M.PL=him   with=bronze-shackles
wayhî   **ṭôḥen**   bəbêt
and=be.YQTL-S.3M.SG   grind.QOT.M.SG   in=house.of
hāʾăsîrîm   wayyāḥæl   śəʿar   rōʾšô
the=prisoners   and=begin.YQTL-S.3M.SG   hair.of   head=his
ləṣammeaḥ   kaʾăšær   gullāḥ
to=grow.INFC   as   be.shaved.QTAL.3M.SG
They bound him with bronze shackles and he **ground** [i.e., he **was set to grinding**] in the prison. But the hair on his head began to grow after it had been shaved. (Judg 16:21–22)

---

4. For a full presentation of the data, see Bergström 2015, esp. 632. See also M.S. Smith 1999, 307, on Late Biblical Hebrew *qotel* that "narrates past action." Not all Smith's examples are best understood as aorist, however. The aorist *qotel* of duration in Late Biblical Hebrew is not entirely comparable to the use of *qotel* for "vivid" narration in Rabbinic Hebrew (Pérez Fernández 1999, 134–35). The latter may be more of a historic present, given that Rabbinic Hebrew has developed a temporal distinction between a present *qotel* and a past *hāyâ qotel* that is much more systematic than in Late Biblical Hebrew, where *qotel* without the copula is normal for expressing past attendant circumstance. Yet, it is possible that the use of *qotel* for vivid narration may predate the development of a tense-prominent verbal system. See Gen 41:2, 3, 5, 6; and Dan 8:3; 9:21, none of which can be considered as aorist *qotel* of duration.

5. Driver 1892, §135.5; Gibson 1994, §136f, rem. 2; Waltke and O'Connor 1990, §37.7.1; Joüon and Muraoka 2009, §121f §; Joosten 2012, 257–58. The copula may also be in the *qatal*, *yiqtol*-L, and volitive *yiqtol*-L, each adding its special temporal and modal character to the *qotel*. On the latter usages, see Joosten 2012, 258–60.

6. Ingressive meaning is the most plausible interpretation in 1 Sam 18:9; 1 Kgs 5:24; 2 Kgs 17:25, 28; Esth 2:15; Neh 1:4 (twice); 4:10 [4:16] (twice); 2 Chr 24:12. Completive meaning for markedly durative events is found in 2 Chr 30:10 (twice). The same aspect occurs in Neh 2:13, 15 (twice), but the events referred to may not stand out in the context for being of particularly long duration, something that is even more true for 2 Chr 21:9.

Biblical Hebrew lacks a separate preparative construction.[7] The predicative *qotel* covers preparative meaning as an extension of its progressivity (see 3.4.2).[8] In the next subsection, we shall see that the construction has even developed so far as to allow temporalized readings. It is to be expected that it is not always easy to draw a clear and definite line between preparative and temporalized, future meanings of *qotel* (see 3.6). Examples of preparatives that clearly refer to a visual preparatory process are not easy to find. Often, intentionality is a very dominant feature (3.4.3), which we can see in the following two examples from present and past contexts:[9]

(5) a. wa'ănî   hinnî   **mebî'**   'æt   hammabbûl
        and=I   behold=me   bring.QOT.M.SG   OBJ   the=flood
        I **am going to bring** floodwaters on the earth. (Gen 6:17)

   b. wayyignōb   ya'ăqōb   'æt   leb
       and=deceive.YQTL(S).3M.SG   Jacob   OBJ   heart.of
       lābān   hā'ărammî   'al   balî   higgîd
       Laban   the=Aramean   in.that not   tell.QTAL.3M.SG
       lô   kî   **bōreaḥ**   hû'
       to=him   that   flee.QOT.M.SG   he
       Jacob deceived Laban the Aramean, in that he did not tell him that he **was going to flee**. (Gen 31:20)

---

7. The construction *hōlek lə* ("be going to") + infinitive is generally used for a literal movement in a certain direction for a certain purpose (Gen 27:25; Num 14:38; Josh 18:8; Judg 14:3; 17:9; 18:14, 17; 1 Kgs 1:3; Isa 30:2; 1 Chr 15:25). An exceptional case with truly preparative meaning seems to be Gen 25:32.

8. This function of the participle falls under the category future, or "instant future" (*futurum instans*) or similar in the literature (Driver 1892, §135.3; Waltke and O'Connor 1990, §37.6f; Joüon and Muraoka 2009, §121e; Joosten 2012, 241–42). Joüon and Muraoka de facto describe the conflation of progressive and preparative meaning, without, however, making a theoretical distinction between preparative aspect and future tense: "The use of the participle to express the near future and the future in general is an extension of the use of the participle as present" (Joüon and Muraoka 2009, §121e). Joosten describes the "immediate future" of punctual verbs in terms that approach my description of the preparative meaning: "The process, which still lies in the future, is represented as contemporaneous with the moment of speaking" (Joosten, 2012, 91). Cook (2012, 232–33) draws attention to the similarity between the instant future (his "expected future") and the prospective aspect expressed by phrases like be going to, but he maintains that the progressive sense of the construction remains.

9. For some more examples, see Gen 9:9; 15:3; 18:17; 19:13, 14; Num 24:14; Josh 3:11; Judg 9:15; 1 Sam 3:11; 1 Kgs 17:12; Neh 6:10. An example of an achievement verb with a natural conflation between the preparative and progressive meaning is *met* ("to die"). See Gen 48:21; 50:5, 24; Exod 12:33; 1 Kgs 12:2; 18:9.

4.1.2. Temporalized qotel

A temporalized, future meaning of *qotel* is rather evident in the next example:[10]

(6) 'im   lōqeaḥ   yaʿăqōḇ   'iššâ   [...]
    if   take.QOT.M.SG   Jacob   woman   [...]
    mibbənôṯ   hā'āræṣ   lāmmâ   lî   ḥayyîm
    from=children.of the=land   why   for=me   life
    If Jacob **takes** a wife from among the women of this land [...] why should I live? (Gen 27:46)

The focused time here is in the future, since the interest is focused around the particular state of affairs that may arise later (life not worth living) rather than what may be going on at speech time (Jacob intending to marry). The stage-aspectual value is overturned because of the semantic reanalysis and focus of attention centers around the salient *telos* of the nuclear event, with the result that the limit-aspect becomes completive (see the discussion about the temporalized resultative in chapter 3, example [46]).

In the following example, the verb (*bô*', "to come") occurs twice. The first occurrence may be interpreted as a pure preparative, but the second time the verb is temporalized by means of an adverbial noun phrase (*laylâ*, "tonight") that pushes the focus of attention toward the future:

(7) niwwā'eḏ   'æl   bêṯ   hā'ælōhîm   'æl
    appoint.YQTL-L.1PL   to   house.of   the=god   to
    tôḵ   hahêḵāl   wənisgərâ   daltôṯ
    middle.of   the=temple   and=shut.YQTL(S).COH.1PL   doors.of
    hahêḵāl   kî   bā'îm   ləhorḡæḵā
    the=temple   for   come.QOT.M.PL   to=kill.INFC.you
    wəlaylâ   bā'îm   ləhorḡæḵā
    and=night=at   come.QOT.M.PL   to=kill.INFC=your
    Let us meet in the house of God, inside the temple, and let us close the temple doors, for they **are coming** to kill you; indeed, during the night they **will come** to kill you. (Neh 6:10)

Without the aid of temporal adverbials, more subtle ways of shifting the temporal focus can be effected. In the next example, the same predication again occurs in two sentences, the second occasion being a restatement of the first.

---

10. The temporalized reading of the preparative *qotel* is treated as instant future in the grammars (see n. 284). See also Gibson and Davidson 1994, §113c.

While a preparative meaning is quite plausible in the first sentence, a future interpretation suggests itself more strongly in the second one. Perhaps this is reflected in the NIV, which in the first sentence chooses the phrase *be about to*, but in the second *be going to*, which is somewhat more of a future and less of a preparative phrase than *be about to*:

(8) hinne__h__ 'ănî **bônæ__h__** bayit ləšem YHWH
behold I build.QOT.M.SG house for=name.of YHWH
[...] wəhabbayi_t_ 'ăšær 'ănî **bônæ__h__** gāḏôl
[...] and=the=house that I build.QOT.M.SG big
kî gāḏôl 'ælōhênû mikkol hā'ælōhîm
for big god=our from=all the=gods
Now I **am about to build** a temple for the Name of the Lord" [...] The temple I **am going to build** will be great, because our God is greater than all other gods. (2 Chr 2:3, 4; [2:4, 5])

The preparative meaning of the first clause may be underlined even more by translating as "I am planning to build." The reason why the second *qotel* does not draw the attention to the preparative stage of building as forcibly is probably that it is already known, hence less interesting, and that the discourse now elaborates more on future matters in mentioning the planned size of the building.

4.1.3. Nonprogressive and Nominal qotel

The participle *qotel* with predicative function is the youngest member of the Biblical Hebrew verbal system. The corresponding forms attested in, for example, Ugaritic, Amarna-Canaanite, and Akkadian do not have the same syntactical properties but are attributive or substantivized.[11] In Biblical Hebrew, there are several uses belonging to this older type. In these positions, *qotel* seems to be unmarked for aspect, and a distinction is instead to be made on the basis of diathesis, something that is also reflected in the designation "active participle," which is often used for *qotel*, in contrast to the passive participle *qatul*.[12] Sometimes, resultative aspect seems to be implied, for example, with the verb *bô'*, "come":

(9) hôṣî'î hā'ănāšîm **habbā'îm** 'ēlayi_k_
bring.out.IMP.2F.SG the=men the=come.QOT.M.PL to=you

---

11. For Ugaritic, see Tropper 2012, §73.43; for Amarna Canaanite (few attestations), Tropper and Vita 2010, §4.7; for Akkadian, Huehnergard 1997, 195–97.
12. See Joüon and Muraoka 2009, §121i; Waltke and O'Connor 1990, §37.5e.

'ăšær   bā'û   ləbêtek
who   come.QTAL.3M.PL   to=house=your

Bring out the men **who have come** to you, the ones who came into your house. (Josh 2:3)

On a few occasions, *qotel* is found with what appears to be resultative meaning even in predicate position. It happens at least once with *bô'* and a few more times with the verb *nāpal*, "fall":[13]

(10) a. wayyišlaḥ   mal'ākîm   'æl   'ăbîmælæk
         and=send.YQTL(S).3M.SG   messengers   to   Abimelek
         [...]   l'emōr   hinneʰ   ḡa'al   bæn   'æbæd
         [...]   QUOT   behold   Gaal   son.of Ebed
         wə'æḥāʸw   **bā'îm**   šəkæmâ
         and=brothers=his   come.QOT.M.PL   Shekem.toward
         wəhinnām   ṣārîm   'æt   hā'îr
         and=behold=them   besiege.QOT.M.PL   OBJ   the=city
         'ālækā
         against=you

He sent messengers to Abimelech [...] saying, "Look, Gaal son of Ebed and his brothers **have come** to Shechem, and they are stirring up the city against you." (Judg 9:31)

b. wəhamælæk   šāb   [...]   'æl   bêt
    and=the=king   return.QTAL.M.SG   [...]   to   house.of
    mišteʰ   hayyayin   wəhāmān   **nōpel**   'al
    drinking.of   the=wine   and=Haman   fall.QOT.M.SG   on
    hammiṭṭâ   'ăšær   'æster   'ālæʸhā
    the.couch   that   Esther   on=it

The king returned to the banquet hall. Haman **had thrown himself** on the couch on which Esther was lying. (Esth 7:8)

These examples could be seen as exceptions to the rule that *qotel* is progressive when it is not nominal, but we should be careful not to draw far-reaching conclusions. Possibly, the verb *nāpal* in (10b) is lexically ambiguous between a telic "fall"/"lay"-meaning and an atelic "lie"-meaning (see 2.2.2 and 4.3.3), and the

---

13. In Ezek 21:12 [21:7], there is another example with the verb *bô'*, unless this is actually a *qatal* that has been misrepresented by the Masoretes. For *nāpal*, see Judg 3:25; 4:22; 19:27; 1 Sam 5:3, 4. The *qotel* in Josh 7:10 can be interpreted as a present progressive, even though the progressive stage of the event, technically speaking, is over (see Joüon and Muraoka 2009, §113d on "actual present" *yiqtol*-L).

participle *bā'îm* in (10a) could perhaps be an instance of a *qotel* for vivid narration (see n. 4 above). In any case, the phenomenon is too marginal to allow us to reject the assumption that *qotel* is part of a progressive-resultative opposition in the Biblical Hebrew verbal system.

As to the nominal *qotel*, it needs to be mentioned that the distinction between the "nominal" and the "verbal," which is always slippery when it comes to participles, is especially so in Biblical Hebrew. In the following sentence, a substantival *qotel* functioning as a subject with nonspecific reference functions at the same time at a subordinate level as a verbal predicate that is coordinated with a finite verb:

(11) **makke**ʰ[14]   'îš   wāmet   môt
     smite.QOT.M.SG   man   and=die.QTAL.3M.SG   die.INFA
     yûmāt
     be.killed.YQTL-L.3M.SG
     Whoever **strikes** a man so that he dies shall surely be put to death.
     (Exod 21:12)

In this generalizing statement, the aspect of the *qotel* is decidedly completive at the microlevel (that is, with regard to the individual instantiations of the general state of affairs; see 3.2), since the verb is telic and represents the event as part of a chain of successive events. The focus of attention is not fixed by any contrasting event but moves through the chain.

A special category is the epithetic *qotel*, which is typically used for both specific historical and recurring nonspecific actions performed by the Lord:

(12) kî   hinneʰ   **yôṣer**   hārîm
     for   behold   form.QOT.M.SG   mountains
     ûḇōre'   ruaḥ   **ûmaggid**
     and=create. QOT.M.SG   wind   and=tell.QOT.M.SG
     ləʾāḏām   maʰśśeḥô   **'ōśe**ʰ   šaḥar
     for=human   what=thought=his   make.QOT.M.SG   dawn
     'êp̄â   wəḏōrek   'al   bāmŏtê   'āræṣ
     darkness   and=tread.QOT.M.SG   on   high.places.of   earth

---

14. This participle is morphologically in the construct state, which marks it as the main word of a genitive relation (The same applies to *'ōśeʰ* in example [12]). The best way to render the substantival nature of the participle in this construction is to use a *nomen agentis*, as in "the maker of the dawn." I have not marked the construct state in the interlinear glossing, since this state is not morphologically distinctive in most masculine singular participles in Biblical Hebrew, which means that there is mostly no paradigmatic way to distinguish a genitive relation ("the doer of x") from a transitive ("the one who does x") in Biblical Hebrew. On nominal *qotel* with direct object, see Waltke and O'Connor 1990, §37.3b; Nyberg 1952, §90b.

YHWH 'ælōhê ṣəbā'ōṭ šəmô
YHWH god.of hosts name=his
He who (1) has formed / (2) formed / (3) forms the mountains, **(1) who has created / (2) created / (3) creates** the wind, **he who reveals** his thoughts to humans, **who turns** dawn to darkness, **who treads** the high places of the earth—the Lord, God of hosts is his name. (Amos 4:13)

The aspecto-temporal meaning of the first two participles in this sentence is very open to interpretation. They may be taken to refer to singular, specific events in the past, with the focus either on (1) the present results of these events or (2) the past events as such. Alternatively, they may refer to (3) typical and nonspecific recurrent events.

In the next example, the epithetic *qotel* has a slightly more verbal morphosyntax. The qualifiers of the first and second participles (*ḥāyil* and *raḡlay*) are clearly direct objects and not objective genitives, and the second and third do not have a definite article, in spite of being coordinated with a participle that does.

(13) kî mî 'æloah mibbal'ădê YHWH ûmî ṣûr
    for who god apart.from YHWH and=who rock
    zûlāṯî 'ælōhênû hā'el ham'**azzəreni**
    except God=our the=God the=strengthen.QOT.M.SG=me
    ḥāyil wayyitten tāmîm darkî
    power and=give.YQTL(S).3M.SG faultless way.my
    məšawwæh raḡlay kā'ayyālōṯ wə'al bāmōṯay
    turn.QOT.M.SG feet.my as=the=deers and=on heights=my
    ya'ămîḏenî **məlammed** yāḏay
    place.YQTL(S).3M.SG=me teach.QOT.M.SG hands=my
    lammilḥāmâ wənihătâ qæšeṯ nəḥušâ
    for=the=battle and=press.QTAL.3F.SG bow.of copper
    zərô'ōṯay
    arms=my

(32) For who is God besides the Lord, and who is the rock except our God—(33) God **who girded** me with strength and made my way safe; (34) **who made** my feet like the feet of a deer and set me on the heights; (35) **who trained** my hands for battle, so that my arms could bend the bow of bronze. (Ps 18:32–35)

The participles in this example are formally a chain of adjuncts to *hā'el* ([the] God) in verse 32, but they gain a quite independent status as they are continued in verse 34 by a series of finite clauses that develop to an entire discourse treating the success story of the speaker and not ending until several verses later (v. 46). Most translators translate the participial clauses with independent, finite clauses.

From here it is not a big step to the formally independent participial clause of the type we find in the song of Hannah in 1 Sam 2:

(14) YHWH **memît** ûməḥayyæʰ
 YHWH let.die.QOT.M.SG and=let.live.QOT.M.SG
 môrîd šəʾôl
 bring.down.QOT.M.SG netherworld
 wayyaʿal
 and=bring.up.YQTL-S.3M.SG
 The Lord [is one who] **causes death** and **keeps alive**; he **brings down** to the grave and raises up. (1 Sam 2:6)

A possible interpretation of these participles is that they are stativized progressives, as proposed by Tania Notarius.[15] However, in view of the resemblances with the epithetic *qotel* in the above-mentioned examples, it is clear that the generalizing meaning could also be easily inferred from a nominal construction (sc. the Lord is "a death-bringing one," etc.). I therefore prefer to see them as basically substantival.[16]

4.2. *Yiqtol*-L

It is assumed in this study that the long variant of the prefix conjugation was originally an ordinary progressive form, regularly used for the expression of ongoing dynamic processes. These are the meanings most often understood as progressive in standard linguistic research. However, within the framework of a stage-based aspectual approach, semantically stative as well as pragmatically stativized predicates may be analyzed as progressives, as opposed to resultatives (see 3.4.2).

4.2.1. Invariant Progressive yiqtol-L

Nongeneralizing progressive *yiqtol*-L is rare in the Hebrew Bible.[17] It occurs more or less sparingly in *wh*-questions (15a), relative clauses (b), causal clauses (d), and with verbs denoting perceptions (d), ability (e), and knowledge (f):

---

15. Notarius 2010, 263.
16. I argue at length for this interpretation in Bergström 2016, 223–26.
17. See especially Joüon and Muraoka 2009, §113d and Joosten 2012, 101–2, 278–80. Also Driver 1892, §39γ; Waltke and O'Connor 1990, §31.3b; Gibson 1994, §63b rem. 3.

(15) a. lāmæʰ **tiḇkî**
why weep.YQTL-L.2F.SG
Why **are you weeping**? (1 Sam 1:8)

b. wəʾôlîḵâ ʾetḵæm ʾel hāʾîš
and=lead.YQTL(S).COH.1SG you to the=man
ʾăšær **təḇaqqəšûn**
who seek.YQTL-L.2M.PL
And I shall lead you to the man **you are seeking**. (2 Kgs 6:19)

c. maʰ lāʿām kî **yiḇkû**
what to=the=people that weep.YQTL-L.3M.PL
What is the matter with the people, that **they are weeping**?
(1 Sam 11:5)

d. ʾerʾænnû wəlōʾ ʿattâ
see.YQTL-L.1SG=him but=not now
ʾăšûrænnû wəlōʾ qārôḇ
behold.YQTL-L.1SG=him but=not near
I see him, but not now; **I behold** him, but not near. (Num 24:17)

e. ʾanaḥnû nišbaʿnû lāhæm [...] lōʾ
we swear.QTAL.1PL to=them [...] not
nûḵal lingoaʿ bāhæm
can.YQTL-L.1PL to=touch.INFC in=them
We have sworn to them [...]. **We can**not **touch** them. (Josh 9:19)

f. wəʾānōḵî naʿar qāṭōn lōʾ **ʾeḏaʿ**
and=I boy young not know.YQTL-L.1SG
ṣeʾṯ wāḇōʾ
go.out.INFC and=come.in.INFC
And I am a little child. **I do** not **know** how to handle this. (1 Kgs 3:7)

In some poetic passages, *yiqtol*-L is used to depict an imagined present situation:

(16) **yəḥalləqû** bəḡāday lāhæm
divide.YQTL-L.3M.PL garments=my for=themselves
wəʿal ləḇûšî **yappîlû** ḡôrāl
and=for clothes=my cast.YQTL-L.3M.PL lot
They divide my garments among themselves, and for my clothes
they cast lot. (Ps 22:19; English: 22:19)

All the examples in (15) and (16) are imperfective. The progressive stage of the event is viewed as continuous around the focalizing event, which is the act of speech. The nuclear event is either continuous, as in (15a–f), or repeated, as in (16) (cf. 3.4.4, fig. 2). Several of the events are prototypical progressives in the sense that they are dynamic, and none of them refer to permanent states. In subsection 5.4.2, we shall return to the question of why *yiqtol*-L can be used for continuous progressives in these particular cases, even though the normal form is *qotel*.

I am not aware of any certain example of an imperfective dynamic present progressive *yiqtol*-L in Late Biblical Hebrew.[18] In past settings, there may be at least two or three with pluractional meaning. Thus, in the following example, the *yiqtol*-L describes an extended process that seems to be developing when the Manassite leaders join David. The verb seems to have specific rather than generalizing meaning:[19]

(17) bəlæḵtô   'æl   ṣîqlaḡ   nāp̄əlû
     in=go.INFC=his to   Ziklag   defect.QTAL.3M-PL
     'ālāʸw   mimmənaššæʰ 'aḏnaḥ   wəyôzāḇāḏ   [...]
     on=him   from=Manasseh Adnah   and=Jozabad [...]
     rā'šê   hā'ălāp̄îm   'ăšær   limnaššæʰ   [...]
     heads.of   the=thousands which   for=Manasseh [...]
     wayyihyû   śārîm   baṣṣāḇā'   kî
     and=be.YQTL(S).3PL   commanders in=the=army for
     lə'ēṯ   yôm   bəyôm   **yāḇo'û**   lə'ozrô
     to=time.of   day   in=day   come.YQTL-L.3M.PL for=help=his
     'aḏ   ləmaḥănæʰ ḡāḏôl   kəmaḥăneʰ   'ĕlôhîm
     until   to=army   big   as=army.of God

When he went to Ziklag, Adnah, Jozabad [...], commanders of the thousands in Manasseh defected to him from Manasseh [...] and they became commanders in the army. Indeed, day after day people **kept coming** to help, until there was a great army, like the army of God. (1 Chr 12:21, 23)

Much more often, *yiqtol*-L expresses habituality or some other generalizing meaning.[20] When there is no other possible contrasting event, the act of speech

---

18. The stative verb *yāḵōl*, "to be able" (negated) does occur, however, even with a transitory meaning (Esth 6:13; Neh 4:4; 6:3). Another example may be *yaḥpōṣ* of the verb *ḥāp̄eṣ*, "to desire," "wish" in Esth 6:6 (see the discussion on example [33]).

19. Other examples are found in Esth 2:11 (*yeʿāśæʰ*) and 4:3 (*yuṣṣaʿ*).

20. See Driver 1892, §30s, 33; Waltke and O'Connor 1990, §31.2b, 3e; Gibson 1994, §63a–b; Joüon and Muraoka 2009, §113c, e; Joosten 2012, 276–77, 280–81.

constitutes a focalizing event against which the state is seen as ongoing. This imperfective perspective testifies to the basic progressive aspect of the form (see 3.4.2):

(18) hălô' zæʰ 'ăšær **yištæʰ** 'ădōnî
Q=not this which drink.YQTL-L.3M.SG master.my
bô
with=it
Is it not this one that my master **drinks** from? (Gen 44:5)

The focalizing event can also be some event mentioned in the context. In the next example, the focalizing event is marked by the predicate *wayyar'* ("and he saw") in the first clause. Before the *yiqtol*-L there is also a progressive *qotel* (*rōbəṣîm* "were lying") that represents a specific, ongoing event:

(19) wayyar' wəhinneʰ bə'er baśśādæʰ
and=see.YQTL-S.3M.SG and=behold well in=the=field
wəhinneʰ šām šəlōšā 'ædrê ṣō'n
and=behold there three herds.of small.cattle
rōbəṣîm 'ālǽhā kî min habbə'er hahî'
lie.QOT.M.PL over=it for from the=well the=this
yašqû hā'ădārîm
water.YQTL-L.3M.PL the=herds
And he saw a well in the field, and three herds were lying near it, for there **they used to water** the herds. (Gen 29:2)

Generic *yiqtol*-L characterizes nonspecific referents and often has a timeless character. It is thus very far removed from the most basic meaning of the progressive type, which involves individuals performing transitory events (see 3.4.2). The only common denominator is that both the generic and the prototypical progressive represent a stage that is extended around a focalizing event. In (20) it is the time of speech:

(20) 'al yera' bə'ênæʸkā 'æt
not be.evil.YQTL-S.JUSS.3M.SG in=eyes=your OBJ
haddābar hazzæʰ kî kāzōʰ wəkāzæʰ
the=thing the=this for as=this and=as=this
tō'kal hæḥāræb
eat.YQTL-L.3F.SG the=sword
Do not let this matter trouble you, for the sword **eats** now one, now another. (2 Sam 11:25)

The question whether progressive *yiqtol*-L can be employed for past aorist meaning, like *qotel* (4.1.1), is very difficult to answer. Free-standing *yiqtol*-forms with past aorist meaning do occur, especially in poetry, but since there are some examples of apocopated forms among them, one has to reckon with the possibility that they actually originate from an old resultative *yiqtol*-S. It is not crucial for the purposes of this study to make a distinction between possible past aorist *yiqtol*-L and *yiqtol*-S, however. I give a couple of examples in the subsection about *yiqtol*-S below (4.4.3), without intending to be too dogmatic on the issue.

It is difficult to point at clear examples of preparative *yiqtol*-L in the present sphere in Biblical Hebrew in spite of the fact that it is probably basically a progressive form.[21] A strong case, however, can be made for the following example:

(21) bārûk YHWH 'ælōhê yiśrā'el [...] 'ăšær
blessed YHWH god.of Israel [...] who
nātan ləḏāwîḏ hammælek ben ḥākām
give.QTAL.3M.SG for=David the=king son wise
yôdea' śekæl ûbînâ 'ăšær
know.QOT.M.SG insight and=discernment who
yibnæʰ bayit laYHWH
build.YQTL-L.3M.SG house for=yhwh
Blessed be the Lord, God of Israel, [...] who has given King David a wise son, gifted with insight and discernment, who **is going to build** a house for the Lord. (2 Chr 2:11 [2:12])

This is king Hiram's reaction to Solomon's request for assistance in his planned building project. The praise for Solomon's intelligence seems to direct focus of attention to the present stage of planning rather than to the future completion of the temple.

Additionally, in the next example, the *yiqtol*-L makes good sense as referring to a present intention, whereas a pure future meaning is less feasible:

(22) 'im **tiḡ'al** gə'āl wə'im
if redeem.YQTL-L.2M.SG redeem.IMP.2M.SG and=if
lō' **yiḡ'al** haggîḏâ lî
not redeem.YQTL-L.3M.SG [sic] tell.IMP.2M.SG for=me
If **you intend to redeem** [her], redeem, but if **you do** not **intend to redeem** [her], tell me. (Ruth 4:4)

---

21. The grammars do not mention any usage corresponding to the "immediate" future *qotel*. The possible preparative *yiqtol*-L in (21) occurs in connection with the *qotel*-clauses with similar function in example (8).

A strong sense of intentionality can sometimes shine through when it is less clear whether the meaning is best understood as preparative or future.[22] The gray zone between these meanings is probably what makes preparative *yiqtol*-L a rather elusive category.

Other examples of preparative meaning in *yiqtol*-L are found in past contexts.[23] In (23), the focused time is set in the past by the verb *wayyiqqaḥ* ("he took"):

(23) wayyiqqaḥ   'æt   bənô   habbəkôr
     and=take.YQTL(S).3M.SG OBJ son=his   the=firstborn
     'ăšær **yimlōḵ**   taḥtāʸw
     who   rule.YQTL-L.3M.SG instead.of=him
     wayyaʿălēhû   ʿōlâ
     and=sacrifice.YQTL(S).3M.SG=him   burnt.offering
     ʿal   hahōmâ
     on   the=wall
     He took his firstborn son, who **was going to rule** after him, and offered him as a burnt offering on the city wall. (2 Kgs 3:27)

From the point of view of the narrator and the reader, the predicate in the relative clause (*yimlōḵ* "was going to rule") can have neither progressive nor relative future meaning, since we know that the king's son is not ruling at the focused time and never ruled afterward. The relative clause clearly refers to a preparatory stage of the event, which is simultaneous to the event marked by *wayyiqqaḥ* ("he took"). In this way it fits the above description of preparative meaning, according to which the focus is on the preparative stage of the event without regard as to whether the nuclear event will actually follow (3.4.3). However, from the point of view of an observer within the story, it would be natural to speak and to think about the future rule of the king's son in future terms. The observer's temporal perspective is always expressed in reported speech and thought in Biblical Hebrew. There is a possibility that this perspective has spread to relative clauses by analogy.[24]

---

22. For some examples, see Num 16:14; Isa 21:12; Jer 44:17, 25.

23. See Driver 1892, 38β, 39β; Waltke and O'Connor 1990, §31.6.2c; Gibson 1994, §64a; Joüon and Muraoka 2009, §113b; Joosten 2012, 281–83. The grammars do not distinguish between past preparative meaning and future in the past.

24. See Joosten (2012, 283) on "prospective" *yiqtol*-L in object-clauses. Among the examples he mentions, preparative meaning is a possible interpretation in Exod 37:16; 1 Kgs 7:7; Eccl 4:15; Ezra 10:8. Joosten argues that past prospective meaning occurs also in main clauses (pp. 133–34), but two of the three examples he offers (1 Sam 13:17–18 and Isa 6:4) are, in my opinion, better taken as past aorist *yiqtol*. The *yiqtol* in 2 Sam 15:37 is the most feasible candidate, but here, too, aorist meaning is an option.

4.2.2. Temporalized **yiqtol-L**

In spite of the somewhat meager evidence of unambiguous and/or semantically motivated preparative meaning of *yiqtol*-L, the occurrences of *yiqtol*-L with prototypically progressive functions support the conclusion that the abundant future use of the form derives from a basic progressive meaning.[25] Moreover, future *yiqtol*-L is less dependent on context for its temporal meaning than present and past *yiqtol*-L are, and it often appears without a focalizing event. This is a natural consequence of temporalization (see 3.6). Thus, future *yiqtol*-L takes on various aspectual meanings depending on *Aktionsart* and contextual factors. Given the predominance of telic verbs in nonpresent discourse, completive aorist meaning is the most common:

(24) hā'āræṣ   'ăšær   'attâ   šōḵeḇ   'ālæʸhā   ləḵā
     the=land   which   you   lie.QOT.M.SG   on=it   to=you
     'ættənænnâ   ûləzar'æḵā
     give.YQTL-L.1SG=it   and=to=offspring=your
     I shall give the land on which you are lying to you and your offspring. (Gen 28:13)

Atelic verbs referring to isolated events naturally have imperfective meaning:

(25) YHWH   **yillāḥem**   lāḵæm   wə'attæm
     YHWH   fight.YQTL-L.3M.SG   for=you   and=you
     taḥărîšûn
     be.still.YQTL-L.2M.PL
     The Lord **shall fight** for you, and you **shall be still**. (Exod 14:14)

However, when the event referred to starts a course of events, atelic verbs may have completive meaning, as in Jacob's objection to his mother's proposal that he should try to swindle his brother out of the fatherly blessing. The verb *māšaš* ("to feel, touch") is atelic, but in this imagined future course of events, the activity of feeling has the implied result that Isaac becomes aware of Jacob's deceit:

(26) hen   'ēsāw   'āḥî   'îš   śā'ir   wə'ānōḵî   'îš
     behold   Esau   brother=my   man   hairy   and=I   man

---

25. On the future *yiqtol* and various associated modal meanings, see Driver 1892, §37α, 38 α, 39 α, 41; Waltke and O'Connor 1990, §31.6.2; Gibson 1994, §64c; Joüon and Muraoka 2009, §113b; Joosten 2012, 266–76.

ḥālāq	'ûlay	**yəmuššenî**		'ābî
smooth	perhaps	touch.YQTL-L.3M.SG=me		father=my
wəhāyîtî		bəʿênāyw	kimtaʿteaʿ	
and=be.QTAL.1SG		in=eyes=his	as=deceive.QOT.M.SG	

Behold, Esau my brother is a hairy man and I am a smooth-skinned man. Perhaps my father **will feel** me and I shall appear in his eyes as deceiving him. (Gen 27:11–12)

The time of speech is not the only possible deictic center for a temporalized meaning of the *yiqtol*-L:[26]

(27)	wæ'ælîšāʿ	ḥālâ	'æt	ḥolyô	'ăšær
	and=Elisha	fall.ill.QTAL3M.SG	OBJ	sickness=his	which
	yāmût	bô			
	die.YQTL-L3M.SG	in=it			

And Elisha fell ill with the illness from which **he was to die**. (2 Kgs 13:14)

In my interpretation, this is an instance of a real future in the past. That is, the verb *ḥālâ* ("fell ill") marks a secondary deictic center that becomes the point of departure for a temporalized reading of *yāmût*. The verb *yāmût* is a future in the past pointing out to the reader that Elisha would die soon afterward. For this posterior event there is no focalizing event. The aspect becomes completive aorist owing to the telic *Aktionsart* of the verb. To decide whether the predicate is a future in the past rather than a past preparative, one can test how easily it can be exchanged with a preterite (*from which he* [later] *died*; see 2.1).

All kinds of modal nuances can go along with the future *yiqtol*-L in Biblical Hebrew. This is no reason to posit a "modal" element in the semantics of the form. A future reference can be pragmatically laden with any secondary modal meaning, but it is hard to see how any particular modal source can lie behind the wide spectrum of possible modal connotations in *yiqtol*-L.

Accordingly, the future utterance in (28) has a secondary modal meaning of epistemic necessity, because Leah reckons that the event will occur on the basis of what she thinks must necessarily follow from the present facts:

(28)	wattahar	ʿôḏ		
	and=conceive.YQTL-S.3F.SG	again		
	wattelæḏ	ben	wattōʾmær	
	and=give.birth.YQTL-S.3F.SG	son	and=say.YQTL-S.3F.SG	

---

26. See n. 299.

116 Aspect, Communicative Appeal, and Temporal Meaning

> 'attâ   happa'am   **yillāwæʰ**   'îšî   'elay
> now   the=time   join.PASS.YQTL-L.3M.SG   man=my   to=me
> kî   yāladtî   lô   šəlōšâ   bānîm
> for   give.birth.QTAL.1SG   for=him   three   sons
>
> And she got pregnant again and gave birth to a son. She said: "Now at last [it must be the case that] my husband **will hold on** to me, for I have given him three sons." (Gen 29:34)

Another modality is implied in the following example, which contains Isaac's response when Esau asks whether Isaac has some blessing for him, too, after having blessed Jacob:

> (29) wayya'an   yiṣḥāq   wayyo'mær
>   and=answer.YQTL-S.3M.SG   Isaac   and=say.YQTL-S.3M.SG
>   lə'eśāw   hen   gəbîr   śamtîw   lāk
>   to=Esau   behold   master   put.QTAL.1SG=him   to=you
>   wə'æt   kol   'æḥāʸw   nātattî
>   and.OBJ   all   brothers=his give.QTAL.1SG
>   lô   lā'ăbādîm   wədāgān   wətîrōš
>   to=him   for=servants   and=grain   and=new.wine
>   səmaktîw   ûləkā   'epô'
>   sustain.QTAL.1SG=him   and=for=you   so
>   **'æ'æśæʰ**   bənî
>   do.YQTL-L.1SG   son=my
>
> Isaac answered and said to Esau: "I have made him your master and given all his brothers as servants to him, and I have sustained him with grain and new wine. So, what **shall I** do for you, my son?" (Gen 27:37)

Isaac's enumeration of what he has done for Jacob is meant to make Esau understand that he has already spent what he has to offer on the younger brother. Thus, Isaac's ensuing question about what he shall do for Esau after this is strongly suggestive of the modality of ability. As the NIV puts it: "What can I possibly do for you, my son?"

Directive speech acts performed by means of *yiqtol*-L are perhaps the most distinct expression of modality of the form in Biblical Hebrew. Often, it occurs in general commands:

> (30) zākôr   'æt   yôm   haššabbāt
>   remember.INFA   OBJ   day.of   the=Sabbath

ləqaddəšô	šešæt	yāmîm	**taʿăḇōḏ**
to=keep.holy.INFC=it	six.of	days	work.YQTL-L.2M.SG
wəʿāśîtā	kol	məlaʾktækā	
and=do.QTAL.2M.SG	all	work=your	

Remember the day of the Sabbath by keeping it holy. Six days **you shall work** and do all your work. (Exod 20:8–9)

There are also specific commands with *yiqtol*-L:

(31) wayyišlaḥ   yaʿăqōḇ   malʾāḵîm   ləp̄ānāʸw
    and=send.YQTL(S).3M.SG Jacob messengers ahead.of=him
    ʾæl   ʿeśāw   [...]   wayṣaw   ʾōṯām
    to   Esau   [...]   and=order.YQTL-S.3M.SG   OBJ=them
    leʾmōr   kōʰ   **tōʾmərûn**   laʾăḏōnî   ləʿeśāw ...
    QUOT   thus say.YQTL-L.2M.PL   lord=my   to=Esau

Jacob sent messengers ahead of him to Esau [...], and he instructed them, saying, "**You shall speak** thus to my Lord Esau." (Gen 32:4–5 [32:3–4])

The directive *yiqtol*-L is probably an example of what Bybee, Perkins, and Pagliuca would call the "imperative" function of futures. Bybee, Perkins, and Pagliuca hypothesize that this function originates in contexts where the speaker has authority over the addressee, and they illustrate with the following example:

(32) You're gonna take off your shoes before you come in here.[27]

The directive meaning of the utterance can be inferred from the assumption that the predicted event is desired by the speaker and that it is taken for granted that the addressee will comply to his/her will. The same inference, I would suggest, has given rise to the directive *yiqtol*-L. There are certain social implications associated with this kind of directive (for which, see 5.2.3 and 5.4.3).

The above examples must suffice to illustrate the rich variety of modal implications that arise in connection with future *yiqtol*-L. Theoretically, the modal meanings of *yiqtol*-L could be semantic, provided that they are regularly used in contexts where there is no ambiguity between future and modal meaning, but in that case, the modal meaning is secondary to the future meaning and not vice versa. An illustration of what a nonfuture modal *yiqtol*-L could look like

---

27. Bybee, Perkins, and Pagliuca 1994, 211.

is example (33) below, but it can just as well be interpreted as a nonmodal real present, or even a generalizing present with an implication of potentiality:[28]

(33) wayyāḇô' hāmān wayyō'mær
and=come.YQTL(S).3M.SG Haman and=say.YQTL-S.3M.SG
lô' hammælæḵ maʰ laʿăśôṯ bāʾîš
to=him the=king what to=do.INFC for=the=man
'ăšær hammælæḵ ḥāp̄eṣ bîqārô
whom the=king desire.QTAL.3M.SG for=honor=his
wayyō'mær bəlibbô ləmî
and=say.YQTL-S.3M.SG in=heart=his for=whom
yaḥpōṣ hammælæḵ laʿăśôṯ yāqār
desire.YQTL-L.3M.SG the=king to=do.INFC honor
yôṯer mimmænnî
other than=me

Haman came in, and the king said to him, "What should be done for someone whom the king wants to honor?" Haman said to himself, "Whom **does** the king **want** [alt. "would the king want"] to honor other than me?" (Esth 6:6)

4.3. *Qatal*

Qatal is a common designation for the verbal form also called the "suffix conjugation" or the "perfect." The latter term indicates that the basic aspectual meaning of the form is resultative. However, within the *qal* stem form, there is a morphological convergence between *qatal* formed on verbal lexemes and *qatal* that are, lexically speaking, inflected adjectives. Here, I shall only consider the detectably verbal *qatal* as part of the resultative-progressive opposition of the Biblical Hebrew verbal system.[29] The adjectival *qatal* is commented upon in the subsection on the so-called "stative" *qatal* below (see 4.3.3). Stative *qatal* also includes a group of *qatal* formed on stative verbs, which is dealt with in the same subsection. I do not claim, however, that the verbal statives of the *qal* stem form constitute a nonresultative category on par with the adjectival stems, since it is possible that the "state" signified in this category is actually the result stage of a dynamic event that is encoded by the lexeme.

---

28. See (8) in chapter 3 above for an example of a generalizing statement with an implication of potentiality.

29. *Pace* Waltke and O'Connor 1990 §22.2.2d: "The Qal stative constructions [sc. of the adjectival roots] mark the situation represented with all the values of a verbal form (aspect, mood, *Aktionsart*)"; see also their n. 10.

4.3.1. Invariant Resultative qatal

The resultative meaning of *qatal* is evidenced by its frequent use with the perfect limit-aspect in present (34a) and past (34b) contexts:[30]

(34) a. ki   'attâ   **hirḥîb**   YHWH   lānû
       For   now   make.big.QTAL.3M.SG   YHWH   for=us
       Now the Lord **has made room** for us. (Gen 26:22)

   b. wayyar'   'ēśāw   kî   **berak**
      and=see.YQTL-S.3M.SG   Esau   that bless.QTAL.3M.SG
      yiṣḥāq   'æt   ya'ăqōb   wəšillaḥ   'ōtô'
      Isaac   OBJ   Jacob   and=send.QTAL.3M.SG   him
      paddænâ   'ărām
      Paddan.toward   Aram
      Esau saw that Isaac **had blessed** Jacob and sent him to Paddan-aram. (Gen 28:6)

Future perfects are also found, as in Moses's ruling about how slaves may be acquired after the Israelites have settled in the promised land:

(35) wəḡam   mibbənê   hattôšāḇîm   haggārîm
     and=also   from=sons.of   the=residents   the=live.QOT.M.PL
     'immākæm   mehæm   tiqnû   'ăšær
     with=you   from.them   acquire.YQTL-L.2M.PL   who
     hôlîdû   bə'arṣəkæm
     be.born.QTAL.3M.PL   in=your=land
     And also from the sons of the temporary residents you shall acquire them [i.e., slaves]—those who [will] **have been born** in your land. (Lev 25:45)

In (34a), the focalizing event that fixes the mutual perception of the event referred to by the *qatal*-form is the speech act; in (34b) and (35) it is the events referred to by the verbs *wayyar'* ("he saw") and *tiqnû* ("you shall/may acquire"). The difference between the Hebrew verbs and their English equivalents in the above examples is that the Hebrew verbs do not mark the temporal relation between the focused time and the utterance—that is, the tense.

---

30. On the perfect meaning in different temporal settings, see Driver 1892, §8, 16, 17; Waltke and O'Connor 1990, §30.3, 5.2; Gibson 1994, 57d, 58a, 59a; Joüon and Muraoka 2009, §112c, e, i; Joosten 2012, 194 96, 205–6, 219–21. Notice, however, that these authors do not distinguish between perfect and relative past meaning (on which, see 2.1).

A special case of invariant resultative meaning is when *qatal* functions as "perfect of persistent situation" (see 3.4.1):[31]

(36) wə'attâ   hinne[h]   **hæḥæ̆yâ**   YHWH   'ōtî
     and=now   behold   keep.alive.QTAL.3M.SG   YHWH   me
     ka'ăšær   dibber   zæ[h]   'arbā'îm   wəḥāmeš   šānâ
     as   say.QTAL.3M.SG   this   forty   and=five   year
     me'āz   dibbær   YHWH   'æṯ   haddāḇār hazzæ[h]
     since   say.QTAL.3M.SG   YHWH   OBJ   the=word   the=this
     And now, the Lord **has kept** me **alive**, as he said, these forty-five years since the time that the Lord spoke this word. (Josh 14:10)

Just like the English perfect, the resultative grammatical marker in this *qatal*-clause has scope over the qualification "for forty-five years," which is to say that it governs not only the verb phrase *to keep alive* but the whole phrase *to keep alive for forty-five years*. The "result" in this event is the time span of forty years. The result stage, accordingly, is present from the moment that the forty-five years has been completed. Since the transition to the result stage precedes the time of speech, the limit-aspect here resembles perfect more than anything else.

The *qatal* of persistent situation behaves like a typical perfect in that the adverbial lies within the scope of the resultative marking. Hence, one would not expect the form to be compatible with the adverbial "still" (3.4.1). However, there may be a difference between dynamic and stative verbs here, since there is at least one example in the Hebrew Bible where a stative *qatal* is combined with an adverbial with this meaning:

(37) 'ōḏ   **šā'ar**   haqqāṭān
     still   be.left.QTAL.3M.SG   the=little
     The little one **is** still **left**. (1 Sam 16:11)

As an experiential perfect, *qatal* expresses one of its most thinned-out forms of resultative meaning:

(38) mî   **šāma'**   kāzō'ṯ
     who   QTAL.3M.SG   like=the=this
     Who **has heard** of such a thing? (Isa 66:8)

---

31. See Waltke and O'Connor 1990, §30.5.1; Joosten 2012, 196.

A generalizing, "gnomic," *qatal* is rather commonly used in a poetical register to express timeless truths. It is best translated with the English present tense:[32]

(39) a. gam   ṣippôr   **māṣəʾâ**   bayit
         even   sparrow   find.QTAL.3F.SG   house
         Even the sparrow **finds** [lit. "has found"] a home. (Ps 84:4 [84:3])

   b. **ʾāmar**   ʿāṣel   ʾărî   baḥûṣ   bətôk   rəḥōbôt
       say.QTAL.3M.SG.   lazy   lion   outside   in   street
       ʾērāṣeaḥ
       be.killed.YQTL-L.1SG
       The lazy one **says** [lit. "has said"]: "There is a lion outside. I shall get killed in the street." (Prov 22:13)

Scholars sometimes compare the gnomic *qatal* with the gnomic aorists or preterites found in many languages, which would mean that the gnomicity of *qatal* is derived from its temporalized, past meaning.[33] But gnomic meaning is also known to develop from perfects, where it can be derived from the perfect of persistent situation or the experiential perfect (see chapter 3, example [13b, c]).[34]

The invariant resultative *qatal* may also have aorist meaning; that is, it may represent the result stage as emergent, rather than continuous (3.5). An example is the performative speech act.[35] The speech act here fixes the focus, with the implication that the result stage of the event begins with the utterance. Thus, the event is viewed at the climactic moment of transition into the *telos* of the lexically denoted nuclear event, which gives the clause completive aorist meaning:

(40) hinneʰ   **nātattî**   lākæm   ʾæt   kol   ʿēśæb
     behold   give.QTAL.1SG   to=you   OBJ   each   herb
     Behold, I **give** you all the herbs. (Gen 1:29)

---

32. Driver 1892, §12; Joüon and Muraoka 2009, §112d; Joosten 2012, 204–5. Some scholars working with the hypothesis that *qatal* is basically stative see gnomicity as a direct expression of the stativity of the form (Meyer 1972, §101.2b; Eskhult 1990, 21; Gibson 1994, §57c); see 2.2.4. The usage is mentioned without explanation in Waltke and O'Connor 1990, §30.5.1c.

33. Kautsch 1909, §106k; Rogland 2003, chapter 2.4; Joosten 2012, 205.

34. See Andrason 2012c, 24–29 (the perfect of persistent situation is here called "inclusive perfect"). Andrason also mentions another possible source of gnomic perfects, the "iterative indefinite perfect" (26), which is very close to the experiential perfect. See also Joüon and Muraoka 2009, §112d.

35. Driver 1892, §10, 13; Waltke and O'Connor 1990, §30.5.1d; Gibson 1994, §57b; Joüon and Muraoka 2009, §112f; Joosten 2012, 202–4.

Qatal may also be aorist in combination with an adverbial that marks a temporal boundary:

(41) mâ   'ănaḥnû   yōšəḇîm   poh   'aḏ   **maṯnû**
     why   we   sit.QOT.M.PL   here   until   die.QTAL.1PL
     Why should we sit here until we **die** [lit. "have died"]? (2 Kgs 7:3)

As we can see, the adverbial in sentence (41) sets the *qatal*-event in the future.

Future meaning can also be inferred in a *qatal* that is juxtaposed with a *yiqtol*-L:

(42) wəḵol   mizra'   yə'ôr   yîḇaš
     and=every   field.of   Egypt   wither.YQTL-L.3M.SG
     niddap̄   wə'ênænnû
     be.scattered.QTAL.3M.SG   and=none.of=it
     Every sown field along the Nile will become parched, **will be scattered** and be no more. (Isa 19:7)

Such unqualified, free-standing *qatal*-clauses with future reference are known as "prophetic perfects," because of their tendency to occur in prophetic texts.[36] The difference between *qatal* and the *yiqtol*-L in (42) is that *qatal* provides no semantic basis for the future inference; contextual factors alone do the job. This is perfectly normal in a form that has aspect, rather than tense, as its basic meaning. The *qatal*-clause does not differ from an atemporal nominal clause in this respect. For comparison, consider example (43), where the tense value of the nominal clause is given by the juxtaposition with the *yiqtol*-L-clause:

(43) lammô'eḏ   'āšûḇ   'elệḵā   kā'eṯ
     for=appointment   return.YQTL-L.1SG   to=you   as=time
     ḥayyâ   ûləśārâ   ben
     living   and=for=Sarah   son
     I shall return to you at the appointed time at this time next year, and Sarah will have a son [lit. "and for Sarah, a son"]. (Gen 18:14)

In some utterances the only cue as to the future meaning of *qatal* is a shared presupposition that the event that is being referred to has not yet occurred and, hence, must be situated in the future. This is at least the common interpretation of several *qatal*-clauses that traditionally have been counted among the prophetic

---

36. Driver 1892, §14; Waltke and O'Connor 1990, §30.5.1e; Gibson 1994, §59b; Joüon and Muraoka 2009, §112h; Joosten 2012, 207–8.

perfects. Since the original context of the utterances is often hard to establish, there is almost always a way to argue that the *qatal* actually refers to a past event, but the following example stands a good chance of being a genuine future *qatal*:

(44) ’ær’ænnû   wəlō’   ‘attâ
     see.YQTL-L.1SG=him but=not now
     ’ăšûrænnû   wəlō’   qārôḇ
     behold.YQTL-L.1SG=him but=not near
     dāraḵ   kôḵāḇ   miyya‘ăqōḇ
     tread.QTAL.3M.SG star   from=Jacob
     I see him, but not now, I behold him but not close. A star **shall come out** of Jacob. (Num 24:17)

In combination with the particles *kî ’îm*, the future *qatal* assumes an asseverative nuance:

(45) nišba‘   YHWH   ṣəḇā’ôṯ   bənap̄šô   kî
     and=swear.QTAL.3M.SG YHWH.of hosts   in=soul=his for
     ’îm **mille’ṯîḵā**   ’āḏām   kayyælæq
     if   fill.QTAL.3M.SG=you   man   as=the=locust
     The Lord of hosts has sworn by himself: "For sure, **I will fill** you with troops like locusts." (Jer 51:14)

Some readers feel that the future *qatal* in general lends an aura of certainty to the proposition that is lacking in *yiqtol*-L-clauses. The knowledge of the future event appears to stem from experience rather than more or less well-informed guesswork, so that the future event is presented "as having already been accomplished."[37] This goes well with the idea that the basic semantic function of the form is to put focus on the result stage of the event.

The existence of future *qatal* without the proclitic *wə*- has been questioned from time to time, most recently and emphatically by Max Rogland, who considers *qatal* to be a true past tense ("either absolutely or relatively").[38] Rogland argues that many of the alleged cases of "prophetic perfects" have been misinterpreted and actually refer to past events. He admits that there is a group of *qatal* that do refer to future events, but these can be explained as referring to past *visions* of future events. That is, the prophet is referring to what he *saw* in the vision, regardless of the fact that the event that is being referred to is supposed

---

37. Joüon and Muraoka 2009, §112h. See also Driver 1892, §14; Joosten 2012, 119.
38. Rogland 2003, 10. His treatment of future *qatal* is found in the third chapter of his book. For similar views, see Nyberg 1952, §8700; Zuber 1986, 153–55, 173–74.

to occur in the future. In Rogland's terms, the temporal value of *qatal* is tied to the time when the event occurred in the vision, "E^{vision}," and not when it occurs in reality, "E^{real}." The argument is supported by the dream and vision narratives from the books of Genesis and Daniel, where dreams and visions referring to a future E^{real} are retold as past E^{vision}. According to Rogland, it became a convention to report prophetic messages as if with reference to a past vision, even if the vision was not mentioned explicitly.[39]

Apart from the historical problems connected with this hypothetical reconstruction of the conventions of the prophetic genre, there is really nothing from the linguistic point of view that precludes *qatal* from having future meaning—except for the preconception that it is a past tense form.[40] First, as we have seen, the contextual indications that some *qatal*-forms have future time reference are very strong indeed. Second, the hypothesis of the past-only *qatal* hinges on the assumption that the consecutive *wəqataltí* is a separate verbal form, although this construction is neither morphologically distinct from nonconsecutive *weqatal* (1.4) nor functionally distinct from asyndetic *qatal* (see examples [53]–[55] in this subsection). Moreover, some of the functions of *wəqataltí* can also be performed by *wayyiqtol* (4.4.1), but no one would suggest that *wayyiqtol* consists of two different forms because of that.

This leads us to the syndetic, consecutive *qatal*—that is, *wəqataltí*.[41] It often occurs in the apodosis of a conditional clause, as in (46):

(46) 'im   'æmṣā'   bisdōm   hămiššîm   ṣaddiqîm
     if   find.YQTL-1.SG   in=Sodom   fifty   righteous
     bətôk   hā'îr   wə**nāśā'tí**   ləkol
     in=midst.of the=town   and=forgive.QTAL.1SG for=all.of
     hammāqôm   ba'ăbûrām
     the=place   because.of=them

---

39. Rogland 2003, 72 n. 55. Rogland admits that he cannot account for the example from Isa 19:7 above; see Rogland 2003, 113 (the same goes for Isa 33:3–5; 34:14–16).

40. The historical problem of Rogland's hypothesis lies in the assumption that prophecy was always visionary. This premise relies on the literal interpretation of one of the terms for prophet, *ḥōzæh* ("seer"), and prophecy, *ḥāzōn* ("vision"). However, visions were hardly the sole source of prophetic knowledge in ancient Israel. Prophetic formulas like *dābār YHWH* ("the word of the Lord"), *nə'ūm YHWH* ("the utterance of the Lord"), and, in particular, *kōh 'āmar YHWH* ("thus says the Lord") speak of messages received by hearing rather than seeing. Even the terms *ḥōzæh* and *ḥāzōn* may be more closely connected with aural than visual experience, in spite of the literal meaning of the words (Jepsen 1977, 825). Furthermore, the traditions preserved in the narrative material, where paradigmatic prophetic figures like Moses and Samuel are reported to have received their messages in spoken form, lend little support to the hypothesis of a predominantly visionary prophetical practice.

41. For the various usages of *wəqataltí*, some of which are illustrated below, see Driver 1892, chapter 8; Waltke and O'Connor 1990, §31; Gibson and Davidson 1994, §§55–60; Joüon and Muraoka 2009, §119; Joosten 2012, 288–308. Among these scholars, Gibson (§69) stresses that there is no semantic difference between *wəqataltí* and ordinary *qatal*.

If I find in Sodom fifty righteous men in the city, **I shall forgive** the whole place because of them. (Gen 18:26)

In apodotic position, the use of *weqataltí* resembles that of the English perfect in example (36b) (chapter 3 [*Sell this estate and you **have made** a fortune*]). Normally, as here, it has an aorist meaning, presenting the resultative stage of the event as emergent.

William L. Moran has shown that the equivalent of the syndetic *qatal* in the Byblian Canaanite of the Amarna letters, *u* + *qatala*, also occurs in apodoses. Since this is the syntactic position in which the Byblian *u* + *qatala* occurs most often when it is not an anterior/perfect or a stative verb, Moran, and others with him, assumes that this is the source context from which the Biblical Hebrew *weqataltí* originates.[42] However, there is no compelling reason to believe that all nonconditional uses of *weqataltí* came about as a result of some kind of syntactic reanalysis of conditional *weqataltí*, since resultative meaning in principle is no less natural in other contexts where the construction occurs in Biblical Hebrew. As I have stressed above, there is nothing strange about resultative forms referring to future events (if there is anything unusual about *weqataltí*, it would be the combination of resultative aspect and active voice in the contexts where it occurs, but this could be said of performative *qatal* as well [3.5], so *weqataltí* is no special case in that regard); thus, there is no need to derive all uses of *weqataltí* from the conditional *u* + *qatala* to account for its future meanings. On the contrary, since nobody has been able to explain how the nonconditional uses of *weqataltí* would have been inferred from the conditional source construction, it is just as plausible to assume that the former arose independently of the latter. Therefore, I treat the conditional *weqataltí* as but one of several types of invariant resultative *qatal* with aorist meaning. The examples (47)–(51) below show a few of the many different clause constellations where *weqataltí* can be found.

The *weqatal* that heads the protasis in (47) is not properly a "consecutive" *qatal*, since it does not express any event continuity between itself and the preceding clause, but it is marked in bold here as it has a similar meaning as the consecutive *qatal*:

(47) wə**ʿāzab**   ʾæṯ   ʾāḇîw
    and=abandon.QTAL.3M.SG   OBJ   father=his
    wā**mēṯ**
    and=die.QTAL.3M.SG
    Should **he abandon** his father, he [the father] **would die**. (Gen 44:22)

---

42. Moran 2003, 215–16; Waltke and O'Connor 1990, §32.1.2b; M.S. Smith 1991, 8; Joosten 2012, 288–90.

In (48) the same construction is used in a past setting.[43] The example also shows that *weqatalti* can be used to continue both the protasis and the apodosis. The quoted text is a part of a larger structure where several *weqatalti*-clauses concatenate—something that occurs very often in Biblical Hebrew:

(48) rōʻæʰ   hāyâ   ʻaḇdəḵâ   lə'āḇîw
     sheperd   be.QTAL.3M.SG   servant=your   for=father=his
     baṣṣōʼn   ûḇāʼ   hāʼărî
     with=small.cattle   and=come.QTAL.3M.SG   the=lion
     wəʼæṯ   haddôḇ   wənāśaʼ   śæʰ
     and=OBJ[44]   the=bear   and=take.QTAL.3M.SG   lamb
     mehāʻeḏær   wəyāṣāʼṯî   ʼaḥărāyw
     from=the=herd   and=go.out.QTAL.1SG   after=him
     wəhikkiṯîw
     and=strike.QTAL.1SG=him
     Your servant used to keep the sheep for his father, and if a lion or a bear **came** and took a **lamb** from the herd, **I went** after it and **struck** it. (1 Sam 17:34–35)

In (49) we see an alternative way of forming the protasis with the conjunction *ʼîm*, "if" instead of the *waw*:[45]

(49) [wəhāyâ]   ʼim   zāraʻ   yiśrāʼel
     and=be.QTAL.3M.SG   if   sow.QTAL.3M.SG   Israel
     wəʻālâ   miḏyān   waʻămāleq   ûḇənê
     and=go.QTAL.3M.SG   Midian   and=Amalek   and=sons.of
     qæḏæm   wəʻālû   ʻālāyw
     east   and=go.up.QTAL.3M.PL   upon=them
     [And it used to be so, that] whenever Israel had sown their crops, the Midianites and the Amalekites and the people of the east **went up** and **came up** against them. (Judg 6:3)

In (50a) and (50b), *weqatalti* continues *yiqtol* in a nonconditional constellation, with future and past habitual meaning, respectively:

---

43. Note that the protasis-apodosis structure can also express *when*-relations (see, e.g., the parallel to example [47] in Gen 29:3: *When they had gathered all the herds, they used to roll the stone from the mouth of the well*).
44. See Gibson and Davidson 1994, §94; Waltke and O'Connor 1990, §10.3.2.
45. The form *wəhāyâ*, "and it used to be" is an anticipatory *qatal*-clause that marks the following *weqatalti*-clauses as habitual. It also occurs with future meaning.

(50) a. 'æt   kol   hā'āræṣ   'ăšær   'attâ   rō'æʰ
       OBJ   all   the=land   which   you   see.QOT.M.SG
       ləkā   'ættənænnâ   [...]   wəśamtî
       to=you   give.YQTL-L.1SG=it [...]   and=put.QTAL.1SG
       'æt   zar'ăkā   ka'ăp̄ār   hā'āræṣ
       OBJ   seed=your   as=the=dust.of   the=earth
       All the land that you see, I shall give to you [...], and **I shall make** your offspring like the dust of the earth. (Gen 13:15–16)

   b. ûmə'îl   qāṯōn   ta'ăśæʰ   lô
      and=robe   little   make.YQTL-L.3F.SG   for=him
      'immô   wəha'alṯâ   miyyāmîm
      mother=his   and=bring.up.QTAL.3F.SG   from=days
      yāmîmâ   ba'ălôṯāh   'æt   'îšāh
      days.toward   in=go.up.INFC=her   with   man.her
      lizbōaḥ   'æt   zæḇaḥ   hayyāmîm
      to=sacrifice.INFC   OBJ   sacrifice.of the=days
      ûḇeraḵ   'elî   'eṯ   'ælqānâ   wə'æṯ
      and=bless.QTAL.3M.SG   Eli   OBJ   Elkanah   and=OBJ
      'îštô
      woman=his
      His mother used to make a little robe for him and **take** it to him each year when she went up with her husband to offer the annual sacrifice, and Eli used to **bless** Elkanah and his wife. (1 Sam 2:19–20)

Weqataltí can also continue the imperative (51a), the cohortative (51b), and the jussive (51c):

(51) a. bō'   'æl   par'ōʰ   wĕ'**āmartā**
       go.IMP.2M.SG   to   pharao   and=say.QTAL.2M.SG
       'elayw   ...
       to=him
       Go to Pharao and **say** to him: ... (Exod 7:26)

   b. 'ălaqŏṭâ   nā'   wə'**āsap̄tî**
      pick.YQTL(S).COH.1SG   please   and=gather.QTAL.1SG
      ḇā'ŏmārîm   'aḥărê   haqqôṣərîm
      in=cut.grains   after   the=harvest.QOT.M.PL
      Please, let me glean and **gather** from the cut grains after the reapers. (Ruth 2:7)

c. yišpōṭ   YHWH   bênî
   judge.JUSS.3M.SG YHWH   between=me
   ûbênækā   **ûnəqāmanî**   YHWH
   and=between=you and=avenge QTAL.3M.SG=me   YHWH
   mimmækkā
   from=you
   May the Lord judge between me and you, and **may** the Lord **avenge** me on you! (1 Sam 24:13 [24:12])

To get a sense of the naturalness by which the resultative aspect of the *qatal* form fits into these different contexts, it is helpful to modify the translations somewhat, using English resultative forms: *If his father should be **abandoned**, he would **be grieved** to death; if a lamb **was attacked** by a lion [...] and taken, it [the lion] would **be pursued** and **struck**; ... whenever Israel had sown, the Midianites [...] **had gone up** and **come up** against them ... ; ... I shall give to you, and your offspring will **be made** ... ; His mother used to make a little robe [...] and have it **brought** to him [...] and they **were blessed** ... ; go to Pharaoh and let it **be known** to him ... ; ... let it **be gathered** ... ; ... may I **be avenged** ...* The difference between these English resultative constructions and the Biblical Hebrew *weqatalti* is that the latter is typically in the active voice and the various temporal and modal values are indicated only by the context rather than by means of auxiliaries. The stage-based resultative aspect, however, is invariant in both.[46]

An explanation for the temporal and modal versatility of *weqatalti* lies in the fact that coordination in Biblical Hebrew can be used for syntactico-semantic relations that, in English (and many other languages), must be expressed by means of various forms of syntactic subordination.[47] An obvious case of this is when *weqatalti* continues substantival forms like the participle:

(52) makkeʰ   ʾîš   wāmet   môṯ
     smite.QOT.M.SG   man   and=die.QTAL.3M.SG   die.INFA
     yûmāṯ
     be.killed.YQTL(L).3M.SG

---

46. I take the resultative meaning of the English past participle clauses as invariant as long as the auxiliary is in the simple present, past or future. When the participle is embedded in a progressive construction (e.g., *a lamb is being attacked*), the resultative force of the participle is overruled (in like manner, the progressive aspect is overruled in the perfect progressive).

47. This is probably what Waltke and O'Connor (1990, §32.2b) have in mind when they say that "the essential meaning [sc. of *weqatalti*] involves clausal subordination," See also Robar's (2014, 123–28) observation that *weqatalti* very often implies what she terms "purpose/result modality." For this reason, Robar uses the subordinating conjunctions "so that" or "in order that" to gloss the interclausal relation expressed by most *weqatalti*-clauses except the conditional ones.

Whoever strikes a man so that **he dies** shall surely be put to death. (Exod 21:12)

A more literal—and ungrammatical—translation of this passage would be [*a person*] *striking a man and he dies shall surely be put to death*. In English it is not possible to coordinate the finite verb with the noun phrase, except by adding an existential "there is," so that the noun phrase becomes the predicate of a clause (*There is a person striking a man, and he dies*). That changes the meaning of the text, however, in that the person who dies becomes the one who strikes rather than the one being struck. In order to render the meaning of the Hebrew correctly, one has to employ a subordinating device, such as the conjunction *so that*, so as to indicate that the event of dying is a consequence of the event of striking (*A person striking a man so that he dies*...). Biblical Hebrew allows all this to be implied by the coordination—presumably because the sentence does not make sense otherwise. The example teaches us that in Biblical Hebrew a complete final clause may be semantically (as opposed to syntactically) embedded in a phrase by means of coordination.

The same principle of semantic embedding, I suggest, applies when *weqatalti* is used to continue finite verbs such as the *yiqtol*-L in (50) and the imperative in (51a). In the case of the former, the embedding of the *weqatalti* in the *yiqtol*-L can often quite easily be rendered in English by including the second clause under the scope of auxiliary of the first clause (cf. [shall [give and make]] as in *I shall give this land to you and make*..., and [used to [make and take up]] as in *Her mother used to make him a robe and take it to him*). In English, it is normal to renew the temporal/modal marking every now and then, especially when there is a subject switch (*His mother **used to** make him a robe and take it to him* [...], *and Eli **used to** bless Elkanah and his wife*). In Biblical Hebrew this is not required; long chains of *weqatalti* can form without any renewal of the modal or temporal marking, the only thing indicating the continued modal/temporal meaning of the chain-initial predicate being the chain as such. Such chains of *weqatalti* are semantically, albeit not syntactically, embedded in the predicate that they continue.[48] In this respect, the whole chain is fully comparable to the single *weqatalti*-clause that is embedded in the noun phrase in (52). The same goes for *weqatalti*-clauses continuing volitives: the *weqatalti*-clause is under the scope of the volitive mood and therefore does not coordinate its own mood with it. Accordingly, we do not read (51a) as an ungrammatical *Go to Pharaoh, and you say* [lit. "have said"] *to him* [...]. Rather, the *weqatalti*-clause

---

48. Any way of rendering this embedding in English would be grammatically irregular, but one could try to get a sense of it by using participles: *His mother used to make a little robe, taking it up to him when she went* [...] *to Bethel* [...], *Eli blessing them*..., etc.

coordinates only the event-representations, while the imperative mood remains superordinate and active, as when we translate using a subordinating device (*Go to Pharaoh, so that you may* [or, "in order to"] *say to him* ...).

In conclusion, it must be acknowledged that Biblical Hebrew uses coordination much more freely than English, in that it allows the virtual embedding of the *weqataltí*-clause under the semantic scope of the construction that it continues, whether it be a substantival (52) protasis, a future (50a) or past habitual (50b) *yiqtol*-L, or a volitive (51a–c). Only if we understand the *weqataltí* as a semantically embedded construction can we satisfactorily explain how it is able to continue such a wide and semantically diverse range of constructions.

If, as I suggest, *weqataltí* has the same basic semantics as *qatal*, the question of how exactly to distinguish between the two is not crucial. It therefore poses no problem for this study that *qatal* without the conjunction can occur in positions where it is functionally equivalent with the *weqataltí*. For those who hold that *weqataltí* and *qatal* are separate forms, however, that fact does pose a problem, although one that seems to be more or less unknown. Without having undertaken a systematic investigation of the matter, I shall here only mention some of the more obvious examples that I have come across. Thus, in (53), the construction *wəḡam* ("and even"), *qatal* appears as a continuation form surrounded by *weqataltí*-clauses:[49]

(53) ûḇeraḵtî   'ōṯāh   wəḡam   **nāṯattî**
     and=bless.QTAL.1SG her   and=even   give.QTAL.1SG
     mimmænnâ   ləḵā   ben   ûḇeraḵtîhā
     from=her   for=you   son   and=bless.QTAL.1SG=her
     wəhāyəṯâ   ləḡôyim
     and=be.QTAL.3F.SG   to=nations
     I will bless her and also **give** you a son by her. I will bless her, and she shall give rise to nations. (Gen 17:16)

The next example shows a *qatal* with future time reference heading the apodosis of a conditional sentence—a position where *weqataltí* could be expected:[50]

(54) lō'   kî   'attâ   titten   wə'îm   lō'
     no   for   now   give.YQTL-L.2M.SG   and=if   not
     lāqaḥtî   bəḥāzəqâ
     take.QTAL.1SG   by=force

---

49. See Isaksson 2013, 663. Van de Sande (2008, 329–33) cites this example as well as a parallel to (55) below under the general heading of nonpast *qatal*-forms, without, however, noting the special functional equivalence to consecutive *weqataltí* (a category that he does not acknowledge).
50. See 1 Sam 6:9, where *weqataltí* is used in the same position.

No, for you must give it now! If not, **I will take** it by force. (1 Sam 2:16)

Within a *weqatalti*-chain, *qatal* can be coordinated disjunctively by means of *'ô*, "or" instead of *wə-*, in which case the clause has the same TAM-value as *weqatalti*:[51]

(55) kî   yiḡnōḇ   'îš   šôr
     if   steal.YQTL-L.3M.SG   man   ox
     ûṭəḇāḥô   'ô   **məḵārô**
     and=slaughter.QTAL.3M.SG=it   or   sell.QTAL.3M.SG=it
     If somebody steals an ox and **slaughters** it or **sells** it ... (Exod 21:37)

It is often claimed that *weqatalti* has the same meaning as *yiqtol*-L and, thus, that it is semantically opposed to *qatal*. However, the fact that it occurs with future and habitual meaning together with *yiqtol*-L does not define its meaning any more than the fact that it conveys volitive meanings with the volitive forms. All those meanings can be seen as pragmatic, as described above. As for the "imperfective" meaning of the *weqatalti*-clauses associated with the habitual *yiqtol*-L, it applies only to the macroevent—namely, the habitual state—which is viewed as continuous at a certain point in time (3.2). At the microlevel, there is also a representation of the individual events that instantiates the habit, and with regard to them, the aspect is aorist.[52] Being embedded in the habituality of the *yiqtol*-L-clause, the resultative *weqatalti*-clauses operates at the microlevel, where they represent the result stage of each event as emergent. They are no more imperfective in themselves than the infinitives in *His mother used to **make** a robe for him and **take** it up*, which convey the imperfective aspect only because they stand under the scope of the auxiliary (*used to*) that they complement.[53]

The particular aorist meaning mostly conveyed by *weqatalti* is the completive, since the "emergence of the result stage" is normally one and the same thing as the reaching of the *telos* in telic events. However, with atelic verbs, the *weqatalti* can have an ingressive meaning.[54] Consider, for example,

---

51. This construction occurs regularly in casuistic law. See, e.g., Exod 22:9, 13; Lev 5:21–22; 25:49; Num 5:14; 30:11. See also Num 11:8 for an example from a narrative text.

52. Carlson 2012, 838–39.

53. The infinitives in the example are, of course, not resultative like *weqatalti*, but the English "used to" is good with resultative forms, too: *a robe used to be made for him and taken to him*.

54. Ingressive future *qatal* is not very common, but other cases can be found in Gen 9:14 (wənir'ătā), Exod 4:14 (wərā'ăḵā, wəśāmaḥ), 2 Chr 6:24, 26, 32, 34, 37 (wəhiṯpallǎlû, wəhiṯhannǎnû).

(56) wîhî   kəbōʾăkā   šām
and=be.YQTL-S.3M.SG   as.come.INFC=your   there
hāʾîr   ûpāḡaʿtā   ḥæbæl   nəbîʾîm
the=town   and=meet.QTAL.2M.SG   procession.of   prophets
[...]   wəṣāləhâ   āléękā   rûaḥ
[...]   and=rush.QTAL.3F.SG   on=you   spirit.of
YHWH   wəhiṯnabbîṯā   ʿimmām
YHWH   and=prophesy.QTAL.2M.SG   with=them
wənæhpaktā   ləʾîš   ʾăḥer
and=be.changed.QTAL2M.SG   to=man   other

As you go into the town, you will meet a procession of prophets. The Spirit of the Lord will overcome you, and **you will prophesy** with them and be changed into a different man. (1 Sam 10:5–6)

The ingressive *weqatalti* displays the same apparent oddity as the perfect of persistent situation (see chapter 3, example [14])—namely, that the emergence of the result does not imply that the activity denoted by the verb has ended. Consequently, the same explanation applies as well: In atelic events, there is no privileged moment for the transition from a progressive to a result stage, as there is no semantically privileged result (i.e., a *telos*) associated with the event. Therefore, the transition can occur equally well at any point in time, from the onset of the event to the end of it. In the example quoted above, the implied result of Saul's prophesying seems to be precisely the event that is referred to in the following clause—namely, that he is turned into another man. Since this transformation takes place at the very moment when he starts to prophesy (the prophesying in itself being an indication of the transformation), the result stage overlaps with the nuclear event. In this way, the resultative is compatible with ingressive aspect.

4.3.2. Temporalized qatal

The next two examples are taken from a victory song commemorating the powerful deeds of the Lord (57a) and a description of an overheard conversation (57b). In both it is fully possible to render the *qatal*-clauses with English perfects. However, the impression is that the present results of the events are not important at the time of speech, and the focus of attention is therefore directed toward the past:

(57) a. YHWH   ʾîš   milḥāmâ   YHWH   šəmô   markəḇōṯ
        YHWH   man.of   war   YHWH   name=his   chariots.of
        parʿōʰ wəḥêlô   **yārâ**   bayyām
        Pharao and=army=his throw.QTAL.3M.SG   in=the=sea

The Lord is a warrior; the Lord is his name. Pharaoh's chariots and his army **he cast** into the sea. (Exod 15:3–4)

b. | hinne^h | **šāmaʻti** | ˀæṯ | ˀāḇîḵā |
behold	hear.QTAL1SG.	OBJ	father=your
məḏabber	ˀæl	ʻeśāw	ˀāḥîḵā	leˀmōr
speaking.QOT.M.SG	to	Esau	brother=your	QUOT

Behold, **I heard** your father speaking to your brother Esau, saying ... (Gen 27:6)

There is no focalizing event for the events *cast* and *heard* in these sentences; hence the exact location of the focus depends on the internal features of the represented events themselves. Both are telic events with salient endpoints—namely, the entering into the sea and the completion of Isaac's utterance to Esau. These endpoints attract attention, and we experience the events as completed. That is, the limit-based aspect is completive.

The completive meaning, which follows as the most natural consequence of the telic *Aktionsart* of the verb, is the most common limit-based aspect meaning with temporalized *qatal*. In the next example, however, the *qatal* must be taken as ingressive:

(58) | wayyeṭ | | mōšæ^h | ˀæṯ | maṭṭehû |
and=strech.out.YQTL-S.3M.SG		Moses	OBJ	staff=his
ʻal	haššāmayim	waYHWH	**nāṯan**	
against	the=sky	and=YHWH	give.QTAL.3M.SG	
qōlōṯ	ûḇārāḏ	wattihălaḵ	ˀeš	ˀarṣâ
thunders	and=hail	and=go.YQTL(S).3F.SG	fire	earth.toward

Moses stretched out his staff toward heaven, and the Lord **sent** thunder and hail, and fire went down on the earth. (Exod 9:23)

The *qatal* here has pluractional meaning, representing a process of continuous lightning and hailing that starts from the moment when Moses lifts his staff. The subsequent verses describe the disasters it causes in the land, until Pharao finally yields and begs for it to cease (in verse 29).

Sometimes it is hard to tell whether a *qatal* in a given context should have a temporalized reading or a nontemporalized present perfect reading (cf. chapter 3, example [45]). This is the case particularly when the result stage is important but is already part of the shared knowledge at the time of speech. The ambiguous temporal status of the last verb in the example below is well illustrated by comparing the NRSV and NIV translations:

(59) bərah   ləkā   'æl   lābān   'āhî   [...]
    flee.IMP.2SG for=you   to   Laban   brother=my [...]
    wəyāšaḇtā   'immô   yāmîm   'ăḥāḏim   [...]
    and=sit.QTAL.2M.SG   with=him days   several   [...]
    'aḏ   šûḇ   'ap̄   'āḥîḵā   mimməḵā
    until   return.INFC anger brother=your   from=you
    wəšāḵaḥ   'eṯ   'ăšær   **'āśîṯā**
    and=forget.QTAL.3M.SG   OBJ   which   do.QTAL.2M.SG
    lô
    to=him

NRSV: Flee to my brother Laban [...] and stay with him for a while [...] until your brother's anger against you turns away, and he forgets what **you have done** to him.

NIV: ... forgets **what you** did to him. (Gen 27:43–45)

The NRSV's choice to render *'āśîṯā* with a perfect ("have done") suggests a nontemporalized interpretation of the form, while the NIV apparently opts for a temporalized reading by means of a simple past tense.

The use of *qatal* for expressing past in the past may result from temporalization of its past perfect meaning:

(60) wayyiqrā'   lāhæn   šemôṯ   kaššemōṯ
    and=call.YQTL(S)3M.SG   for=them   names   as=the=names
    'ăšær   **qārā'**   lāhæn   'āḇîw
    which   call.QTAL.3M.SG   for=them   father=his
    And he called them with the names that his father **had called** them.
    (Gen 26:18)

The verb *qārā'* ("had called") in this sentence is a real relative past and not a perfect in the past. That is to say, it does not direct the focus of attention to the result stage of the event obtaining at the time marked by the verb *wayyiqrā'* ("he called"). Rather, the focus of attention is turned to a time that is anterior to the time marked by these verbs. However, it is difficult to exclude the possibility that the past preterite meaning in example (60) can arise solely from our knowledge that the subject referent of the subordinate clause was dead at the time of the event referred to by the main clause, since that knowledge alone would suffice to make us infer a past preterite meaning event with a simple past form in the same context (as if we substitute the pluperfect in the English translation with a preterite *called*). In the latter case, the temporalized interpretation of the *qatal*-form takes its point of departure from the primary deictic center marked by the speech act rather than from the secondary deictic center marked by the main clause predicate *wayyiqrā'*. Such an analysis is precluded in the English pluperfect, where the secondary deictic center is marked by the auxiliary "had."[55]

A not so common variety of the temporalized *qatal* is the past specific aorist *weqatal*—not to be confused with the past habitual *weqataltí*:[56]

(61) wayyeṣeʼ   'ěhûḏ   hammisdərônâ
     go.out.YQTL(S).3M.SG Ehud   the=vestibule.toward
     wayyisgōr   daltôṯ   hā'ăliyyâ
     and=shut.YQTL(S).3M.SG   doors.of the=upper.room
     ba'ăḏô   wənā'āl
     behind=him   and=lock.QTAL.3M.SG
     Ehud went out to the vestibule and closed the doors of the upper room and **locked** them. (Judg 3:23)

In this example, the *weqatal* is not part of a past habitual chain and, therefore, clearly not a consecutive *weqataltí*. We must note, however, that past habitual/generalizing meaning alone may not be a feature by which to safely distinguish consecutive *qatal* from temporalized *qatal*-forms. In the example below, generalizing meaning is expressed with what seems to be temporalized *qatal*:

(62) wayya'aś   'eṯ   hakkiyyôr   nəḥōšæṯ   wə'æṯ
     and=do.YQTL-S.3M.SG   OBJ   the=basin   bronze   and=OBJ
     kannô   bəmar'ōṯ   haṣṣōbə'ōṯ   'ăšær
     stand=its   in=mirrors.of   the=serve.QOT.F.PL who
     ṣāḇə'û   pæṯaḥ   'ōhæl   mô'eḏ
     serve.QTAL.3PL   entrance.of   tent.of   meeting
     He made the basin in bronze and its stand in bronze, from the mirrors of the women who **served** at the entrance of the tent of meeting. (Exod 38:8)

It is a moot question whether there is also a temporalized past *weqatal* with generalizing meaning in Biblical Hebrew, and, if so, how it can be distinguished from the invariant resultative past generalizing *weqatal* (i.e., *weqataltí*). As long as there are clear syntactic analogies with nonpast uses, as in the case of the conditional *weqataltí* and the *weqataltí* continuing *yiqtol*-L in the previous

---

55. See the treatment of this issue in Declerck 2006, 446.
56. Driver 1892, chapter 10; Waltke and O'Connor 1990, §32.3; Gibson and Davidson 1994, §84; Joüon and Muraoka 2009, §119z–za (where the construction is regarded as an anomalous *weqataltí*); Joosten 2012, 223–28.

subsection, the matter is fairly straightforward, but that is not always the case. The example below differs quite significantly from what we have seen so far:

(63) wayyibḥar mōšæʰ ʾanšê ḥayil mikkol
and=choose.YQTL(S).3M.SG Moses men.of valor from=all
yiśrāʾel wayyitten ʾōṯām rāʾšîm ʿal
Israel and=set.YQTL(S).3M.SG them heads over
hāʿām [...] **wəšāp̄əṭû** ʾeṯ
the=people [...] and=judge.QTAL.3M.PL OBJ
hāʿām bəkol ʿeṯ ʾeṯ haddāḇār haqqāšæʰ
the=people in=all time OBJ the=matter the=hard
yəḇîʾûn ʾæl mōšæʰ wəkol haddāḇār
bring.YQTL-L.3M.PL to Moses and=all the=matter
haqqāṭōn yišpûṭû hem
the=little judge.YQTL-L.3M.PL they
wayyišlaḥ mōšæʰ ʾeṯ ḥōṯnô
and=send.YQTL(S).3M.SG Moses OBJ father.in.law=his
Moses chose capable men from all Israel and appointed them as leaders of the people [...]. **They judged** the people at all times; difficult cases they would bring to Moses, but any minor case they judged themselves. Then Moses let his father-in-law depart. (Exod 18:25–26)

In contrast to the embedded *weqatalti*-clauses continuing the substantival *qotel*, the *yiqtol*-L, and the imperative, which all continues the TAM meanings of the preceding clauses, this *weqatal*-clause apparently indicates a shift from specific to generalizing meaning. It differs also from the conditional *weqatal*-clauses, being neither a protasis nor an apodosis. The state of affairs that it represents (together with the two elaborative *yiqtol*-L-clauses) is a consequence of the event represented by the previous clause, but it is also posterior to the event represented by the following clause, thus being out of phase with the progression of the storyline.[57]

If the *weqatal*-clause in (63) is a consecutive *weqatalti*, we should take it as embedded in the preceding *wayyiqtol*-clause, roughly the equivalent of a final clause (... *appointed them as leaders* [...], *in order that they should judge*..., etc.).[58] In this interpretation, it resembles a future *weqatalti*-clause that continues a nonfuture clause with an implication of finality and/or consequence, as in (64):

---

57. For similar uses of *weqatal*, see also 2 Kgs 12:10; 25:29 (= Jer 52:33); Ezra 8:36. The token in 2 Kgs 25:29 follows after what looks like a past aorist specific *weqatal*-clause.

58. Or, with resultative morphology: ... *in order that the people be judged by*..., etc.

(64) lāḵen   'attâ   šaḇnû   'elêḵā
     nevertheless now   turn.QTAL.1PL to=you
     wəhālaḵtā   'immānû
     and=go.QTAL.2SG   with=us
     Nevertheless, we have now come back to you so that **you may go**
     with us. (Judg 11:8)

Against this explanation, I would caution that it is not altogether clear that the *weqatal*-clause in (64) is really embedded rather than an independent confident future (and you will go [lit. "will have gone"] with us; cf. [44]–[45]), nor that (64) is a clear analogy to (63).

If (64) could possibly be read as a case of semantic embedding, (65a–b) probably cannot:

(65) a. wayhî   'îš   'æḥāḏ   min
         and=be.YQTL-S.3M.SG   man   one   from
         hārāmāṯayim   [...]   ûšəmô   'ælqānâ   [...]
         the=Ramathaim [...]   and=name=his   Elkanah   [...]
         wəlô   štê   nāšîm   šem   'aḥaṯ
         and=to=him   two.of women   name.of   one
         ḥannâ   wəšem   haššēnîṯ   pəninnâ
         Hannah   and=name.of the=second Peninnah
         wayhî   lipninnâ   yəlāḏîm
         and=be.YQTL-S.3M.SG   for=Peninnah   children
         ûləḥannâ   'ên   yəlāḏîm   wə**'ālâ**
         and=to=Hannah   none.of   children and=go.up.QTAL.3M.SG
         hā'îš   hahû'   me'îrô   miyyāmîm   yāmîmâ
         the=man   the=he from=town=his   from=days   days.toward
         ləhištaḥăwōṯ   [...]   bəšilô   wəšām   šənê
         to=worship.INFC   [...]   in=Shilo and=there   two.of
         bənê   'elî   ḥopnî   ûpinḥās   kōhănîm
         sons.of   Eli   Hophni   Phinehas priests
         There was a certain man from Ramathaim [...] and his name was Elkanah [...] He had two wives; the name of the one was Hannah, and the name of the other Peninnah. Peninnah had children, but Hannah had no children. This man **used to go up** year by year from his town to worship [...] at Shiloh. There, the two sons of Eli, Hophni and Phinehas, were priests. (1 Sam 1:1–3)

     b. wayyišpōṭ   Šəmû'el   'æṯ   yiśrā'el   kol
         and=judge.YQTL(S).3M.SG Samuel   OBJ   Israel   all

yəmê	ḥayyāʸw	wəhālak̲		middê
days.of	life=his	and=go.QTAL.3M.SG		from=enough
šānâ	bəšānâ	wəsā̲b̲ab̲		bêt̲ ʾel
year	in=year	go.around.QTAL.3M.SG		Bet el
wəhaggilgāl		wəhammiṣpâ	wəšā̲p̲aṭ	
and=the=Gilgal		and=the=Mizpah	and=judge.QTAL.3M.SG	
ʾæt̲	yiśrāʾel	ʾet̲	kol hammǝqômôt̲	hāʾellæʰ
OBJ	Israel	OBJ	all the=places	the=these

And Samuel judged Israel all the days of his life. He **went** year by year and **went around** to Bethel, Gilgal, and Mizpah, and he **judged** Israel in all these places. (1 Sam 7:15–16)

It cannot be completely ruled out that these *weqatal*-clauses belong to some of the types mentioned in the subsection about the invariant resultatives; (65a) may be a past perfect of persistent situation (*This man had gone up year by year*), and (65b) perhaps a temporal protasis-apodosis relation (*As he went from year to year and went around* [...], *he judged*), but if so, they are rather untypical, especially (65b). The more removed (syntactically or semantically) from similar nonpast uses of *weqatalti* the past generalizing *weqatal*-clauses get, the more likely it becomes that they are to be understood not as invariant resultatives but rather as temporalized *qatal*. I leave it an open question as to whether or not the distinction was always upheld.

In combination with the particle *lû*, "if only," and *lûlê* (alt. *lûleʾ*), "if not," *qatal* expresses counterfactual meaning with regard to the past (66a, c) and the present (66b).[59] The construction occurs both in independent sentences and in the protases of conditional periods. With *lû* (sometimes written *lûʾ*), it often gets an optative meaning:

(66) a. lû **matnû** bəʾæræṣ miṣrayim
if.only die.QTAL.1PL in=land.of Egypt
Would that we **had died** in Egypt! (Num 14:2)

---

59. Driver 1892, §140, 143–45; Waltke and O'Connor 1990, §30.54b, 38.2e; Gibson and Davidson 1994, §69c, 122a; Joüon and Muraoka 2009, §163c, 167k; Joosten 2012, 211–12. The present counterfactual meaning of *lû qatal* is quite poorly represented in the Hebrew Bible, almost to the point where it could be questioned, were it not for the existence of present counterfactual *qatal* without *lû* (see example [67]). Andrason's claim that *lû qatal* is almost as frequent as the past counterfactual meaning (Andrason 2013a, 32) is not backed by solid evidence. His example from Gen 23:13 is actually not a *qatal* but an imperative, and if stative *qatal*-forms are eliminated, very few cases are left. Apart from the occurrence in (66b), Mic 2:11 probably belong to the category (if we take the participle *hōlek̲* as a complement to the subject rather than a predicate). There is also a negated present counterfactual *qatal* in the apodosis in Judg 8:19.

b. lû'   qāra'tā   šāmayim   **yāradtā**
    if.only   tear.QTAL2M.SG   heavens   go.down QTAL2M.SG
    mippānǽkā   hārîm   **nāzollû**
    in.front.of=you mountains   quake.QTAL.3M.PL
    Oh, that you **would tear** the heaven and **come down**, and the
    mountains **would tremble**! (Isa 63:19 [64:1])

c. lûle'   **ḥăraštæm**   bə'æḡlātî   lō'
    if.not   plow.QTAL.2M.PL   with=heifer=my   not
    məṣā'tæm   ḥîdātî
    find.QTAL.2M.PL   riddle=my
    If you **had** not **plowed** with my heifer, you would not have found
    out my riddle. (Judg 14:18)

Another context for *qatal* with present counterfactual meaning is found in questions like (67) below:[60]

(67) mî   **mānâ**   'ăp̄ar   ya'ăqōb̠
     who   count.QTAL.3M.SG   dust.of   Jacob
     Who **can count** the dust of Jacob? (Num 23:10)

The present counterfactual meaning expressed by *qatal* may derive from the past meaning of the form, since past meaning is associated with counterfactuality in many languages. In his study on mood and modality, F. R. Palmer recognizes the significance of this phenomenon and treats counterfactuals based on past tense forms as a special modal type.[61] Why past tense gives rise to this particular inference is difficult to say. Palmer discusses a few attempts at explanations that have been suggested, without coming up with a conclusive answer.[62] I shall content myself by stating that there is enough crosslinguistic evidence to suggest that the counterfactual *qatal* may be historically derived from an underlying past meaning, which, in turn, is based on the resultative aspect of the form. I also concur with Andrason's assumption that the past counterfactual meaning of *qatal* derives from its relative past meaning—an assumption that is

---

60. Driver 1892, §19; Gibson and Davidson 1994, §59b; Joosten 2012, 209; Joüon and Muraoka 2009, 112j.

61. Palmer 2001, 209–18. Palmer's translation of one of his Greek examples (216: "Had I such strength!") illustrates the fact that counterfactual inferences of the past tense can be made in English as well. Joosten (2012, 208), too, suggests that the modal uses of *qatal* derives ultimately from the past meaning, but I am skeptical to his idea that the gnomic meaning serves as an intermediate stage.

62. Palmer 2001, 218–21. Hendel (1996, 171–72) refers to Palmer's discussion in his treatment of the counterfactual *qatal*.

corroborated by the use of the pluperfect for that meaning in several languages, including English (as illustrated by [66c]).[63]

The disputed so-called precative *qatal* can, if it exists, be classified as yet another category of counterfactual *qatal*.[64] The problem with this category is that the alleged occurrences are almost exclusively restricted to poetry, which is notoriously open-ended when it comes to the meaning of the verbal forms, and there is hardly any case where a declarative meaning is not also possible:

(68) hôšî'enî   mippî   'aryeʰ
save.IMP.2M.SG=me   from=mouth.of   lion
ûmiqqarnê   remîm   **'ănîtānî**
and=from=horns.of   wild.oxen   rescue.QTAL.2M.SG=me
Save me from the mouth of the lion, from the horns of the wild oxen **rescue** me (alt. "from the horns of the wild oxen you have rescued me"). (Ps 22:21)

Perhaps the most convincing example of a precative *qatal* comes from a prose passage in First Chronicles, where the speaker (David) prays to God concerning the blessing that he has been promised (69a). The precative interpretation is strengthened by the fact that the parallel passage in Second Kings has a marked volitive (imperative) in the same position (69b). Whether this single example is enough to settle the problem with regard to the instances in the poetic texts is disputable:

(69) a. wə'attâ   YHWH   'attâ   hû'   hā'ælōhîm
and=now   YHWH   you   he   the=God
wattədabber   'al   'abdəkā   haṭṭôbâ
and=talk.YQTL(S).2M.SG   about   servant=your   the=good
hazzō't   wə'attâ   **hô'altā**   ləbārek
the=this   and=now   be.willing.QTAL.2M.SG   to=bless.INFC
'æt   bêt   'abdəkā   lihyôt   lə'ôlām
OBJ   house.of   servant=your   to=be   forever
ləpānæ̂kā
before=you
And now, Lord, you are God, and you have told this good thing concerning your servant. Therefore, **may it please you** to bless the house of your servant, that it may continue forever before you. (1 Chr 17:26–27)

---

63. Andrason 2013a, 46–47.
64. For an explanation along these lines, see Andrason 2013b. On precative *qatal*, see also Driver 1892, §20; Waltke and O'Connor 1990, §30.54c–d, 38.2e; Gibson and Davidson 1994, §69c, 122a; Joüon and Muraoka 2009, §112k; Joosten 2012, 211–12.

b. wattəḏabber   'æl   'aḇdəḵā
   and=talk.YQTL(S).2M.SG   to   servant=your
   haṭṭôḇâ   hazzō't   wə'attâ   **hô'el**
   the=good   the=this   and=now   be.willing.IMP.2M.SG
   uḇāreḵ   'æṯ   bêṯ   'aḇdəḵā
   and=bless.IMP.2M.SG   OBJ   house.of servant.your
   and you have promised this good thing to your servant. Therefore, **be willing** and bless the house of your servant. (2 Sam 7:29)

4.3.3. Adjectival and Verbal Stative qatal

The stative *qatal*, consists, in terms of lexical content, of two main groups: inflected adjectives like *kāḇēḏ* ("to be heavy/rich/glorious") and *qāṭōn* ("be small"), on the one hand, and verbal statives, which express emotions, mental states, ability, and posture like *āhaḇ* ("to love"), *yāḏa'* ("to know"), *yāḵōl* ("to be able"), *yāšaḇ* ("to sit"), on the other. Of these, the inflected adjectives are not to be considered as proper resultatives.

The verbal stative *qatal* is normally translated with present tense forms in English. It could be understood as an original resultative formed on a dynamic verb that has lost its resultative force through reanalysis (thus, *āhaḇ* = "he has fallen in love [with]" < "he loves"; *yāḏa'* = "he has perceived" < "he knows"; *yāḵōl* = "he has taken hold of" < "he can"; *yāšaḇ* = "he has sat down" < "he is sitting / he lives"). This would not be unique from a cross-linguistic perspective. In fact, several verbs in Germanic languages that now belong to the present tense paradigm originate from resultative (i.e., perfect) forms.[65] If this explanation is valid, the difference between the stative *qatal* and the stative *qotel* is not one of resultative versus progressive meaning. Rather, the difference would be that the stative *qotel* imparts more dynamicity to the constructions, in a similar way to when the English progressive is used with stative verbs instead of the simple present (*I'm liking her very much* vs. *I like her very much*).[66] However, it is doubtful whether dynamicity alone is the distinctive factor here. It is not evident that *qotel* of mental verbs like *'āhaḇ* is generally more dynamic than the same verb in *qatal*.[67] As for posture verbs like *'āmaḏ* ("stand") and *yāšaḇ* ("sit"), it is hard to imagine how they could possibly have different degrees of dynamicity. Furthermore, the simple fact that in Biblical Hebrew the stative *qatal*-forms belong to the *qatal* paradigm also speaks against a typological affiliation of the verbal stative *qatal* with the English simple present tense. At least in those

---

65. Maslov 1988, 71; Bybee, Perkins, and Pagliuca 1994, 77–78.
66. Thus, Dobbs-Allsopp 2000, 38–39.
67. Compare, e.g., 1 Sam 18:28 and 1 Sam 20:17 with Gen 25:28 and 1 Sam 18:16.

cases where the stative verbal root can be conjugated as both *qotel* and *qatal*, it is likely that the *qatal* conveys some shade of resultative meaning. In this respect, the *qatal/qotel*-contrast of the Biblical Hebrew verbal statives more resembles the kind of synonymity we have in the English *has hidden / is hiding*, both of which refer to a present state of hiding.[68] It was suggested earlier (2.2.2) that such verbs are semantically ambiguous between a telic meaning (*hide* = "go into hiding") and an atelic meaning (*hide* = "be in hiding"), the perfect being formed on the basis of the former and the progressive on the latter. The same explanation could be valid for the verbal statives in Biblical Hebrew.

4.4. *Yiqtol*-S

Yiqtol-S is here taken to be an old resultative (2.5). It has two main functions whose morpho-syntactical realizations are normally distinguishable and therefore are treated as distinct forms in the standard description of the Biblical Hebrew verbal system: the preterite (or some other term) and the jussive. Here, I shall use the terms declarative *yiqtol*-S and volitive *yiqtol*-S. The declarative *yiqtol*-S includes the free-standing variant and *wayyiqtol*. The volitive *yiqtol*-S includes the so-called jussive and the cohortative (1.4).

4.4.1. Invariant Resultative yiqtol-S: wayyiqtol

Wayyiqtol sometimes have present perfect meaning, representing the result stage as continuous around speech time. Often, there is a certain ambiguity as to whether a past meaning or a present perfect meaning is intended, but the perfect meaning is still very evident in many instances.[69] Typically, *wayyiqtol* has perfect meaning when it continues a perfect *qatal* (70a), but the preceding construction does not have to be a *qatal*-clause (70b), or even have perfect meaning (70c):

---

68. The same contrast can be expressed with the simple present, e.g., *has understood / understands*.

69. The usage is treated by Waltke and O'Connor 1990, §33.3.1c; Gibson and Davidson 1994, 81b, 82b; Joosten 2012, 185–86. The other grammars I have checked do not mention it specifically, but see Driver 1892, §76a, 79 for some examples that are translated with perfects. The rather small number of examples in the grammars can make the present perfect *wayyiqtol* appear as a more marginal phenomenon than it actually is. The following references contain *wayyiqtol*-clauses that, in my opinion, are better translated with the present perfect than the simple past: Gen 16:5 (two occurences); 19:9, 13, 19; 24:37; 26:27; 30:27; 32:5, 6 (two); 44:20; Exod 1:18; 3:8; 31:3; 32:8 (three); 35:31; Num 23:4; Deut 13:14; Lev 10:19; 20:17, 26; Josh 22:2; Judg 6:13; 10:10; 1 Sam 13:14; 15:23; 25:21, 35; 28:16; 2 Sam 7:9 (two); 14:5; 16:8; 19:42; 1 Kgs 1:19 (two), 44 (two), 45 (three); 19:10; 21:14; 2 Kgs 2:16; 3:23; 7:12; 21:11, 15; 22:9, 17; Isa 2:7 (two); 30:12; Jer 5:23, 27; 33:24; 35:8; Ezek 8:17; 9:9; Ezra 9:9; 2 Chr 13:9; 21:13 (three); 24:20; 29:8 (two); 34:16.

(70) a. wayyōʼmar   ʽæḇæḏ   ʼaḇrāhām
       and=say.YQTL(S).3M.SG servant.of   Abraham
       ʼānōḵî   waYHWH   beraḵ   ʼæṯ
       I   and=YHWH   bless.QTAL.3M.SG   OBJ
       ʼăḏōnî   məʼōḏ   **wayyiḡdāl**
       master=mine much   and=be.great.YQTL(S).3M.SG
       wayyittæn   lô   ṣōʼn   ûḇāqār
       and=give.YQTL(S).3M.SG   to=him sheep   and=cattle
       [...]   **wattelæḏ**   śārâ   ʼešæṯ
       [...]   and=give.birth.YQTL(S).3M.SG   Sarah   wife.of
       ʼăḏōnî   ben   laʼḏōnî
       master=my   son   for=master=my
       He said: "I am Abraham's servant. The Lord has blessed my master abundantly and he **has become rich**. He **has given** him sheep and cattle [...]. And Sarah, my master's wife, **has borne** a son to my master." (Gen 24:34–36)

   b. hinneʰ   hāʽām   hayyōṣeʼ   mimmiṣrayim
      behold   the=people   the=go.out.QOT.M.SG   from=Egypt
      wayḵas   ʼæṯ   ʽên   hāʼāræṣ
      and=cover.YQTL-S.3M.SG   OBJ   surface.of the=land
      ʽattâ   ləḵâ   qoḇâ   lî   ʼōṯô
      now   go.IMP.2M.SG   curse.IMP.2M.SG   for=me   OBJ=it
      Behold, the nation who **has** gone out of Egypt and **covered** the whole land, go now and curse them for me. (Num 22:11)

   c. mî   ʼattæm   [...]   ăḥê   ʼăḥazyāhû   ʼănaḥnû
      who   you   [...]   brothers.of   Ahaziah   we
      wannerǽḏ   lišlôm   bənê
      go.down.YQTL(S).1M.PL   for=peace.of   sons.of
      hammælæḵ   ûḇənê   haggəḇîrâ
      the=king   and=sons.of   the=lady
      "Who are you?" [...] "We are relatives of Ahaziah, and **we have come down** to visit the sons of the king and the queen mother." (2 Kgs 10:13)

With the focused time set in the past, the perfect *wayyiqtol* regularly continues the perfect *qatal* for the representation of courses of events:[70]

---

70. Waltke and O'Connor 1990, §33.3.1c; Gibson and Davidson 1994, §81b; Joüon and Muraoka 2009, §118d; Joosten 2012, 175–77. Driver (1892, §76a, 79) and Joüon and Muraoka (2009, §118d

(71) wayyuggaḏ   lišlōmō^h   kî
and=be.told.YQTL(S).3M.SG   to=Solomon   that
hālaḵ   šimʿî   mîrûšālaim   gaṯ
go.QTAL.3M.SG Shimei   from=Jerusalem Gath
wayyāšōḇ
and=return.YQTL-S.3M.SG
And Solomon was told that Shimei had gone from Jerusalem to Gath and **returned**. (1 Kgs 2:41)

Wayyiqtol can refer to continuous emotional or cognitive states in the present (example [72a]) and the past (example [72b]).[71] I assume that this use may have the same rationale as when *qatal* is formed on such verbs—that is, the basic, resultative meaning of the form is applied to a telic reading of the lexically ambiguous verbal root (see 4.3.3):[72]

(72) a. wəʾêḵ   tāšîḇ   ʾeṯ   pənê
and=how   repulse.YQTL-L.2M.SG   OBJ   face.of
p̄aḥaṯ   ʾaḥaḏ   ʿaḇdê   ʾăḏōnî   haqqəṭannîm
governor   one.of   servants   lord=my   the=small
wattiḇṭaḥ   ləḵā   ʿal miṣrayim
and=put.trust.YQTL(S).2M.SG   for=you on   Egypt
ləræḵæḇ   ûləp̄ārāšîm
for=chariot   and=for=horsemen
How can you repulse even one of the least of my lord's governors, although **you have put your trust** in Egypt for chariots and horsemen? (2 Kgs 18:24)

b. wayyōʾmær   lāḇān   ləyaʿăqōḇ   [...]
and=say.YQTL-S.3M.SG   Laban   for=Jacob   [...]
haggîḏâ   lî   ma^h maśkurtæḵâ
tell.IMP.2M.SG   for=me   what   wages=your
ûləlāḇān   štê   bānôṯ   šem   haggəḏōlâ
and=for=Laban   two   daughters   name.of   the=big
leʾâ   wəšem   haqqəṭannâ   rāḥel   [...]
Leah   and=name.of   the=small   Rachel   [...]
wayyæʾӕ̈haḇ   yaʿăqōḇ   ʾӕṯ   rāḥel
and=love.YQTL(S).3M.SG   Jacob   OBJ   Rachel

---

n. 2) seem to object to the idea of a pluperfect *wayyiqtol*, but the point they are actually making is that *wayyiqtol* cannot have the value of a pluperfect unless preceded by a *qatal*.

71. Waltke and O'Connor 1990, §33.3.1b; Joüon and Muraoka 2009, §118p; Joosten 2012, 186.

72. See, however, the alternative interpretation of (72b) as a temporalized *wayyiqtol* in example (83) below.

Laban said to Jacob, [...] "Tell me what your wages shall be."
Now, Laban had two daughters—the name of the elder was Leah,
and the name of the younger was Rachel—and Jacob **loved**
[i.e., approximately, "had fallen in love with"] Rachel. (Gen
29:15, 16)

The perfect meaning of *wayyiqtol* is also evident in the following atemporal relative clause. Here, an adverbial infinitive (*bəṣe'tô*, "in its coming out") represents a focalizing event set within the result stage of the event referred to by the *wayyiqtol* (*wayye'ākel*, "is eaten"):

(73) 'al   nā'   təhî   kammet   'ăšær
     not   please   be.YQTL-S.3F.SG   as=dead   which
     bəṣe'tô   meræḥæm   'immô
     in=go.out.INFC=it   from=womb.of   mother=its
     wayye'ākel   ḥăṣî   bəśārô
     and=eat.PASS.YQTL(S).3M.SG   half.of   flesh=its
     Let her not be like a stillborn, whose flesh **is** half **eaten** when it
     comes out of her mother's womb. (Num 12:12)

Apparently, *wayyiqtol* can also have the meaning of a perfect of persistent situation in combination with the adverbial "until now / this day":

(74) hišmîḏ   'æt   hahōrî   mippənêhæm
     destroy.QTAL.3M.SG   OBJ   the=Horites   before=them
     wayyîrāšum   **wayyešəḇû**
     and=dispossess.YQTL(S).3M.PL=them   and=live.YQTL(S).3M.PL
     taḥtām   'aḏ   hayyôm   hazzæʰ
     instead.of=them   to   the=day   the=this
     He destroyed the Horites before them, and they dispossessed them
     and **have lived** in their place to this day. (Deut 2:22)

However, this kind of expression is inconclusive as to the intrinsic resultative meaning of *wayyiqtol*, since the adverbial is also used with ordinary past aorist *wayyiqtol*. In this case, the adverbial evidently qualifies not the *wayyiqtol* but rather some implicit predicate like the one added within square brackets in the translation below:

(75) **wayyittənem**   yəhôšua'   bayyôm
     and=give=them.YQTL(S).3M.SG   Joshua   in-the=day
     hahû   ḥōṭəḇê   'ēṣîm   wəšō'ăḇê   mayim
     the=that   cutters.of   wood   and=carriers.of   water

> lā'ed̠â ûləmizbeaḥ YHWH 'ad̠
> for=the=congregation and=for=the=altar.of YHWH until
> hayyôm hazzæʰ
> the=day the=this
>
> On that day Joshua **made** them woodcutters and water carriers for the congregation and for the Lord's altar[. And they have remained as such] until this day. (Josh 9:27)

Just like *qatal*, *wayyiqtol* may have an inferred gnomic meaning, typically in contexts where the latter continues the former:[73]

> (76) ṣaddîq miṣṣārâ næḥǽlāṣ
> righteous from=trouble be.rescued.QTAL.3M.SG
> **wayyāb̠ō'** rāšā' taḥtāʸw
> and=come.YQTL(S).3M.SG wicked instead.of=him
>
> The righteous person is rescued from trouble, and the wicked **gets into** it instead. (Prov 11:8)

Numbers 31:50 (example [77a]) has been cited as evidence of a performative *wayyiqtol*.[74] If this reading is correct, it is another case of invariant resultative *wayyiqtol*, and a parallel to the performative *qatal*. It could also have present perfect meaning, as suggested by the translations in the NIV and NRSV, but there are some other candidates as well, based on verbs of speech (example [77b]):

> (77) a. 'ăb̠ād̠ǽk̠ā nāśə'û 'æt̠ rō'š 'anšê
> servants=your count.QTAL.3M.PL OBJ head men.of
> hammilḥāmâ 'ăšær bəyād̠ēnû wəlō'
> the=war which in=hand=our and=not
> nip̄qad̠ mimmænnû 'îš
> miss.PASS.QTAL.3M.SG from=us man
> **wannaqreb̠** 'æt̠ qorban YHWH
> and=bring.YQTL-S.1PL OBJ offering.of YHWH
>
> Your servants have counted the warriors under our command and not one man of us is missing. **We bring** [alt. "have brought"] the offering to the Lord. (Num 31:49–50)

---

73. Driver 1892, §80; Waltke and O'Connor 1990, 33.3.1b; Gibson and Davidson 1994, §82a; Joosten 2012, 186–87.

74. Joüon and Muraoka 2009, §1180; Joosten 2012, 187. The latter also mentions Ps 119:106; 1 Chr 17:10. See also Exod 3:17; Isa 49:6; and perhaps Isa 29:13.

b. rā'ô   rā'înû   kî   hāyâ   YHWH
   see.INFA   see.QTAL.1PL   that   be.QTAL.3M.SG   YHWH
   'immāk   **wannō'mær**   təhî   nā'
   with=you   and=say.YQTL-S.1PL   be.YQTL-S.3F.S please
   'ālâ   bênôṯênû   bênênû uḇênæḵā
   oath   between=us   between=us   and=between=you
   wənikrəṯâ   bərît   'immāk
   and=cut.YQTL-S.COH.1PL   covenant   with=you

   We have clearly seen that the Lord has been with you. **We say**, let there be an oath between us, between us and you, and let us make a covenant with you. (Gen 26:28)

The rare future *wayyiqtol* is restricted to poetic discourse.[75] Taken as an atemporal resultative, the future meaning of *yiqtol*-S is an altogether context-dependent inference, just like future *qatal*. Here, three *wayyiqtol* continue an asyndetic prophetic perfect:

(78) 'āsōp̄   'æ'æsōp̄   ya'ăqōḇ   kullāḵ   [...]
     gather.INFA   gather.YQTL-L.1SG Jacob   all=you   [...]
     'ăśîmænnû   kəṣō'n   boṣrâ   [...]
     set.YQTL-L.1SG=him   as=sheep.of   fold   [...]
     'ālâ   happōreṣ   lip̄nêhæm
     go.up.QTAL.3M.SG   the=break.QOT.M.SG   before=them
     pārəṣû   **wayya'ăḇōrû**   ša'ar
     break.QTAL.3PL   and=pass.YQTL(S).3M.PL   gate
     wayyēṣə'û   bô   **wayya'ăḇōr**
     and=go.out.YQTL(S).3M.PL   in=it   and=pass.YQTL(S).3M.SG
     malkām   lip̄nêhæm
     king=their   before=them

   I shall surely gather all of you, Jacob [...] I shall make him like sheep in the fold [...] One who breaks through will go before them, they will break out and **pass** the gate and **walk out** through it; their king **will pass** through before them. (Mic 2:12–13)

Wayyiqtol can also be used in coordination with past habitual *weqatalti*.[76] Given that *wayyiqtol* is a resultative, this type can be understood exactly in the

---

75. Driver 1892, §81; Waltke and O'Connor 1990, §33.3.1d; Gibson and Davidson 1994, §82c; Joüon and Muraoka 2009, §118s; Joosten 2012, 188–89.

76. Also after past stativized *yiqtol*-L (e.g., Judg 12:5) or nominal clause (2 Sam 15:2). Examples are found in Joüon and Muraoka 2009, §118n, and Joosten 2012, 177–78.

same way as *weqatalti* with the corresponding function, which means that the invariantly resultative construction is semantically embedded in the generalizing meaning transmitted from the previous clauses:

(79) wəhāyâ   'im   zāra'   yiśrā'el
     and=be.QTAL.3M.SG if   sow.QTAL.3M.SG   Israel
     wə'ālâ   miḏyān   wa'ămāleq   ûḇənê
     and=go.QTAL.3M.SG Midian   and=Amalek   and=sons.of
     qæḏæm   wə'ālû   'ālayw
     east   and=go.up.QTAL.3M.PL   against=him
     wayyaḥănû   'ălêhæm
     and=encamp.YQTL(S).3M.PL   against=them
     wayyašḥîtû   'æṯ   yəḇûl   hā'āræṣ
     and=destroy.YQTL(S).3M.PL OBJ   produce.of   the=land
     [And it used to be so, that] whenever Israel had sown their crops, the Midianites and the Amalekites and the people of the east went up. And they went up and **encamped** against them and **destroyed** the produce of the land. (Judg 6:3)

That *wayyiqtol* really is fully integrated in the *weqatalti*-chain and analyzable in the same way as *weqatalti* is plausible also in the light of the fact that *wayyiqtol*, just like *weqatalti*, can be coordinated with, and semantically embedded in, a nonfinite form. We have already seen an example of a *wayyiqtol*-clause continuing an infinitive construct in (73). In the following example, a *wayyiqtol*-clause followed by a chain of *weqatal*-clauses is embedded in a substantival participle:

(80) waḏōnāy   YHWH   haṣṣəḇā'ôṯ   hannôḡea'
     and=lords=my   YHWH.of   the=hosts   the=touch.QOT.M.SG
     bā'āræṣ   **wattāmôḡ**   wə'āḇəlû
     on=the=earth   and=melt.YQTL-S.3F.SG   and=mourn.QTAL.3PL
     kol   hayyôšəḇê   bāh   wə'ālətâ
     all   the=sit.QOT.M.PL   in=her   and=rise.QTAL.3F.SG
     ḵay'ōr   kullāh   wəšāqə'â   kî'ōr
     like=the=Nile   all.of=her   and=sink.QTAL.3F.SG   as=Nile.of
     miṣrāyim
     Egypt
     And my lord, the Lord of hosts, he who touches the earth [lit. "the one touching"] and **it melts**, and all who live in it mourns, and all of it rises like the Nile and sinks like the Nile of Egypt. (Amos 9:5)

4.4.2. Temporalized wayyiqtol

In the vast majority of cases, *wayyiqtol* has preterite meaning.[77] The existence of *wayyiqtol* with perfect meaning indicates that the preterital meaning arose as a result of the temporalization of the resultative meaning of *yiqtol*-S. Aspectually, the past *wayyiqtol* is predominantly completive, but atelic predicates tend to highlight the initial limit of the events when they occur in temporal succession:

(81) wayyiššaq   yaʿăqōḇ ləraḥel
  and=kiss.YQTL(S).3M.SG Jacob to=Rachel
  wayyiśśaʾ   ʾæṯ qōlô
  and=raise.YQTL(S).3M.SG OBJ voice=his
  wayyēḇk   wayyaggēḏ
  and=weep.YQTL-S.3M.SG and=tell.YQTL-S.3M.SG
  yaʿăqōḇ ləraḥel kî ăḥî ʾāḇîhā hûʾ
  Jacob for=Rachel that brother.of father=her he
  Jacob kissed Rachel and **began to weep**. And Jacob told Rachel that he was a relative of her father. (Gen 29:11–12)

The verb in the above sentence is naturally understood as ingressive because the predicate is atelic, and the context indicates that it may well continue at the onset of the next event. There is no total correspondence between atelicity and ingressive aorist aspect in the *wayyiqtol*, however. An atelic *wayyiqtol* may be completive if there is some contextual indication that the event actually has ended before a subsequent event starts. Thus, in example (82), we understand that the eating and drinking come to an end before the rising in the morning:

(82) wayyaʿaś   lāhæm mištæh
  and=did.YQTL-S.3M.SG for=them feast
  wayyōʾḵəlû   **wayyištû**
  and=eat.YQTL(S).3M.PL and=drink.YQTL(S).3M.PL
  wayyaškîmû   babbōqær
  and=raise.early.YQTL(S).3M.PL in=the=morning
  He made a feast for them and **they ate** and **drank**. In the morning they rose early. (Gen 26:30)

Although temporalized forms in general are not necessarily restricted to aorist meaning (see the German perfect, section 3.6), the existence of the progressive

---

[77] Driver 1892, §78; Waltke and O'Connor 1990, §33.2.1–2, 4; Gibson and Davidson 1994, §78–81; Joüon and Muraoka 2009, §118c; Joosten 2012, §164–78.

predicative *qotel* in the Biblical Hebrew verbal system in practice restricts the aspectual value of the temporalized *wayyiqtol*. It is therefore very difficult to find clear instances of imperfective *wayyiqtol* referring to specific events. However, some exceptions could be made if we assume that the *wayyiqtol* of some stative roots like *'hb* in example (83a) or the copula *hāyâ* in (83b) below really are atelic verbs, meaning *to love* and *to be* rather than *to fall in love* and *to become* (see the analysis of example [72] above). In that case, the focused time, marked by *wayyō'mær* ("he said," example [83a]) and *wannibnæʰ* ("we built," example [83b]), falls within the limits of the nuclear events, and the aspect is imperfective:

(83) a. wayyō'mær   lābān   ləya'ăqōb [...]
       and=say.YQTL-S.3M.SG   Laban   for=Jacob   [...]
       haggîdâ   lî   maʰ   maśkurtǣkā̂
       tell.IMP.2M.SG   for=me   what   wages=your
       ûləlābān   štê   bānôt   šem   haggədōlâ
       and=for=Laban   two   daughters name.of   the=big
       le'â   wəšem   haqqətannâ rāḥel   [...]
       Leah   and=name.of the=small Rachel [...]
       wayyæ'ǣhab   ya'ăqōb   'æt   rāḥel
       and=love.YQTL(S).3M.SG   Jacob   OBJ   Rachel
       Laban said to Jacob, [...] 'Tell me what your wages shall be.'
       Now, Laban had two daughters—the name of the elder was Leah, and the name of the younger was Rachel—and Jacob **loved** Rachel. (Gen 29:15, 16)

b. wannibnæʰ   'æt   hahômâ
   and=build.YQTL(S).1PL   OBJ   the=wall
   wattiqqāšer   kol   hahômâ   'ad
   and=be.joined.YQTL(S).3M.SG   all   the=wall unto
   ḥæṣyāh   **wayhî**   leb   lā'ām
   half=its   and=be.YQTL-S.3M.SG   heart for=the=people
   la'ăśôt
   to=work
   We built the wall and it was all joined together up to half of its height, for the people **were** devoted to the work. (Neh 3:38 [4:6])

Generalizing meaning can be expressed with temporalized *wayyiqtol*, even with imperfective aspect, although it seems very exceptional.[78] In (84), the verb

---

78. See Joosten's examples of *wayyiqtol* for "iterative processes" (2012, 174). Of these examples, however, most are best understood as aorist, representing temporally successive events (Gen 30:39;

wayyāḇe' ("he brought") is habitual. The habitual state is viewed against the focalizing event marked by the mainline *wayyaḥălōm* ("had a dream"):

(84) yôsēp̄   bæn   šəbaʿ   'æśreʰ   šānâ   hāyâ
     Joseph   son.of   seven   ten   year   be.QTAL.3M.SG
     rōʿæʰ   'æṯ   'æḥāyw   baṣṣōʾn
     shepherd.QOT.M.SG   with   brothers=his   in=the=small.cattle
     [...]   wəhûʾ   naʿar   'æṯ   bənê   bilhâ
     [...]   and=he   servant   with   sons.of   Bilhah
     wəʾæṯ   bənê   zilpâ   nəšê   'āḇîw
     and=with   sons.of   Zilpah   wives.of   father=his
     wayyāḇe'   yôsēp̄   'æṯ   dibbāṯām   rāʿâ
     and=bring.YQTL-S.3M.SG   Joseph   OBJ   gossip=their bad
     'æl   'āḇîhæm   [...]   wayyaḥălōm   yôsēp̄
     to   father=their [...]   and=dream.YQTL(S).3M.SG   Joseph
     ḥălôm   wayyaggeḏ   ləʾæḥāyw
     dream   and=tell.YQTL-S.3M.SG   for=brothers=his

Joseph was seventeen years old and was sheperding with his brothers. He was the helper of Bilhah's sons and Zilpah's sons, and he **brought** bad reports about them to their father [...] And Joseph had a dream and he told it to his brothers. (Gen 37:2, 5)

4.4.3. Free-Standing Declarative yiqtol-S

Some of the free-standing *yiqtol* in the Hebrew Bible are often considered as *yiqtol*-S comparable with preterite *wayyiqtol*.[79] Due to the absence of the characteristic *wa*C-C/*wā*-C-pattern, their identification in most cases depends entirely on contextual cues. Morphology comes into play in the analysis when the *yiqtol* in question is apocopated. The best evidence is when the same verb occurs at the same place in parallel texts, once as a *wayyiqtol*, and once as an apocopated *yiqtol*. Psalm 18 and 2 Sam 22 have two examples of this switch (*wayyāšēṯ*/*yāšæṯ*, *yarʿem*/*wayyarʿem*) in quite close sequence:

Exod 16:21; Judg 9:25; 1 Sam 18:13; 2 Sam 8:6; 1 Kgs 12:30), or else they are stative, comparable to examples (83a–b) (thus Gen 6:11; 41:56; Num 15:32; 1 Sam 14:25). The possible cases of temporalized imperfective *wayyiqtol* in Joosten's list are found in Judg 4:5; 1 Sam 8:3; 13:20; 1 Kgs 8:27. As with *weqatal*, it is not always entirely clear how to distinguish between temporalized and invariant past resultative *wayyiqtol*, especially when they occur in atypical past habitual *weqatal*-constellations, as, e.g., in 1 Sam 27:8–9, where a whole chain of habitual *weqatal*- and *wayyiqtol*-clauses is initiated by a generalizing *wayyiqtol*.

79. Waltke and O'Connor 1990, §31,1d; Gibson and Davidson 1994, §62; Joosten 2012, 287. In Driver's day, the idea of the different historical roots of the *yiqtol*-form were not known, but see his comments on preterite *yiqtol* in Driver 1892, §83–84 and his appendix II.

(85) a. **wayyāšæt**   hōšæk   səbîbōtā_yw   sukkôt
       and=set.YQTL-S.3M.SG darkness   around=him   canopy
       [...] **yarʿem**   min   šāmayim   YHWH
       [...] thunder.YQTL-S.3M.SG   from   heavens   YHWH
       And he **made** darkness his canopy around him [...] The Lord
       thundered from the heavens. (2 Sam 22:12, 14)

   b. **yāšæt**   hōšæk   sitrô   səbîbōtā_yw
       set.YQTL-S.3M.SG   darkness   covering around=him
       [...] **wayyarʿem**   baššāmayim   YHWH
       [...] and=thunder.YQTL-S.3M.SG   in=the=heavens YHWH
       And **he made** darkness his covering around him [...] The Lord
       thundered in the heavens. (Ps 18:12, 14)

The adverbial *ʾāz* ("then") in past settings is probably an indicator that a subsequent *yiqtol* is an original *yiqtol*-S, although one would expect a higher rate of apocopated forms in the cases where this is possible, the only example being the following:[80]

(86) āz   **yaqhel**   šəlōmô   ʾæt   ziqnê
     then   gather.YQTL-S.3M.SG   Solomon   OBJ   elders.of
     yiśrāʾel
     Israel
     Then Solomon **gathered** the elders of Israel. (1 Kgs 8:1)

Some scholars assume that the past *yiqtol* following *ʾāz* is a *yiqtol*-L.[81] However, that is not very likely considering that *yiqtol*-L generally has meanings similar to those of the progressive *qotel*, whereas *yiqtol*-S parallels the resultative *qatal*, and the construction *qatal* plus *ʾāz* in past contexts is used in the same way as *ʾāz* plus *yiqtol*.[82] The very rare combination of *ʾāz* and *qotel*, by contrast, is decidedly imperfective, just as one might expect of a progressive form:[83]

(87) wayhî   rîb   bên   rōʿê
     and=be.YQTL-S.3M.SG   strife   between   herdsmen.of
     miqneh   ʾabrām   ûbên   rōʿê   miqnê   lôt
     cattle.of   Abram   and=between   herdsmen.of   cattle.of Lot

---

80. See Cook 2012, 263.
81. Rundgren 1961, 97–99; Rabinowitz 1984, 53; Joüon and Muraoka 2009, §113i n. 3; Joosten 2012, 110–11.
82. *Pace* Rabinowitz 1984, 53–54.
83. The only other example I have found is Jer 32:2.

wəhakkəna'ănî wəhappərizzî 'āz **yōšeḇ**
and=the=Canaanite and=the=Perizzite then live.QOT.M.SG
bā'āræṣ
in=the=land
There arose a strife between the herdsmen of Abram's cattle and the herdsmen of Lot's cattle. The Canaanites and the Perizzites **were** then **living** in the land. (Gen 13:7)

Other possible cases of temporalized free-standing declarative *yiqtol*-S have to be established on the sole basis of extratextual knowledge (3.1), whether it be general knowledge, as in the case of the fact that the birth of a speaking person is always past (88a), or specific knowledge of what has happened in Israel's history (88b):

(88) a. yō'ḇaḏ yôm 'iwwālæḏ
      perish.YQTL(S).JUSS.3M.SG day be.borne.YQTL(S).1SG
      bô
      in=it
      May the day perish on which **I was born**. (Job 3:3)

   b. 'a'ălæʰ 'æṯkæm mimmiṣrayim
      bring.up.YQTL(S)1SG OBJ=you from=Egypt
      wā'āḇî' 'æṯkæm 'æl hā'āræṣ
      and=bring.in.YQTL(S).1SG OBJ=you to the=land
      'ăšær nišba'tî la'ăḇōṯêkæm
      which swear.QTAL.1SG for=fathers=your
      I brought you up from Egypt and led you into the land that I had promised to your forefathers by oath. (Judg 2:1)

Evidence that free-standing *yiqtol*-S can also have gnomic meaning, is found for, instance, in Psalm 90:[84]

(89) **tāšeḇ** 'ænôš 'aḏ dakkā'
      turn.back.YQTL-S.2M.SG human to dust
      wattō'mær šûḇû ḇənê 'āḏām
      and=say.YQTL-S.2M.SG return sons.of human
      You turn humans **back** to dust and say: "Return, children of humankind." (Ps 90:3)

---

84. Driver 1892, §84; Waltke and O'Connor 1990; Gibson and Davidson 1994, §62, rem. 2.

The fact that this *yiqtol* is apocopated, clause-initial, and coordinated with a *wayyiqtol*-clause representing a subsequent event indicates that this is a *yiqtol*-S.

Although the verb-subject word order in examples (85)–(89) helps to identify the verbs as *yiqtol*-S, in analogy with *wayyiqtol*, there is no saying that *yiqtol*-S could not also appear in second position. Thus, the *yiqtol* in the following example has aorist meaning and is continued by *wayyiqtol*-forms. It is hard to see why it should not be a *yiqtol*-S rather than a *yiqtol*-L:

(90) ûḇəśeʿîr   yāšəḇû   haḥōrîm   ləp̄ānîm
     and=in=Seir   live.QTAL.3M.PL   the=Horites   before
     ûḇənê   ʿēśāw   **yîrāšûm**
     but=sons.of   Esau   dispossess.YQTL(S).3M.PL=them
     wayyašmîḏûm   mippənêhæm
     and=destroy.YQTL(S).3M.PL=them   in.front.of=them

The Horites formerly lived in Seir, but the sons of Esau **dispossessed** them and destroyed them. (Deut 2:12)

Free-standing declarative *yiqtol*-S is considered as an archaic or archaizing trait. It occurs mainly in poetic texts, but it is generally acknowledged that there are some traces of it in prose too, some of the most-cited examples being the ones above. A radical way of coming to terms with this problematic use is to deny the existence of genuine past aorist *yiqtol*-S in prose altogether and to classify possible cases as "local anomalies, to be explained on an ad hoc basis," as suggested by Jan Joosten.[85] A more appropriate starting point, perhaps, would be to analyze each instance carefully from the point of view of their textual function and see whether some pattern appears. Such an investigation would have to consider a number of cases that tend to be classified as *yiqtol*-L in order to settle whether or how they actually differ in terms of their textual function.[86] Comparative Semitic studies would also be helpful.[87] However, this is outside the scope of the present study. For our purposes, it is enough to state that the free-standing declarative *yiqtol*-S has detached itself from the resultative subsystem in Biblical Hebrew, since it is not found with unambiguously clear resultative meaning (i.e., with perfect aspect) and is no longer morpho-syntactically distinctive.

---

85. Joosten 2012, 287.
86. Cases belonging to this group of possible free-standing *yiqtol*-S are found in Gen 37:8; 48:17; Exod 8:20; 19:19; 1 Sam 13:17–18; 2 Sam 15:37; 23:10; 1 Kgs 7:8; 20:32–33; 21:6; 2 Kgs 3:25; 8:29; 9:15; 20:14; Isa 6:4; Jer 52:7; Neh 3:15; Ezra 9:4; Dan 8:12.
87. Notarius (2013, 313–17) argues that Biblical Hebrew free-standing aorist *yiqtol*-clauses are mainly *yiqtol*-L on the basis of comparisons with Ugaritic, which according to Greenstein and others, uses its corresponding form, *yaqtulu*, as a narrative form (in epic poetry). See, however, section 1.4, n. 42, on the different opinions about the Ugaritic narrative.

4.4.4. Volitive yiqtol-S

In spite of the strong evidence in favor of a common origin for the volitive (i.e., jussive/cohortative) and the declarative *yiqtol*-S, there is no trace of resultative meaning in the volitive *yiqtol*-S in Biblical Hebrew, just as there is no progressive form that could serve as its paradigmatic counterpart.[88] Furthermore, the volitive *yiqtol*-S is neutral with regard to limit-based aspectual distinctions and will be interpreted as aorist or imperfective depending on *Aktionsart* and context. Most often, the predicates used are telic, and aorist meaning is implied, but when markers of telicity or boundedness are missing, the volitive *yiqtol*-S may instead be understood as imperfective, even though the aspectual interpretation, in the absence of focalizing events that can fix the focus of attention on a particular part of the event, is always somewhat loose. The next example contains two jussives, the first atelic and most easily taken as imperfective, the second telic and suggestive of completive meaning:

(91) wə'attâ **yešæḇ** nā' 'aḇdəḵâ
and=now sit.YQTL-S.JUSS.3M.SG please servant=your
taḥat hanna'ar 'æḇæḏ la'ḏōnî wəhanna'ar
instead.of the=boy servant for=lord=my and=the=boy
ya'al 'im 'æḥāʸw
go.up.YQTL-S.JUSS.3M.SG with brothers=his

And now, please, **let** your servant **stay** instead of the boy as servant for my lord, and **let** the boy **return** with his brothers. (Gen 44:33)

It is most unlikely that the volitive meaning of the *yiqtol*-S underlies the various declarative meanings demonstrated in the previous subsections. Conversely, there is no lack of evidence that the development can go in the other direction. As I mentioned above, preterites are used with counterfactual and optative meanings in many languages (4.3.2). Andrason has demonstrated the typological parallels between the Biblical Hebrew volitive *yiqtol*-S and various non-Semitic resultative-preterite forms as well as the Semitic suffix-conjugation, including the Biblical Hebrew counterfactual and precative *qatal*.[89] In short, the same explanation is valid for the volitive use of the *yiqtol*-S as for the counterfactual/precative *qatal*: it stems from an underlying past meaning, which, in turn is based on the resultative aspect of the form. Special for the volitive *yiqtol*-S,

---

88. On the usage of the jussive and the cohortative, see Driver 1892, §44–58; Waltke and O'Connor 1990, §34; Gibson and Davidson 1994, §67–68; Joüon and Muraoka 2009, §114, 116; Joosten 2012, 319–26, 333–47.

89. Andrason 2012b, 329–33. See also Andrason 2013b, 20–27.

of course, is that word order has become a more important distinguishing factor than morphology. Thus, from the synchronic point of view, volitive *yiqtol*-S is practically speaking nothing but a volitive *yiqtol*, which means that the connection with the resultative/preterite basis is lost.

4.5. Summary

This chapter has provided examples, which, given our theory, indicate that stage-aspectual meanings are basic to the Biblical Hebrew verbal forms. The overall picture is that *qatal* and *yiqtol*-S—in the shape of *wayyiqtol*—have resultative meaning whereas *qotel* in predicative position and *yiqtol*-L have progressive meaning. Preparative meaning seems also to be expressed by the latter forms, especially by *qotel*. Resultative meaning is relatively rare in *wayyiqtol* however, and the same can be said for dynamic progressive meanings in *yiqtol*-L. As for the latter, this tendency seems to be even stronger in Late Biblical Hebrew.

The aspectual meanings of all the forms can be shown to be invariant in present and nonpresent contexts, which is an indication of the basic aspectual, nontemporal character of the verbal system. The basicness of stage-aspect is further confirmed by the fact that the predominant temporal meanings expressed by the forms are such that can be inferred from their respective stage-aspectual meaning. Thus, *qatal* and *yiqtol*-S are likely to have developed past meaning from their resultative meanings, whereas *qotel* and *yiqtol*-L derive their future meaning from their progressive/preparative meaning. Further, it has been suggested in this section that the modal meanings of *yiqtol*-L are pragmatic inferences based on the future meaning of the form and that the volitive (jussive/cohortative) meanings of *yiqtol*-S derive from its past meaning, although that derivation can only be made by reconstructing the history of the form. As for the modal meanings of *qatal*, the counterfactual meaning (possibly including the precative) has, in all likelihood, developed similarly to the volitive meanings of *yiqtol*-S. As I have not provided any explanation as to how the counterfactual meaning is inferred from past meaning, the counterfactual meaning of *qatal* will have to be considered as semantic, but I view this as a provisional conclusion. By contrast, the volitive meanings of *weqatalti* are not inferred from the semantics of the form. The basic resultative meaning of *qatal* is here invariant.

Finally, the investigation in this chapter has highlighted the variety of limit-aspectual meanings that can arise in different contexts, both in relation to invariant and temporalized uses. This shows the inadequacy of simple oppositions as imperfect–perfect or imperfective–perfective for a full description of the aspectual nature of the Biblical Hebrew verbal system. An aspectual approach needs to integrate the whole complexity of the data in order to become more plausible.

CHAPTER 5

Communicative Appeal and the Semantics of the Biblical Hebrew Verb

IN THE PREVIOUS CHAPTER, the Biblical Hebrew verbal system was described in terms of the basic semantic categories progressive(/preparative) and resultative. According to this description, the forms *qotel* and *yiqtol*-L belong to the progressive, and *qatal* and *yiqtol*-S to the resultative. As we saw, in spite of some examples to the contrary, the *yiqtol*-L and the *yiqtol*-S are used with derived meanings to such an extent that they can hardly be considered as synonyms with their partners, *qotel* and *qatal*. Having stated that, we could, of course, exempt the *yiqtol*-forms altogether from the progressive-resultative opposition and try somehow to redefine them on the basis of the more frequent, derived meanings (e.g., *yiqtol*-L = stativized progressive/future; *yiqtol*-S = past), but that would leave us with meaning labels that are not sufficiently basic to explain the entire semantic range of the forms. Moreover, the considerable functional overlap existing between the forms within the progressive and resultative subsystems and the nature of the verbal system as a whole would not be given proper recognition. Therefore, I shall maintain that the progressive and resultative aspects are basic meanings for the two *yiqtol*-forms, although they are relatively infrequent in them (especially in Late Biblical Hebrew). The question then arises how to account for the semantic differences within the progressive and resultative subsystems.

So far, my semantic analysis has been developed in close dialogue with research on verbal typology and grammaticalization. In this chapter, however, I shall look beyond the conceptual framework that is used within such studies. Drawing on semiotic theory, I shall investigate the concept of *communicative appeal* (for short: "appeal") to see whether it can be used as a semantic feature by which to distinguish between the *yiqtol*-forms, on the one hand, and *qatal* and *qotel*, on the other hand.

The present chapter is divided into sections as follows: Section 5.1 presents the concept of communicative appeal within the framework of semiotics and grammar, suggesting that human language has grammatical means to make a distinction between reduced appeal and full appeal. Section 5.2 describes the criteria for full appeal. Section 5.3 argues that some verbal forms in English default for full appeal, whereas other forms are marked for reduced appeal. Finally, in section 5.4, the theory is applied to Biblical Hebrew.

5.1. The Semiotic Foundations for a Theory of Appeal in Language

Semiotics is the study of signs. A *sign*, according to semiotic theory, is a physical phenomenon that stands for something else.[1] This phenomenon can be many things: a word, a traffic sign, an animal call, a pathological symptom, etc. Thus, human language is just one of the study objects of semiotics, and linguistics can be considered as a subdiscipline within this general science.

In subsection 1.3.1, I wrote about the three basic semiotic functions that, according to Bühler, are mediated through linguistic utterances—namely, expression, appeal, and representation. Expression has to do with what the utterance reveals about the sender, appeal is the effect on the receiver, and representation is the knowledge that is exchanged between them. All three aspects are present in all utterances, but their relative importance varies from one kind of utterance to another. For example, with regard to the verbal moods in Latin, it was suggested that the dominant function of the indicative is representation, whereas appeal is relatively more important in the imperative, and expression in the subjunctive (in the sense of optative). The overall tendency in language, however, is that representation is conventionalized to a higher degree than the other functions—something that is particularly evident from the number of nouns and verbs in our vocabulary. Thus, even if the relatively dominant function in an utterance consisting of the single word "wolf" may be appeal (in a warning), expression (in an exclamation), or representation (as a piece of information), the representational function of representing a particular species of animal is invariant in all contexts, by virtue of the lexical meaning of the noun. Similarly, irrespective of mood, a specific verb always denotes the same kind of event. An indirect proof of the importance of representation in language is that the linguistic discipline that investigates the meaning of linguistic expressions, *semantics*, has mainly been devoted to the study of representation (see 1.3.1).

In Bühler's model of linguistic communication, the utterance is called by different names depending on which primary function it fulfills: as *symptom*, it performs its expressive function, as *signal*, it appeals to the receiver, and as *symbol* it represents objects and events. *Symptom*, *signal*, and *symbol* are known in semiotics as designations for different classes of signs.[2] It is important to bear

---

1. Sebeok 2001, 3–6.
2. Sebeok 2001, chapter 3.

in mind that when Bühler uses these terms, he applies them to *complete utterances*, rather than individual words, although he also counts words as "signs."[3]

Bühler's recognition of the many-sidedness of the linguistic sign—that is, the fact that it always is simultaneously sender-oriented (symptom) receiver-oriented (signal) and "environment-oriented" (symbol)—is a hallmark of his semiotic theory.[4] Another approach has been to stress the distinctiveness of a certain function of the sign to the exclusion of others. Thus, symbols have been said to belong entirely to human language and signals have been ascribed to animal communication. Linguistic utterances are then called symbols because human interpreters are able to abstract their meaning away from particular sensory inputs in particular situations and to use them with reference to imagined phenomena rather than perceptions, or, in more holistic terms, to a conceived, "symbolic universe" rather than the given, material world.[5] Animal language, on the other hand, consists of signals, because animals lack the abstracting ability characteristic of human semiosis. However, such a distinction says more about the cognitive abilities of humans and animals than the actual function of signs in communicative situations. The function of the symbol, as defined by Bühler, is not exclusively to refer to mentally conceived phenomena; the phenomenon referred to may just as well be something in the physical environment, like rain tapping on the window. Some sorts of animal communication are of this type, such as food-associated calls and alarm calls.[6] To acknowledge this is not to state anything about the cognitive abilities of animals but merely to say that animal communication can be at least "functionally referential."[7] At the same time, such a statement does not preclude that food-associated calls and alarm calls among animals can be understood first and foremost as signals, because the axiom of the many-sidedness of the sign allows appeal and representation to function in one and the same utterance.

We may therefore retain the idea that there is a qualitative difference between human and animal semiosis, in spite of some functional similarities that do exist. One way to describe the difference would be to state that appeal is a more dominant feature in animal communication. Animal communication is never concerned with purely mental representations, as human speech often is. Even

---

3. See Bühler's (1965, 25) example: "Es regnet." In his figure on p. 28, this utterance is supposed to take the place of "the (complex) linguistic sign" ("des [komplexen] Sprachzeichens"). On words as signs, see, e.g., p. 33.

4. Bühler 1965, 33.

5. For an orientation, see Nöth, 2000, 179, 190. For particular statements along these lines, see Cassirer 1944, 24–25; Benveniste 1966a, 25–27.

6. Wildgen 2004, 30–31 (quoting Fischer and Hammerschmidt).

7. See Evans and Marler 1995, 347–48; restatement by McAninch, Goodrich, and Allen 2009, 128.

when it is referential, it functions primarily to affect the receiver's behavior.[8] In this respect, it illustrates very well Thomas Sebeok's definition of signal, which states that the function of the signal is to *"trigger some reaction on the part of a receiver."*[9] Our conclusions about what animals do or not do in their communication, of course, follow naturally from the fact that humans cannot "share thoughts" with animals by means of some "animal language" in the way they do it with other humans. We can understand animal communication only by observing their behavior. This makes the criterion of reaction-triggering always applicable, and, as a consequence, animal calls appear as prototypical signals.[10] This is true not only of the declarative-like warning signals and food-associated signals but also of communication that more resembles imperative speech acts, such as the sound a cat makes when it wants its owner to open the door.[11] In contrast, a human utterance referring only to a mental representation may seem to elicit no reaction at all, for which reason the appeal in such an utterance is much less evident. On the other hand, human utterances aimed at immediately influencing the receiver's behavior are indeed comparable to animal signals in terms of their communicative appeal, notwithstanding the fact that they are also related to a symbolic universe. Consider, for example,

(1) a. Wolf!
    b. Come!

Here, I shall say that prototypical signals such as these are characterized by the property of *full appeal*, as opposed to utterances with *reduced* appeal.

By way of clarification, the term "appeal" is used in a somewhat restricted sense in this study, since there are actually different kinds of appeal, triggering different kinds of reactions. The kind of appeal that is of interest for this study triggers world-oriented action; that is, some kind of motoric adjustment to and/or manipulation of the physical environment. This is the adequate response to signals like the warning and the command in example (1). By contrast, this study draws no conclusions as to the *emotional* side of the appeal. An utterance like *You're fantastic!* may cause a strong emotional reaction in the receiver, but since there is no call for an action to be performed, it is not a prototypical signal with regard to the action-directed dimension of the communication.[12] Furthermore, we are not concerned with the special appeal of vocative expressions, greetings,

---

8. See Rendall and Owren 2002, 310–11.
9. Sebeok, 2001, 44 (emphasis added).
10. See Bühler 1965, 31.
11. This is Vauclair's (2003, 14) example of a "protoimperative signal."
12. See Bühler (1965, 32) on the appeal of endearment and abuse.

and conversational fillers (yeah, I see, and so on), which only aims at establishing and maintaining communication.

The fundamental importance of communicative appeal for the physical welfare and survival of both animals and humans is self-evident. It also stands to reason that the ability to distinguish between different degrees of appeal is very useful in human communication, which actually more often than not serves other purposes than to trigger immediate behavioral reaction. These facts are much forgotten in linguistic studies—perhaps they are "too basic" to receive attention—but it should come as no surprise if a distinction between full and reduced appeal is actually reflected in grammar.

This brings us back to Harald Weinrich's claim that the verbal systems of all languages contain one set of verbal forms for "relaxed speech" and one for "tense speech" (2.4)—his two "linguistic attitudes" (*Sprechhaltungen*). It is intuitively plausible to associate Weinrich's notion of tense speech with full appeal, and relaxed speech with reduced appeal. Turning again to the examples from section 2.4, we find that this correspondence is partly confirmed:

			Linguistic attitude acc. to Weinrich	Communicative appeal
(2)	a.	A wolf *is coming*.	Tense speech	Full appeal
	b.	A wolf *has come*.	Tense speech	Full appeal
	c.	A wolf *came*.	Relaxed speech	Reduced appeal

The sentences (2a) and (2b) are here ascribed the property of full appeal, since they are typically used in situations where the listeners are called to act immediately with regard to the event that is being referred to. The third sentence, by contrast, is designed to turn the listeners' attention from the real circumstances of the speech situation to the mental image of a nonpresent event, which makes the appeal to action much less pressing.[13] These things will be discussed in more detail in the next section.

Traditional grammar, of course, describes the difference between the sentences in example (2) in terms of the temporal semantics of the verbs: the first two are in the present tense (some dispute may arise concerning [2b]; see 2.1) and the third in the preterite. This does not have to exclude the possibility that the factor of communicative appeal is also involved. One may just ask what factor is the more fundamental. If it were temporal semantics, one would perhaps expect the verb to contain some morpheme that was originally a temporal adverbial, like "before," "yesterday," "now," "today," "afterward," or similar,

---

13. The same holds true for sentences with futural or habitual meaning, although Weinrich does not support that claim (see 2.5).

but this is not so in the case of the English verbs, nor in most of the languages in the world.[14] Hence, while Weinrich's dismissal of temporal semantics in verbal forms might be a bit too radical, his case for the linguistic attitudes does deserve some reconsideration.

5.2. Criteria for Full Communicative Appeal

A fundamental question that needs to be dealt with is on what basis it is possible to distinguish between full and reduced appeal. Ideally, of course, the answer to that question should involve verification by psychological experiments. While that is beyond the scope of this study, the goal of the present section is nonetheless to propose an answer that is sufficiently theoretically consistent and consonant with linguistic data to provide a first step for a grammar of communicative appeal. The principles that I am going to discuss are illustrated mainly with English examples, but I assume them to be universal.

The question of how to distinguish between full and reduced appeal will here be answered by first establishing criteria for full appeal and then explaining reduced appeal as the result of the failure to meet those criteria. Thus, on the premise that we are dealing with an action-triggering, world-oriented kind of appeal as described in the previous section, it is possible to identify three main criteria for full appeal, which typically apply in utterances like the above example (1)—namely, first, a world-oriented criterion of *imminence*, second, a listener-oriented criterion of *nonexpectancy*, and, third, a sign-oriented criterion of *efficiency*.

5.2.1. Imminence

Imminence pertains to the stimulus of the utterance, which can be the represented event as such (declarative utterances; see [1a]) or the need for the represented event/action to be carried out (imperative utterances; see [1b]).[15] In the former case, imminence means that the perceived event is in the proximal

---

14. See Comrie 1985, 12. Heine and Kuteva (2002) mention some languages that have grammaticalized future tense from the adverbs "then" and "tomorrow," but comment that, in spite of being "semantically plausible," these pathways appear to be "far less common compared to other pathways leading to the rise of future tense markers" (Heine and Kuteva 2002, 293–94, 299). They also note that past tense markers derived from "yesterday" seem to be confined to some languages in Africa and conclude, "Conceivably, this is a conceptually plausible but possibly areally induced pathway of grammaticalization" (315–16).

15. For convenience, "event" here stands for anything that is predicated, including states (see 3.2).

zone—the "here and now"—of the listener; in the latter, it means that the need is affecting one or more individuals at speech time. In both cases, there is an appropriate behavioral reaction to the signal that would be beneficial to either or any of the participants of the speech situation. The reaction has to be immediate, for the opportunity is passing and nothing is gained by delaying action.

The criterion of imminence is typically not met in utterances with future and past tense, since such forms direct focus of attention to nonpresent events—that is, outside the proximal zone (but see example [12] below). A similar reduction of imminence happens in commands where the need is located in the future (*Come back tomorrow!*).

In the present tense, the criterion of imminence is not met in utterances referring to permanent states (3a) and generalizing predicates (3b–c):

(3) a. The cat is white.
    b. Jimmy plays hockey.
    c. Birds fly.

Being a permanent state, an event like the one in (3a) is unlikely to be felt as something that has to be dealt with immediately. As for the generalizing predicates in (3b) and (3c), they combine the elements of permanence and nonproximity, since they refer to more or less permanent habits or properties associated with events that are not necessarily being observed in the speech situation.

Some transitory states, too, are naturally nonimminent. This is particularly the case with inert perceptions, cognitions, and attitudes:

(4) a. I hear music.
    b. I understand what this means.
    c. I enjoy being here.

As nonovert, subjective experiences, these states concern the experiencer in an exclusive way and do not directly affect anyone else. Furthermore, for reasons to be explained below (see example [11]), although the object of these experiences may be imminent, the mere mention of it as being experienced reduces the appeal of the utterance.

5.2.2. *Nonexpectancy*

This criterion has to do with the mental state of the receiver. A signal with full appeal is one that is designed to affect the listener's behavior regardless of his/her general state of alertness, and regardless of where his/her focus of attention is oriented. The signal is able to shift both the attention and the intention of the listener.

The criterion of nonexpectancy fails if the stimulus of the utterance is part of the so-called *common ground*. The common ground is the knowledge, beliefs, attitudes, etc. that the speaker and addressee assume that they share as a basis for their communication.[16] An example of common ground material is the relative clause in the following sentence:

(5) Here is the man **that you're looking for**.

All the new information in (5) lies in the main clause. The common ground between the speaker and the listener consists (among other things) of their mutual awareness that the latter is looking for a particular man, and the function of the relative clause is to anchor the information of the main clause in this common ground. In other words, it works the opposite way to a prototypical signal: it keeps the attention within an already established frame.[17]

Even reaction-triggering signals may fall short of the requirements for full appeal if the stimulus is part of the common ground. Consider the following example:

(6) Go!

The stimulus of the start signal (i.e., the need to start the race) is common ground because the start signal is part of a script that all the participants are following. So, even though the signal will trigger an immediate reaction in the participants of the race, its appeal is less profound than that of a prototypical signal, which is intended to totally reorient the attention of the listeners. The start signal requires the listeners to be already on their marks in order for listeners to respond to it adequately; it does not have the force, for instance, of an unexpected *Run for your lives!*

Linguistic communication abounds with start-signal-like signals. They may not always be quite as predictable as the real start signal in (6), but they all have in common that the listener is already alert and ready to act. Moreover, the listener's readiness to act itself is part of the common ground, and this affects how the signal can be shaped. In the next example, the "start-signals" consists of the last utterance in the respective dialogue:

---

16. Clark 1992, 3.
17. In (6) the common ground is situation-specific and already within the listener's attention. Common-ground-material can also be nonsituation-specific and, as such, unexpected (*Here is the man who fell off the roof the other day*), but in this case it fails the criterion of imminence and will for that reason not trigger a reaction by the listener.

(7) a. [A: Fire! B: Where? A:] In the barn!
   b. [A: A hotdog, please! B: With or without mustard? A:] With!

As the example illustrates, not only verbs or nouns, but, in principle, any part of speech can have the function of a start signal, provided that there is enough information stored in the common ground for the listener to fill in the missing pieces.

A very rich set of assumptions forms the common ground in the running commentary (typically of a sports event; see chapter 3, example [34]). Even before it starts, the running commentary presupposes that the listeners have their attention directed toward the stimulus, which is the ongoing game. As opposed to the start signal, the running commentary has no intended reaction-triggering effect; the reader is supposed to be entertained, not to take action, even if the stimulus-events take place in the proximity of the listener.

5.2.3. Efficiency

An efficient signal is direct and simple. It directs the listener's focus of attention to the stimulus, and to this only. In linguistic communication, however, signals are often indirect, which reduces their appeal. Exactly why this is so is a somewhat complicated question, which requires different answers depending on whether the indirect signal is of a conventional or nonconventional type. To illustrate, consider the following examples:

(8) a. Give me some water!
   b. Can you give me some water?
   c. Are you able to give me some water?

(8a) is a direct and simple request designed to direct the listener's focus of attention to what the listener wants to be done and nothing else. (8b) and (8c) are indirect requests of a conventional and a nonconventional type, both of which, I assume, are less efficient than (8a), given that we consider each expression within its appropriate context. In the case of the nonconventionalized indirect request in (8c), the lack of efficiency stems from the fact that the listener first has to consider the literal meaning of the signal before s/he can infer that the question is to be taken not literally but as a request. The motivation for using such a slow-processed signal to obtain one's goal would be to put less pressure on the listener by giving him/her the option to fulfill the speaker's need as if on his/her own initiative. This makes the listener appear in a good light, but also the speaker, who purposefully created the opportunity. Due to the high value associated with cooperativeness in human social affairs, this way of communicating is more socially beneficial to the participants than a straight command/compliance interaction.[18]

As for the *Can you*-type in (8b), it has become so conventional that the listener can immediately comprehend the indirect meaning without first having to process the literal meaning.[19] Nevertheless, the literal meaning is also available, as evidenced by the fact that listeners often respond with *Yes I can* or similar before performing the request.[20] This means that, although the indirect meaning is processed very quickly, the expression conveys the same implication as it did before it was conventionalized—namely, that the performace of the request is conditioned on the kindness of the listener (for that reason, *Can you*-requests are considered *polite*). Put differently, the indirect request is cognitively more demanding than the direct request in that it directs the listener not simply to perform a certain action but to do so while maintaining a certain understanding of the social conditions within which the performance of the desired action is taking place and by which it is motivated. This, I suggest, is what reduces the appeal of indirect requests.[21]

The idea that indirect requests are more cognitively demanding than direct requests has yet to be confirmed by empirical psychological research, but pending that, I believe that the explanation presented here remains a cogent one.[22] Furthermore, it is intuitively very hard to argue against the idea that an imperative is more efficient than an indirect request in eliciting a prompt response and that it will be preferred over the latter in situations of emergency. This is not altered by the fact that direct requests may be as inefficient as, or even less effient than indirect requests in situations where there is no call for urgency. Thus, in everyday requests for favors, where a certain level of politeness is anticipated, an imperative as in (8a) may come across as rude and cause some disturbance in the interaction. However, the more urgent the need (e.g., if the speaker has just chewed a chili pepper), the more appropriate the imperative and the less appropriate the indirect expression.

The same appeal-reducing principle should apply also in other kinds of indirect requests, for example, the directive future that we saw earlier (chapter 4, example [32]):

---

18. See Tomasello 2008, 84, 206–7 on the prosocial function of polite requests, or, as he terms it, "cooperative imperatives."

19. This has been shown in experiments by Gibbs (1983, 531).

20. To acknowledge the literal meaning of an indirect request in this way is called "the literal move" by Clark and Schunk (1980, 113).

21. Another reason why polite indirect requests reduce the appeal of the utterance is the fact that part of being polite is to allow the listener to perform the request on his/her own terms. However, this does not explain the reduced appeal of indirect requests in general, since it does not apply to nonpolite indirect requests.

22. See the overview in Ruytenbeek 2017, 317–18.

(9) You're gonna take off your shoes before you come in here.

The literal meaning of this message is that the speaker knows that the listener is going to take off his/her shoes, whereas the indirect meaning is that the speaker wants the listener to do so. Moreover, it is understood that the speaker expects the listener to comply because s/he has authority over the latter. This accords with the above-mentioned principle that indirect requests are aimed at maintaining a certain understanding of the social situation surrounding the desired event. Therefore, nonpolite indirect requests, too, reduce the appeal of the utterance. As we shall see, the directive future may be used with other implications in other contexts (5.4.3).

A performative utterance is another type of speech act that depends on an awareness of the social situation in order to be meaningful. In some contexts, moreover, its function is precisely that of an indirect request, which means that its efficiency as a signal is restricted in the same way (10a). In more ritualized, scripted settings, the recognition of the social situation is presupposed, which entails a degree of anticipation that gives the speech act a "start-signal"-like character (10b; see also 54.2):

(10) a. I give you ten seconds to get out of here!
     b. I declare the Olympic Games of London open!

In declarative utterances, verbs of inert perception (*see*, *hear*, *smell*, etc.) and verbs of cognition (*know*, *understand*, *remember*, etc.) form a special group of appeal-reducing verbs. Thus, consider

(11) a. I see a wolf.
     b. I know a wolf is coming.

In these sentences, the stimulus (the approaching wolf) is represented as mediated through somebody's perception or cognition. The listener, accordingly, must not only attend to the stimulus but also evaluate the import of the speaker's experience of it. Because of this complexity, the reference becomes less efficient as a signal than a direct representation, as in *Wolf!* or *A wolf is coming*.

The next example—in Swedish—illustrates what we may call an "alerting preterite." Like the above-mentioned start-signal and indirect request, this construction functions as a signal with slightly reduced appeal. It is used, for example, when you witness somebody drop something without being aware of it, and you want to alert him/her to the fact, so that s/he can do something about it:[23]

---

23. The alerting preterite does not exist in Biblical Hebrew, which has no semantically marked preterite form, but the category is interesting as an illustration of how reduced appeal can be used

(12) Du   tappade   din   plånbok!
    you   drop.PST   your   wallet
    You dropped your wallet!

In a typical case, an utterance like this is sure to trigger a reaction by the listener. The function of the preterite is thus similar to that of the perfect in the warning signal (see example [2b]), in that the preterite calls the listener's attention to a present result of a past event—in this case, a wallet being lost.[24] However, the alerting preterite differs from the prototypical warning signal in one important respect: the semantic function of the preterite is to direct focus of attention to a past event; hence the reference to the present result is only implied. The question is what is added to the message by this detour to the past event. Why not focus directly on the present result by means of a perfect? The explanation probably lies in the fact that the preterite suggests a higher degree of knowledge on the part of the speaker. By directing the focus of attention to the event preceding the result, the speaker indicates that s/he observed it as it happened, or at least knows about somebody else who did. If the speaker does not know anything about the circumstances under which the accident happened but only notices that the listener's wallet is missing, the perfect is the appropriate form to use in Swedish, rather than the preterite (Swedish: *Du **har tappat*** [PFCT] *din plånbok*, "You have dropped your wallet").

There can be little doubt that the indirectness of the reference in example (12) reduces the appeal of the signal. By using the preterite to indicate that there is a witness to the preceding event, the speaker also gives to understand that there is somebody who already has assessed what action is most appropriate to take; that is, whether to intervene him/herself or alert the listener. In other

---

in a form belonging to an advanced stage of the resultative path (on the origin of the Germanic preterites, see Meid 1971, 5). As for English, the situation seems to be more diversified than for Swedish. Based on what I have found by asking native speakers, the alerting preterite seems natural to American English speakers, whereas British English speakers prefer using the perfect in the same situations (cf. *You have dropped your wallet!*). The reason why I do not use the American English formulation "You dropped your wallet" for my example of the alerting preterite is that the American English preterite does not signify past tense as unequivocally as the Swedish preterite (see the next footnote).

24. I assume that the meaning of the British English simple past is unequivocally past when used as in example (12), but, as mentioned in the previous footnote, the preterite does not seem to be preferred in such contexts in British English. In American English, the aspecto-temporal semantics of the same form is somewhat more complicated. According to Sempere-Martinez (2008, 126–27, 131–32), several uses of the preterite form in American English are remnants from an earlier phase where the perfect did not exist and perfect meaning was regularly expressed by the preterite (e.g., American English *Did you sell your tape-recorder yet?*; cf. British English *Have you sold your tape-recorder yet?*). Whether this means that the American English preterite has perfect meaning and/or is not marked for reduced appeal in utterances like *You dropped your wallet* is doubtful but cannot be dealt with here.

words, the listener can conclude that the situation is more or less under control and that there is no cause for great alarm. In the case of the lost wallet in (12), the action taken by the one who witnessed the accident may have been only to notify the owner of the wallet, so that s/he could fetch it again. Alternatively, the witness may have fetched the wallet him/herself and then notified the owner with the same words. In either case, the understood message would be that the situation is under control. By contrast, the use of the perfect to alert somebody to a wallet being lost would suggest lack of control and would most probably cause some anxiety on the part of the listener.

The implication of control associated with the preterite can have different effects in different contexts (without, however, changing the fact that the appeal is reduced). Thus, when it comes to wallets, the witness may often feel that the most appropriate option is to let the owner take care of it, but the opposite situation can also be the case. A chivalrous gentleman seeing a lady dropping her handkerchief would consider it inappropriate to say *Du tappade* [PST] *din näsduk* ("You dropped your handkerchief") without picking it up for her first, because that would imply that he deliberately refrained from doing her a courtesy when he had the opportunity. Again, the perfect (*Du **har tappat*** [PFCT] *din näsduk*, "You have dropped your handkerchief") would not have the same effect, since it does not imply that the speaker is in control and is able to help.

A general conclusion from this overview of the criteria for full appeal is that the use of signs that do not match the criteria requires rather advanced cognitive abilities by the communicators in terms of reflecting on nonpresent events and nonovert, subjective experiences (example [4]), maintaining a common ground of discourse ([6]–[7]), and conveying indirect messages ([8b]–[10a], [12]) and hierarchical ordering of information (11). It is very telling, then, that the same kind of mental excercises are not performed by animals, whose communication is geared toward full appeal. Animals only refer to present events, they do not conceive of communication as a cooperative enterprise in the way that is necessary to establish a common ground of discourse or to convey indirect requests, and they do not have anything like the syntax of human language.[25]

---

25. Tomasello (2008), states that the establishment of common ground in linguistic discourse as well as the use of indirect requests ("cooperative imperatives"), are made possible thanks to the capacity for "shared intentionality"—a cooperative strategy that is species-unique to humans (see especially pp. 72–75). And Hockett, in an oft-cited study, describes reference to nonpresent events ("displacement") and hierarchical organization ("duality of patterning") as two of several "design features" that, according to him, are found almost exclusively in human communication (Hockett 1960, 90–91). More recently, Slobodchikoff, Perla, and Verdolin (2009, 85–87), have claimed that nearly all of Hockett's design features can be found in the calls of Gunnison's prairie dog. However, they misunderstand the design feature of displacement when they take it to mean reference to distant but visible events. They also claim that the vocalizations of Gunnison's prairie dog has hierarchical organization because it contains phonetic elements analogous to phonemes, but this is something very remote from the complex hierarchical organization of semantic units in human speech.

5.3. Communicative Appeal and Verbal Grammar: The Case of the English Progressives

Every language, I submit, must contain a set of verbal forms that can be used to convey full appeal, including indicative forms used for referring to events occurring in the here-and-now sphere, as well as some volitive form used for prototypical commands. Within their respective functional domain, these forms may contrast semantically or pragmatically with forms that are marked for reduced appeal. The forms used to express full appeal only default for this feature and are not semantically marked for it.

From what we know about diachronic paths of progressives and resultatives, it appears that reduced appeal typically becomes a semantic feature of a verbal form in the later stage of its evolution. Thus, in English, the preterite and the simple present are good candidates for being semantically marked for reduced appeal, as opposed to the present perfect and the present progressive, which represent earlier stages of their respective diachronic path. As for the preterite, it has lost its resultative meaning altogether and is used exclusively for representing nonpresent events. Even the alerting preterite has reduced appeal, although it triggers behavioral reaction. The simple present, on the other hand, is interesting in that it is used for a number of very diverse functions, which all have the factor of reduced appeal in common. Particularly intriguing is the fact that the form never seems to meet all the criteria for full appeal described in the previous section, even though it can refer in various ways to events that are ongoing at speech time, thus fulfilling the minimal requirement of imminence.[26] Thus, we have seen that the simple present can refer to permanent (specific or general) states (13a–b) and nonovert subjective experiences (13c) and that it can be used for performative utterances (13d) as well as for running commentaries (13e):

(13) a. The cat is white.
　　 b. Birds fly.
　　 c. I see a wolf.
　　 d. I pronounce you husband and wife.
　　 e. Ibrahimovic picks up the ball.

---

26. Obviously, the copula, consisting of a finite form of the verb "to be," is an exception from the rule that the simple present has reduced appeal, since it is an integral part of the progressive construction. The copula can also be a full-appeal predicate in locative expressions (*The enemy is here!*). The copula of "to be" is syntactically and semantically unique among present tense forms, and its association with full appeal does not affect the semantic status of the simple present as a whole.

A couple of other real present uses, discussed by Anna Granville Hatcher, also deserves mention.[27] Thus, consider

(14) a. You walk as if your feet hurt.
b. Oh look, it leaks!

Hatcher assumes that the present form *walk* in (14a) is used to deemphasize the involvement of the subject referent in the activity. I suggest instead that indicates reduced appeal, since the event of walking is mutually manifest to both speaker and listener at the time of speech and therefore is part of the common ground.[28]

In (14b) the verb does indeed refer to an event that is ongoing at speech time, but at the same time it can be understood in a generalizing sense as referring to an event that is characteristic of the subject referent (a bucket). The result of this generalization is a slight reduction in the appeal of the utterance. As Hatcher observes, a progressive in the same context would make the leaking appear as a more imminent problem: "*It's leaking* seems to ask for some such comment as *We'd better get a rag to wipe it up*. [...] But we would feel something of a non-sequitur in [...] *Oh look, it leaks; we'd better get a rag* ... (rather, We'll have to find another bucket—as a result of its condition, not as a result of the dripping water)."[29] Thus, even though the same event causes reactions in both scenarios, it does so less directly in Hatcher's second example (i.e., with the simple present). Here, the dripping water is not a problem in itself but an indication that the bucket does not serve its purpose well enough. When the problem is the dripping water, however, the situation is more urgent, and the simple present is not used.

The contrast in appeal between the progressive and the simple present can be felt also in a relative sense. Thus, although utterance (15a) is not as efficient a signal as (2a) above, it has a much stronger action-triggering appeal than (15b):

(15) a. I just heard that a wolf is attacking the sheep (right now).
b. I just heard that a wolf attacks the sheep (every now and then).

In the past tense, the progressive can contrast with other forms by conveying a sense of appeal on behalf of others:

(16) a. They were told that a wolf was attacking the sheep.
b. They were told that a wolf used to attack the sheep.

27. Hatcher 1951, 274, 276.
28. See Clark 1992, 38–39 on "physical copresence" as a basis for common ground.
29. Hatcher 1951, 279.

The following example, borrowed from Comrie, illustrates what could perhaps be understood as a very abstract application of the distinction in appeal:

(17) a. She always buys far more vegetables than they can possibly eat.
b. She is always buying far more vegetables than they can possibly eat.

Both (17a) and (17b) refer to permanent habitual states, but, according to Comrie, the progressive has "a greater emotive effect."[30] The same phenomenon is described in different words by Rena Torres Cacoullos. She suggests that one of the basic functions of the progressive, in English as well as in Spanish, is to stress the involvement on the part of the speaker—what she calls the "experiential" use. In this function, she writes, the progressive expresses "the speaker's viewpoint on the situation as noteworthy and/or personally experienced."[31] In terms of communicative appeal, the "experiential" or "emotive" meaning can be understood as a result of a higher degree of appeal in the progressive as compared to the simple present—the problem somehow appears more imminent with the progressive.[32]

5.4. Communicative Appeal in the Biblical Hebrew Verbal System

We now turn to the evidence for grammatically marked reduced appeal in the Biblical Hebrew verbal system.

As we saw in examples (2a–b), prototypical signals can contain both progressive and resultative verbs. The present section investigates the expression of appeal in the Biblical Hebrew progressive and resultative subsystems, using the criteria of full appeal developed in section 5.2.

---

30. Comrie 1976, 37. It should be clear that I understand Comrie's "emotive effect" as an effect of reaction-triggering properties of the prototypical signal. As I said earlier (5.1), utterances may have emotional appeal for other reasons as well.

31. Torres Cacoullos 2000, 14; see also 177, 209–13, 216–21.

32. It can be safely assumed that relative degrees of appeal can be expressed in all languages. The English data are presented here for the sake of the theory, but I have not investigated the matter in any detail in Biblical Hebrew. In brief, I am not aware that minimal pairs corresponding to those in (15) and (16) are found in the Hebrew Bible. But *yiqtol* with generalizing meaning can be used in object-clauses similar to (15b) (Gen 44:15; Exod 4:14; Num 22:6), and *qotel* can be used in representing imminent events in past contexts, whether it be within an object-clauses, as the English progressive in (16a) (Gen 42:23; see also *qotel* with preparative meaning in Gen 31:20) or a clause with the particle *hinneh* (Gen 24:63; 26:8; 33:1; 37:25; Josh 5:13; Judg 9:43; 2 Sam 13:34; 2 Kgs 11:14). In all likelihood, *yiqtol* would also be the form to use in context (16b), and *qotel* would be the choice in context (15a). It is difficult to assess whether Biblical Hebrew also made a distinction corresponding to the one expressed in example (17a–b). The possible existence of generalizing experiential/emotive *qotel* in Biblical Hebrew is discussed briefly in Bergström 2015, 610.

Since the function of appeal operates in *directive* speech acts as well, a survey of appeal in Biblical Hebrew verbs must also involve the imperative form and the jussive/cohortative *yiqtol*-S, which complements the imperative within the volitive paradigm.

5.4.1. The Resultative Subsystem

Since *qatal* is the closest equivalent to the English present perfect, we should expect that it can serve as a vehicle for full appeal in Biblical Hebrew. The requirements are met in example (18). King Saul is on the hunt for David when Doeg the Edomite comes to him and says:

(18) **bā'**   dāwiḏ   'æl   bêṯ   'ăhîmælæk
     come.QTAL.3M.SG David   to   house.of   Ahimelek
     David **has come** to Abimelek's house. (Ps 52:2)[33]

A special type of signal is used when the speaker wants to direct the listener's attention to what s/he has to say:

(19) šāmaʻtî   'eṯ   'ăšær   'āmərû   hannəḇî'îm
     hear.QTAL.1SG   OBJ   which   say.QTAL.3PL   the=prophets
     hannibbə'îm   bišmî   šæqær   le'mōr
     the=prophesying in=name=my   lie   QUOT
     ḥālamtî   **ḥālamtî**
     dream.QTAL.1SG   dream.QTAL.1SG
     I have heard what the prophets have said, who prophesy falsehood in my name, saying, **I have dreamed, I have dreamed!** (Jer 23:25)

By calling out "I have dreamed!" the prophets direct the focus of attention to a present fact—that is, that they have a message to deliver. Those who hear should pause and pay heed.[34]

In the overwhelming majority of cases, however, the *qatal*-clauses that we encounter in the Hebrew Bible have no full appeal because they refer to nonpresent events, or are part of the common ground of the discourse. There is no point in burdening the reader with more examples of nonpresent *qatal*; we simply conclude from them that *qatal* is unmarked with regard to full appeal, since it

---

33. Other examples of *qatal*-claues aimed at prompting immediate action are Judg 13:10 (*nir'â*); Jer 40:14 (*šālaḥ*). See also 1 Kgs 1:18 (*mālak*), 43 (*himlîk*), although here, the action is temporarily suspended by the subsequent discourse (see below, example [22]).

34. For more examples of the attention-getting type, see Exod 3:13 and 16 (*šəlaḥanî*), Judg 7:13 (*ḥālamtî*).

occurs with both full and reduced appeal. The interesting thing to note in this connection is the crucial role that shifts in communicative appeal may have for the process of temporalization. This is well illustrated by such *qatal*-clauses that are ambiguous between a present perfect and a temporalized preterite meaning. We had an example in 4.3.2 above, where the ambiguous *qatal* (*'āśîtā*, "have done / did") is part of the common ground between speaker and listener (quoted again here with the translations from the NRSV and the NIV):

(20) bəraḥ ləkā 'æl lābān 'āḥî [...]
flee.IMP.2M.SG for=you to Laban brother=my [...]
wəyāšabtā 'immô yāmîm 'āḥādim [...]
and=sit.QTAL.2M.SG with=him days several [...]
'ad šûb 'ap 'āḥîkā mimməkā
until return.INFC anger brother=your from=you
wəšākaḥ 'et 'ăšær **'āśîtā**
and=forget.QTAL.3M.SG OBJ which do.QTAL.2M.SG
lô
to=him

NRSV: Flee to my brother Laban [...] and stay with him for a while [...] until your brother's anger against you turns away, and he forgets what **you have done** to him.
NIV: ... forgets what you **did** to him. (Gen 27:43–45)

The temporally ambiguous clause in (20) belongs to the common ground of the utterance, which means that the full appeal interpretation of the *qatal* is canceled. As a consequence, mutual focus on the present, result stage of the event is no longer required. Which stage of the represented event the focus of attention is directed to is of no importance for the effectiveness of the communication. There is no breach of any cooperative principle if the Hebrew listener (Jacob) thinks back on what happened the other day rather than keeping his mind on the present state of affairs that result from it. This, I suggest, is the reason why the English translator may use either the simple past or the present perfect to render the text.

Performative utterances have present tense, but their appeal is reduced by the fact that their efficiency as signals always ultimately depends on the participants' recogniction of the social conditions surrounding the speech act (5.2.2). In Biblical Hebrew, *qatal* is typically the form to use:

(21) rə'e habbāqār lā'ōlâ
see.IMP.2M.SG the=cattle for=the=burnt.offering
wəhammōriggîm ukəlê habbāqār
and=the=threshing.sledges and=yokes.of the=cattle

```
lā'eṣîm          hakkōl    nātan           'ărawnâ
for=the=woods    the=all   give.QTAL.3M.SG  Araunah
[...]            lammælæk
[...]            to=the=king
```
Here you have the oxen for the burnt offering and the threshing sledges for wood. All of it Araunah **gives** ... to the king.
(1 Sam 24:22–23)

Declarative *yiqtol*-S, in the shape of *wayyiqtol*, sometimes has present perfect meaning in Biblical Hebrew (4.4.1). However, the function of expressing full appeal is canceled by the mere fact that the construction is dependent on the preceding linguistic context for conveying this meaning. It cannot, as *qatal*, be used in the kind of independent, isolated utterance that the prototypical signal consists of, utterances that draw the attention to some new and unforeseen intruding event that demands to be dealt with. Even when it has present perfect meaning, *wayyiqtol* is a continuation form that only develops a given theme. In other words, when the *wayyiqtol*-clause enters the stage, the attention of the listener is already alerted. In this respect, it resembles the start-signals in example (7), although in this case the utterance delays action rather than triggers it, since it makes the speaker's signal longer and more complex. The example below is taken from the episode where the usurper Adonijah and his supporters are told by their comrade Jonathan that Solomon has risen to the throne, an event that has taken place whithin earshot of the company and poses a fatal threat to all of them:

```
(22) bō'                  kî      'îš       ḥayil    'attâ      waṭôb
     enter.IMP.2M.SG      for     man.of    valor    you        and=good
     təbaśśer                                         wayya'an
     announce.YQTL-L.2M.SG                            and=answer.YQTL-S.3M.SG
     yônātān     wayyō'mær                 la'ădōniyyāhû    'ăbāl
     Jonathan    and=say.YQTL-S.3M.SG      to=Adoniyah       alas
     'ădōnênû    hammælæk      dāwiḏ      himlîk
     lord=our    the=king      David      make.king.QTAL.3M.SG
     'æṯ         šəlōmoʰ       wayyišlaḥ                    'ittô
     OBJ         Solomon       and=send.YQTL(S).3M.SG       with=him
     hammælæk     'æṯ      ṣāḏôq      [...]    wə'æṯ      nāṯān    [...]
     the=king     OBJ      Zadoq      [...]    and=OBJ    Natan    [...]
     ûbənāyâhû        [...]    wəhakkərēṯî          wəhappəlēṯî
     and=Benaiah      [...]    and=the=Kerethites   and=the=Peletites
     wayyarkībû                          'ōṯô         'al    pirdaṯ
     cause.to.ride.YQTL(S).3M.PL         OBJ=him      on     mule.of
```

hammælæk
the=king

"Come in, for you are a good man and you will bring good news."
And Jonathan aswered and said: "Alas, no, for our lord, the king
David, has made Solomon king. And the king **has sent** with him
Zadok [...], Nathan [...], Benaiah [...], the Kerethites and the Pele-
tites, and they **have made** him **ride** on the king's mule." (1 Kgs
1:42–44)

If the first *qatal* in this utterance (i.e., *himlîk*, "has made king") calls for some kind of action by the listeners, everything that follows has the effect of delaying it. In other words, the *wayyiqtol*-forms diminish the efficiency, and hence the appeal, of the utterance. In the story, the speech goes on even further, containing among other things a couple of more *wayyiqtol*-clauses, before everybody rushes away in great fear.[35]

5.4.2. The Progressive Subsystem

The following example (repeated from above), shows the progressive *qotel* with full appeal:

(23) wayyar'   ga'al   'æt   hā'ām
     and=see.YQTL-S.3M.SG   Gaal   OBJ   the=people
     wayyō'mær   'æl   zĕbûl hinneʰ 'ām
     and=say.YQTL-S.3M.SG   to   Zebul behold people
     yôred   merā'šê   hæhārîm
     go.down.QOT.M.SG   from=tops.of   the=mountains
     wayyō'mær   'ēlāʸw   zəbûl   'et   ṣel
     and=say.YQTL-S.3M.SG   to=him   Zebul   OBJ   shadow.of
     hæhārîm   'attâ   rō'æʰ   kā'ănāšîm
     the=mountains   you   see.QOT.M.SG   as=men

Gaal saw the troops and said to Zebul: "Look, people **are coming down** from the mountain tops." But Zebul said to him, "It is the shadow on the mountains that you mistake for men." (Judg 9:36)

In this passage, Gaal, the son of Ebed, is started by the sight of an approaching company, which, for all that he knows, might have hostile intentions. His addressee, Zebul, who has secretly called upon the men to come and attack Gaal,

---

35. For similar examples, see Exod 32:8 (three *wayyiqtol*-clauses); 2 Sam 19:2; 1 Kgs 1:19 (two); 21:14; 2 Kgs 22:9.

tries to thwart the appeal to action by suggesting that there is nothing but shadows to be seen (the fact that the event is actually expected by the listener in this example is irrelevant from a linguistic point of view, since the speaker does not know it and therefore assumes nonexpectancy on his part).

It appears that full appeal in connection with *qotel* typically involves the particle *hinne^h* (translated as "Look" in the example).[36] However, the following example shows a *qotel*-clause without *hinne^h*, where the criteria of imminence, nonexpectancy, and efficiency are all met:

(24) wayyāroṣ   hanna'ar   wayyagged
     and=run.YQTL-S.3M.SG the=servant and=tell.YQTL-S.3M.SG
     ləmōšæ^h wayyō'mar   'ældād   ûmêdād
     to=Moses   and=say.YQTL(S).3M.SG   Eldad   and=Medad
     mitnabbə'îm   bammaḥănæ^h wayya'an
     prophesy.QOT.M.PL   in=the=camp   and=answer.YQTL-S.3M.SG
     yəhôšua'   bin   nûn   məšāreṯ   mōšæ^h mibbəḥuraʸw
     Joshua   son.of Nun   servant.of   Moses   from=youth=his
     wayyō'mær   'ăḏōnî   mōšæ^h
     and=say.YQTL-S.3M.SG   lord=my   Moses
     kəlā'em
     stop.IMP.2M.SG=them

And a young man ran and told Moses, "Eldad and Medad **are prophesying** in the camp." Joshua, son of Nun, who had been a servant of Moses since his youth, said, "My lord Moses, stop them!" (Num 11:27–28)

In accordance with the principle that full appeal is not semantically marked in language (5.3), *qotel* can just as well have reduced appeal; we may recall the various examples of nonpresent and stativized uses in section 4.1. There are also many real present *qotel*-clauses with reduced appeal in common-ground material, such as the relative clause in this sentence:

(25) hā'āræṣ   'ăšær   'attâ   **šōḵeḇ**   'ālǽhā   ləḵā
     the=land   which   you   lie.QOT.M.SG   on=it   to=you
     'ættənænnâ
     give.YQTL(L).1SG=it

I shall give you and your descendants the land on which you **are lying**. (Gen 28:13)

---

36 See also Gen 38:13; 48:1, 2 (could also be *qatal*); Judg 9:37 (two occurrences); 1 Sam 14:11; 2 Sam 19:9; 1 Kgs 18:44.

When the other Biblical Hebrew progressive, *yiqtol*-L, refers to the present, it almost always has some kind of generalizing meaning (4.2.1), hence failing the criterion of imminence (5.2.1). Imminence is also lacking in a special kind of fictive present *yiqtol*-L, where the form is used to describe in a symbolic way how the speaker/author experiences a situation:

(26) yəḥalləqû   bəḡāday   lāhæm
     divide.YQTL-L.3M.PL   garments=my   for=themselves
     wə'al   ləḇûšî   **yappîlû**   ḡôrāl
     and=for   clothes=my   cast.YQTL-L.3M.PL   lot
     They divide my garments among themselves and for my clothes
     they cast lot. (Ps 22:19 [22:18])

If this would have been a real speech situation, the participle would most certainly have been used. Interestingly, English translations employ the simple present here.

As for the occasional real present *yiqtol*-L, we may consider again the examples from subsection 4.2.1:

(27) a. lāmæʰ   tiḇkî
        why   weep.YQTL-L.2F.SG
        Why **are you weeping**? (1 Sam 1:8)

     b. wə'ôlîḵâ   'ætḵæm   'æl   hā'îš
        and=lead.YQTL(S).COH.1SG   OBJ=you to   the=man
        'ăšær   **təḇaqqəšûn**
        who   seek.YQTL-L.2M.PL
        And I shall lead you to the man **you are seeking**. (2 Kgs 6:19)

     c. maʰ   lāʿām   kî   **yiḇkû**
        what   to=the=people   that   weep.YQTL-L.3M.PL
        What is the matter with the people, that **they are weeping**?
        (1 Sam 11:5)

     d. **'ær'ænnû**   wəlō'   'attâ
        see.YQTL-L.1SG=him   but=not   now
        'ăšûrænnû   wəlō'   qārôḇ
        behold.YQTL-L.1SG=him but=not   near
        I see him, but not now; **I behold** him, but not near. (Num 24:17)

     e. 'anaḥnû   nišbaʿnû   lāhæm   […]   lō'
        we   swear.QTAL.1PL   to=them   […]   not

> **nûḵal** lingoaʻ bāhæm
> can.YQTL-L.1PL to=touch.INFC in=them
> We have sworn to them [...] We **can**not touch them. (Josh 9:19)

> f. wəʾānōḵî naʻar qāṭōn lōʾ **ʾeḏaʻ**
> and=I boy young not know.YQTL-L.1SG
> ṣeʾṯ wāḇōʾ
> go.out.INFC and=come.in.INFC
> And I am a little child. I do not **know** how to handle this. (1 Kgs 3:7)

Based on the criteria developed in section 5.2, none of these real present *yiqtol*-L clauses have full appeal: the *wh*-question in (27a) and the subordinate clauses in (27b–c) refer to the common ground, and the cognitive and perceptional verbs in (27d–f) represent nonimminent events.[37]

A unique example of a real present dynamic progressive *yiqtol*-L is found in the Song of Deborah. It is the answer given to Sisera's mother, when she wonders why her son does not return from the battlefield:

> (28) hălōʾ **yimṣəʾû** **yəḥalləqû** šālāl
> Q=not find.YQTL-L.3M.PL divide.YQTL-L.3M.PL spoil
> Surely, **they are finding** and **dividing** the spoils. (Judg 5:30)

The compound phrase consisting of the question particle *hă* and the negation *lōʾ* in the beginning of this sentence may have an asseverative function. If so, it is appropriate to translate it as an assertion, as above. Even as an assertion, however, it is understood that this utterance lacks empirical foundation and that it is more of a guess than a factual statement. There is a tacit "don't you think" / "trust me" in it that puts the actuality of the event into question, and, hence, reduces its imminence. As far as I have been able to find, there is no case in the Hebrew Bible where *yiqtol*-L with *hălōʾ* refers factually to an ongoing, dynamic event.[38] *Qotel* with *hălōʾ*, by contrast, does.[39]

---

37. The fact that (27e–f) are negated of course means that the events do not exist, which, if possible, makes them even less imminent. However, negation does not automatically reduce the appeal of an utterance, since nonexistence sometimes can be as imminent as existence (*Everyone is not on board!*).

38. Stative and generalizing present meanings of *yiqtol*-L with *hălōʾ* occur in 2 Sam 3:28; Isa 43:19; Jer 2:17; Ezek 18:25, 29; Mic 2:7; Ps 94:9–10; Job 12:11; Chr 32:13. There are also instances where the temporal meaning is unclear.

39. See Gen 37:13; 1 Sam 23:19; Ps 54:1; Prov 26:19; 2 Chr 32:11. The fact that *qotel* refers factually to ongoing, dynamic events in these passages is a precondition for full appeal, but it does not entail it.

180   Aspect, Communicative Appeal, and Temporal Meaning

On a final note, full appeal is, of course, compatible not only with progressive and resultative but also with preparative meaning (*Your son is about to pull the cat's tail again*), which is expressed by the progressive forms in Biblical Hebrew. I shall not go into much detail on this point, since *yiqtol*-L only very exceptionally has an unambiguously preparative meaning. Of the examples quoted in subsection 4.2.1 above, (22) and (23) refer to nonimminent hypothetic and past events and (21) refers to the common ground.

5.4.3. The Volitive Subsystem

As we have seen in subsections 4.2.2 and 4.4.3, both *yiqtol*-forms are used as directives. In this capacity they are brought into contrast with the imperative. Since the directive speech act, or command, constitutes its own type of signal alongside the declarative type (5.1), some comments on communicative appeal in the volitive subsystem are called for.[40] In particular, the claim that the *yiqtol*-forms marks reduced appeal needs to be substantiated by looking at examples of their volitive use.

In Biblical Hebrew the form employed for commands with full appeal is the imperative:

(29) **himmāleṭ**   'al   napšækā
     flee.IMP.2M.SG   because.of   soul=your
     Flee for your life. (Gen 19:17)

Commands have reduced appeal when the action is not meant to be carried out immediately but after a while (30a) or on a general basis (30b). In such cases, the stimulus of the utterance (i.e., the need that the represented event has to satisfy; see 5.2) is nonimminent. Imperatives are used in these functions, too:

(30) a. 'ôḏ   šəlōšæṯ   yāmîm   wəšûḇû   'ēlāy
       yet   three   days   and=return.IMP.2M.PL   to=me
       Return to me in three days. (2 Chr 10:5)

   b. **kabbeḏ**   'æṯ   'āḇîkā   wə'æṯ
      honor.IMP.2M.SG   OBJ   father=your   and=OBJ
      'immækā   ləma'an   ya'ărîkûn
      mother=your   in.order.that   be.lengthened.YQTL-L.3M.PL

---

40. The term "command" here applies to all kinds of directive speech acts. Elsewhere in this subsection, "request" is also used for modest commands.

> yāmǽkā   'al   hā'ăḏāmâ   'ăšær   YHWH   'ĕlōhǽkā
> days=your   on   the=land   which   YHWH   god=your
> nōṯen   lāk
> give.QOT.M.SG   for=you
>
> **Honor** your father and your mother so that your days will be long in the land that the Lord, your God, is going to give you. (Exod 20:12)

The *yiqtol*-L complements the imperative in both these functions. Thus, in section 4.2.2, we saw the following examples:

> (31) a. wayyišlaḥ   ya'ăqōḇ   mal'āḵîm
>   and=send.YQTL(S).3M.SG   Jacob   messengers
>   ləp̄ānāʸw   'æl   'ēśāw   [...]   wayṣaw
>   ahead.of=him   to   Esau   [...]   and=order.YQTL-S.3M.SG
>   'ōṯām   le'mōr   kōʰ   **tō'mərûn**   la'ḏōnî
>   them   QUOT   thus   say.YQTL-L.2M.PL   to=lord=my
>   lə'ēśāw   ...
>   to=Esau
>
> Jacob sent messengers ahead of him to Esau [...], and he instructed them, saying, "**You shall speak** thus to my lord Esau ..." (Gen 32:4–5 [32:3–4])

> b. zāḵôr   'æṯ   yôm   haššabbāṯ
>   remember.INFA   OBJ   day.of   the=Sabbath
>   ləqaddəšô   šēšæṯ   yāmîm   **ta'ăḇōḏ**
>   to=keep.holy.INFC=it   six.of   days   work.YQTL-L.2M.SG
>   wə'āśîṯā   kol   məla'ḵtæḵā
>   and=do.QTAL.2M.SG   all   work=your
>
> Remember the day of the Sabbath by keeping it holy. Six days **you shall work** and do all your work. (Exod 20:8–9)

Of the two forms, the *yiqtol*-L is more geared toward uses like (31a–b), whereas the imperative predominates in commands where the need is imminent—a distribution that can be expected if *yiqtol*-L is marked for reduced appeal.[41]

---

41. With regard to the function of the imperative and the directive *yiqtol*-L I agree in principle with Dallaire (2014), even though I believe that her conclusion is somewhat too strongly stated as far as the "atemporal" quality of the declarative *yiqtol*-L is concerned (see examples [32] and [34] in the present chapter, and example [31] in chapter 4). Thus, she writes, "The imperative is the unmarked form used to express various types of commands that require immediate attention. It is

It was argued above (4.2.2) that the directive function is not semantic in *yiqtol*-L, since it is always compatible with its future meaning. In other words, directive *yiqtol*-L is a form of indirect request. Thus although *yiqtol*-L is also used occasionally to satisfy more imminent needs than the ones in (31a–b), it does not have the efficiency of the imperative.[42]

Unlike some other forms of indirect requests, like the *can you*-request (5.2.3), the directive *yiqtol*-L is not intended to be polite; rather, it is intended to signal that the speaker takes the execution of the command for granted. As a rule, this presumption is based on the fact that the speaker is socially superior to the listener, but in the following example, the directive *yiqtol* is used in an interaction between equals (Abraham and Abimelech) who are negotiating a covenant:

(32) 'æṯ   šæḇaʿ   kəḇāśîm   **tiqqaḥ**   miyyāḏî
     OBJ   seven   lambs   take.YQTL-L.2M.SG   from=hand=my
     baʿăḇûr   tihyæʰ   lî   ləʿeḏâ   kî
     in.order.that   be.YQTL-L.2M.SG   for=me   to=witness   that
     ḥāp̄artî   'æṯ   habbəʾer   hazzōʾṯ
     dig.QTAL.1SG   OBJ   the=well   the=this

The seven lambs you **shall accept** from my hand so that you may be a witness for me that I dug this well. (Gen 21:30)

The implication of the *yiqtol*-L in this context seems to be that the request is made from a strong bargaining position. Abimelech is given to understand that Abraham has the right to expect him to accept the deal. From the point of view of the narrative, the fact that Abraham is able to speak with such authority to the local king serves to reinforce the theme of God's blessing on Abraham.

It is also possible to use the directive *yiqtol*-L from an inferior position. In the next example, the construction occurs together with an imperative:

(33) halləṣenî   YHWH   meʾāḏām   rāʿ
     rescue.IMP.2M.SG=me   YHWH   from=human   evil
     meʾîš   ḥămāsîm   **tinṣərenî**
     from=man.of   violence   keep.YQTL-L.2M.SG=me

---

used in social dynamics of 'greater to lesser,' 'lesser to greater,' and between equals. The imperfect, on the other hand, is marked for commands that affect the long-term behaviour of the listener(s). It is found mostly in social contexts of 'greater to lesser,' typically appears in legal material, and often addresses the whole community rather than a single individual. Commands expressed by the imperfect are atemporal, while the commands given by the imperative are time related" (Dallaire 2014, 127).

42. See, e.g., Josh 3:8 (especially *taṣawwæʰ*, "you shall command"; Judg 19:24 (*lōʾ taʿăśû*, "you shall not do") 1 Sam 2:16 (*titten*, "you shall give"); Isa 20:2. See also example (32).

Rescue me, Lord, from evil people; **keep** me [lit. "you shall keep"] me from men of violence. (Ps 140:2 [140:1])

In this passage, the initial imperative expresses a direct request. The *yiqtol*-L-clause, by contrast, is an indirect directive, containing a prediction that the listener will comply with the will of the speaker. The prediction is based on the conviction that the speaker has the favor of the listener.

In the following example, the speakers (the people of Israel) are not really justified to expect the listener (Samuel) to comply with their will; hence their use of a self-confident predictive-directive *yiqtol*-L appears rather audacious:

(34) wə'attæm   hayyôm   mə'astæm   'æṯ   'ælōhêḵæm
     and=you   the=day   despise.QTAL.2M.PL   OBJ   God=your
     'ăšær   hû'   môšîaʿ   lāḵæm   mikkol   rāʿôṯêḵæm
     who   he   save.QOT.M.SG   to=you   from=all disaster=your
     wəṣārôṯeḵæm   watto'mərû   lō'   kî   mælæḵ
     and=distress=your   and=say.YQTL(S).2M.PL   no   for   king
     tāśîm   ʿālēnû
     set.YQTL-L.2M.SG   over=us

But today, you have rejected your God, the one who saves you from all your disasters and distresses. You have said, "No, **you shall set** a king over us!" (1 Sam 10:19)

In sum, the indirect, predictive-directive function is common for all kinds of directive *yiqtol*-L. Semantically speaking, the function is declarative, but pragmatically, it is directive. This type of directive does not only impose the speaker's will on the listener; it also implicates a certain set of expectations, deriving from the status of the communicators, which motivate that the desired action be performed. In so doing, it takes on a level of complexity that makes it a less efficient directive than the imperative (5.2.3).

The volitive uses of *yiqtol*-S can be divided into two main groups: one consisting of positive or negative commands and wishes concerning the third- and first- person, and one consisting of negative commands in the second-person.[43] The first group, in turn, can be divided in two: the "jussive" for third person reference and the "cohortative" for the first person (1.4). On the basis of morphology, the variant for negative commands in the second person may also be called "jussive," although, in terms of its function, it is the equivalent of an imperative.

---

43. I shall here only comment on the independent usages of the volitive *yiqtol*-S. The forms also appear as "indirect" volitives in syndetic clauses, but then the function of expressing independent volitive speech acts is weakened and becomes subordinate to the discourse function of expressing purpose or consequence (Joüon and Muraoka 2009, §114a, 116).

The third-person jussive and the cohortative can be broadly described as wish forms. Like the imperative, they express the will of the speaker, but without imposing it directly on a listener. Sometimes they are not directive but more prototypically optative, expressing a hope that certain events will occur, as in blessings.

The directive jussive often expresses something that the speaker wants a third person to do, or something s/he wants to happen to a third person. The intended listener is not addressed directly but is supposed to understand that s/he is the one that can see to that it happens. Being an indirect form of request, the jussive can be assumed to be a less efficient signal than a direct, imperative command. Moreover, since the third person typically is not present in the speech situation, the action is normally not expected to be carried out immediately. In other words, the stimulus (i.e., the need for the event to occur) is nonimminent. For an example, consider

(35) **tikḇaḏ** hā'ăḇôḏâ 'al hā'ănāšîm
    be.heavy.YQTL(S).3M.SG the=work on the=men
    Let heavy work **be laid** on the men. (Exod 5:9)

As with the directive *yiqtol*-L, the social implications of a directive jussive depends on the status of the participants. It may reinforce the superiority of the speaker, as in example (35), but it is also used as a deferential directive, when the speaker does not want to address the listener in the second person:

(36) **yāqum** 'āḇî
    rise.YQTL(S).JUSS.3M.SG father=mine
    wěyō'ḵal miṣṣêḏ běnô ba'ăḇûr
    and=eat.YQTL(S).JUSS.3M.SG from=game son=his in=order
    těḇārăḵannî nap̄šæḵā
    bless.YQTL(L).3F.SG=me soul=your
    Let my father **get up** and eat of his son's game, so that your soul may bless me. (Gen 27:31)

The only time that the third person directive jussive is not indirect is when nobody else is supposed to sense the appeal and perform the action:[44]

(37) wayyō'mær 'ælōhîm **yəhî**
    and=say.YQTL-S.3M.SG God be.YQTL-S.JUSS.3M.SG

---

44. Besides the other jussives used by God for creation throughout Genesis 1, see 2 Kgs 1:10, 12.

'ôr   wayhî   'ôr
light   and=be.YQTL-S.3M.SG   light
God said, "**Let** there **be** light," and there was light. (Gen 1:3)

As for the cohortative, it is used for expressing intentions and wishes concerning the first person.[45] The role of the listener, or listeners, in the speech act is often to consent to something; not to obey. In the first person singular there is often a precative modal nuance:

(38) **'ălaqŏṭâ**   nā'   wə'āsaptî
     pick.YQTL(S).COH.1SG   please   and=gather.QTAL.1SG
     bā'ŏmārîm   'aḥărê   haqqôṣərîm
     in=cut.grains   after   the=harvest.QOT.M.PL
     Please, **let me glean** and gather from the cut grains after the reapers. (Ruth 2:7)

Cohortative meaning in the real sense of the word occurs when the listener or listeners are encouraged to join the speaker in some action:

(39) ləkâ   nā'   **wənāsûrâ**
     go.IMP.2M.SG   please   and=turn.aside.YQTL(S).COH.1PL
     'æl   'îr   haybûsî   wənālîn
     to   town   the=Jebusite   and=spend.the.night.YQTL-L.1PL
     bāh
     in=it
     He said, "**Let us turn aside** to this Jebusite town and spend the night in it." (Judg 19:11)

This is as close to a command as one gets with the Hebrew cohortative. However, there is still an element of consent-requesting that reduces the appeal of such utterances. If a speaker really wants to prompt the listener to joint action without negotiation, the imperative is needed, as when Lot urges his family to flee with him in order to escape the coming destruction of Sodom:

(40) **qûmû**   ṣə'û   min   hammāqôm
     raise.IMP.2M.PL   go.out.IMP.2M.PL   from   the=place
     hazzæʰ   kî   mašḥît   YHWH   'æt   hā'îr
     the=this   for   destroy.QOT.M.SG   YHWH   OBJ   the=city

45. Driver 1892, §49, 51–53, Waltke and O'Connor 1990, §34.5.1; Gibson and Davidson 1994; Joüon and Muraoka 2009, §114b–f; Joosten 2012, 319–26.

Up, get out of this place, for the Lord is about to destroy the city. (Gen 19:14)

The Biblical Hebrew imperative cannot be negated. In negative commands, therefore, it is always supplemented by the second person jussive. Negative commands can have full appeal when they are intended to immediately stop somebody from completing an action that is ongoing or just about to begin:

(41) wayyō'mær   nəḥæmyâ   [...]   hayyôm
     and=say.YQTL-S.3M.SG Nehemiah [...] the=day
     qāḏōš hû' lYHWH   'ĕlōhêḵæm 'al
     holy   it   for=YHWH god=your   not
     tiṭ'abbəlû   wə'al
     mourn.YQTL(S).JUSS.2M.PL   and=not
     tiḇkû   kî   bôḵîm   kol
     weep.YQTL(S).JUSS.2M.PL for   weep.QOT.M.PL all
     hā'ām
     the=people

And Nehemiah said [...], "This day is hallowed to the Lord, your God. **Do not mourn**, and **do not weep**!"—for the whole people was weeping. (Neh 8:9)

Uses like (41) may seem to contradict the claim that *yiqtol*-S is marked for reduced appeal. But the negated second person jussive is syntactically distinct from the assertive jussive through the obligatory negation *'al* and should therefore be considered a separate form. One may compare with the English imperative, which is morphologically identical with but syntactically distinct from the simple present, which is a form marked for reduced appeal.

5.5. Summary

On the basis of the semiotic theories of Bühler and others, it has been suggested in this chapter that *yiqtol*-L and *yiqtol*-S are distinguished from *qotel* and *qatal* with regard to their *appeal*. *Full* appeal characterizes utterances that prompt the listeners to immediate action. Verbal forms available for full appeal in Biblical Hebrew are *qatal* and *qotel*, as well as the imperative. By contrast, the appeal to action in utterances employing *yiqtol*-L and *yiqtol*-S was found to be invariably nonexistent, or mitigated, failing at least one of the criteria of imminence, nonexpectancy, and efficiency. Hence, it is concluded that *reduced* appeal is a distinguishing semantic feature in the prefix forms.

Especially in the case of *yiqtol*-L, it becomes clear that reduced appeal cannot be regarded as a mere entailment of temporalization and stativization. If this were the case, it would be a mystery why *yiqtol*-L has reduced appeal in all its nonreanalyzed uses. Conversely, however, it makes sense that these uses are preserved if the form is marked for reduced appeal. Moreover, the striking similarities with the English present tense give reasons to assume that the emergence of reduced appeal is a common crosslinguistic phenomenon in the evolution of verbal systems. We may hypothesize that the capacity for full appeal is a common feature of the prototypically progressive construction. When a new progressive is grammaticalized, the older progressive, which is increasingly being used in various functions lacking full appeal, is associated with these contexts to the extent that reduced appeal is regarded as intrinsic to the form. A parallel development, we may assume, occurs within the resultative subsystems.

As for the Biblical Hebrew *wayyiqtol*, it has reduced appeal even when it has perfect aspect and conveys new information about present events. In this case, the reduced appeal follows from the fact that the *wayyiqtol* is a continuation form that develops a given theme, thus postponing the reaction. However, as in the case of *yiqtol*-L, the reduced appeal is not a mere entailment on another linguistic function, since *wayyiqtol* is not always a continuation form but may start a narrative sequence.[46] In that case, however, past meaning is intended.

The directive and optative/cohortative functions of the prefix forms have reduced appeal because they express the volition of the speaker in indirect ways. The exception is in negative commands, where *yiqtol*-S supplements the imperative. As ’*al yiqtol*-S, however, it is syntactically distinct from the assertive forms and should be considered as a separate form.

---

46. See Jonah 1:1; Ruth 1:1; Esth 1:1.

CHAPTER 6

Conclusion

STARTING FROM THE FACT that there are significant correlations between the Biblical Hebrew verbal forms and certain temporal meanings, this study has sought to explore the semantic factors behind these correlations. As the formulation of this task reveals, an initial assumption was that there are meanings that might be more basic to the forms than tense—meanings from which the temporal meanings can be derived. Another assumption was that basic meanings can be established by reconstructing the semantic evolution of the forms, since a derived meaning has to be younger than the meaning it is derived from. A suitable conversation partner in this respect has been the so-called evolutionary, or grammaticalization approach, which makes such reconstructions on the basis of a large amount on comparative data. In this thesis, I have benefited from grammaticalization studies for a synchronic application of the approach, making my own assessment on certain points in the reconstruction of the semantic evolution of the Biblical Hebrew forms (see 2.5) where there is no full consensus. I stated that the favored tense meanings of the Biblical Hebrew finite verbal forms (minus the imperative) have evolved along two diachronic pathways: the future meaning of *yiqtol*-L and *qotel* has a progressive source, and the past meaning of the *qatal* and the *yiqtol*-S has a resultative source. It was made clear that this classification alone was not a sufficient answer to the question of how to define the meanings of the Biblical Hebrew verbal forms. For one thing, a basic meaning is not necessarily an original meaning; that is, it should not only be the rational source for the various uses of a verbal form—it should also be an existing meaning in a synchronic perspective (see 1.3.1, 1.3.2). Even more important, fundamental semantic problems like the meaning of the term "aspect," and its applicability to the progressive and resultative verbal types, had to be settled and the inferential process from aspect to tense-meanings had to be outlined.

The task was divided into different parts: The first was to define the concept of aspect in such a way as to make clear how it relates to various aspecto-temporal notions and/or grammatical types, such as relative tense, completed/uncompleted, perfective/imperfective, perfect, and progressive/resultative. The second task was to describe in general terms how future meaning is related to progressive meaning and how past meaning is related to resultative. The third was to apply this theory to Biblical Hebrew. Finally, the fourth part of the investigation was to analyze the semantic difference between those forms in the Biblical Hebrew verbal system that have developed from the same source domain—that is, *yiqtol*-L and *qotel*, on the one hand, and *qatal* and *yiqtol*-S, on the other.

Aspect was defined as the localization of the speaker's and the listener's mutual focus of attention on the event represented by the verb. Instead of the focus of attention, we could also speak about the "focused content of the event" or the "focused time." *Tense* concerns the temporal relation between the focused time and a deictic center (typically the time of speech). *Mutatis mutandis*, this explanation is in agreement with modern Reichenbach-inspired theories that consider "reference time," "topic time" (= focused time) or similar to be crucial for the definition of both tense and aspect. However, inspired by Declerck and Klein, I have taken care to distinguish between focused time and deictic center, which are often confused in the scholarly literature. Through consistent adherence to this distinction, it was shown that the relative tense or taxis approach, which has been applied to Biblical Hebrew, tends to confuse aspect and tense, with the result that it cannot adequately describe the difference between, for example, past perfect meaning (*By the time the dinner was ready, I **had set** the table*) and a true past in the past (*She knew that I **had set** the table the day before*) but calls both meanings "anteriority." By the same logic, one would have to state that there is no difference between simple past meaning (*I set the table yesterday*) and present perfect meaning (*I have set the table*), since both forms must be said to express "anteriority" with regard to the time of speech.

The present study has introduced the notion of *stage-based* aspect. This aspectual category assumes an extended event model, in which the lexically denoted, nuclear event is embedded in stages—that is, the progressive, the resultant, and the preparatory stages. Depending on which stage is in focus, the aspect becomes *progressive* (*The gate is closing*), *resultative* (*The gate is closed*), or *preparative* (*The gate is about to close*). Stage-based aspect, in other words, defines what stage of the event is in the focus of attention. Within this framework, the terms "resultative" and "progressive" have much wider application than they have within standard linguistic typology. Thus, according to my definition, the resultative aspect is expressed by transitive perfect constructions (*I have closed the door*), and the progressive aspect may be expressed even with the "nonprogressive" English present tense, for example, in clauses with verbs of inert perception as predicates (*I hear music*). The resultative and progressive aspects differ from imperfective and perfect meanings in that they are compatible with aorist meaning (normally called "perfective"). For example, in performative utterances resultative forms represent the marked stage as *emergent* (as in *You are excused*), whereas progressive forms represents it as transient (*I am hereby declaring...*). In other words, both the resultative and the progressive meanings are invariant in performatives. The same is valid for several other uses with aorist meaning.

The development of tense meanings from resultative and preparative constructions was described as the result of inferences from the aspectual meanings of the forms. Thus, past meaning is inferred from a resultative form when the focus of attention is no longer directed to the result stage of the event but is directed to the preceding nuclear event. Correspondingly, the inference of future meaning from prospectives involves a shift of focus from the preparatory stage of the event to what ensues. I have called this process temporalization. Since the focus on a particular stage of the event is what defines stage-based aspect, temporalization is a kind of reanalysis that overturns the aspectual meaning of the form. As long as the aspectual meaning is also used, however, it remains the basic meaning (see the criterion of cognitive precedence, described in subsection 1.3.2).

In connection with the discussion of temporalization, it was pointed out that there is a semantic overlap between the progressive and the preparative aspects in the case of achievement verbs like *to win*. More exactly, progressive meaning in such verbs de facto equals preparative meaning (thus, *Carl is winning the race* is more or less synonymous with *Carl is about to win the race*). This implies that a temporalized future reading is possible also with the progressive. I argued that the preparative meaning of the progressive can spread also to durative verbs, and, with that, the possibility for temporalization. Thus, the general tendency of progressives to take on future meaning in many languages is not only contextually motivated; it can be inferred by the same kind of reanalysis as operates on preparatives as soon as preparative meaning is generalized from the progressive. This inferential process plays a particularly important role in languages like Biblical Hebrew, which do not have a separate grammaticalized preparative construction and therefore must cover this semantic domain by means of progressive forms.

The investigation of the Biblical Hebrew data showed that the progressive and the resultative aspects are frequently expressed by predicative *qotel* and *qatal*, respectively. The stage-aspectual meanings of *qatal* and *qotel* are invariant with aorist meaning in certain contexts. With regard to *qatal*, this is the case, for example, in performative and future uses, including the consecutive *weqatalti*, and the so-called prophetic perfect. A variant of aorist, transient progressive in Biblical Hebrew is found in the rare narrative *qotel*. *Yiqtol*-L retains progressive aspect mainly in stativized meanings like the habitual, and only to a very limited extent in dynamic progressive meaning. *Yiqtol*-S, in the form of

Conclusion

wayyiqtol, occurs sparingly with resultative aspect. All forms occur with temporalized meanings, but the two *yiqtol*-variants do so to a significantly higher degree than *qatal* and *qotel*. Meanings stemming from inferences drawn from temporalized meanings include the various modal nuances of *yiqtol*-L and the modal meanings of *qatal* and *yiqtol*-S. Since the future meaning of *yiqtol*-L is not negated by the modal uses such as the directive, modality was classified as altogether pragmatic in this form.

On the whole, *qotel* and *qatal* are the most prototypical in terms of stage-based aspectual meanings, even though they have other functions as well. *Yiqtol*-L and *yiqtol*-S are mainly used in functions involving reanalysis of the stage-aspectual meanings, but they may at times also be used with invariant aspectual meanings. For this reason, the *yiqtol*-forms may be said to have stage-aspect as their most basic meanings, although this meaning is more predominant in *qotel* and *qatal*.

As for the semantic difference between the forms on the same diachronic path, it was suggested the *yiqtol*-forms are distinguished from *qotel* and *qatal* by the semantic feature of *reduced appeal*. The theoretical foundations for the notion of appeal were taken from the semiotics of Bühler and adapted for the analysis of verbal forms via a radical reinterpretation of Weinrich's theory of linguistic attitude (*Sprechhaltung*). Appeal manifests itself as the listener's reaction to a signal—a signal being defined as a sign, for example, an utterance, in its capacity for appeal. The prototypical signal has *full* appeal and is designed to immediately affect the listener's behavior with regard to his/her physical environment. The nature of the appeal differs, for instance, in *warnings*, which prompt the listener to take due measures with regard to the event being referred to, and direct *commands*, which impel him/her to perform the event referred to by means of the verb. *Reduced appeal* characterizes utterances that, compared to prototypical signals, are less efficient, less unexpected, or motivated by stimuli that are less imminent.

It is a striking fact in language that younger resultative and progressive forms are typically used with reference to real phenomena in the physical environment, something that is characteristic of signals with full appeal, whereas older forms are increasingly used with past, future, generalizing, and modal meanings, all of which have reduced appeal, being more detached from the here and now of the speech situation. I assumed that this development is connected with a semantic change whereby the older resultative or progressive becomes marked for reduced appeal. This seems to have happened with Biblical Hebrew *yiqtol*-L and *yiqtol*-S. These forms are used mainly with reference to nonpresent events, and in those cases where they do refer to present events, it can plausibly be argued that the appeal is reduced for other reasons, for example, that the event referred to belongs to the common ground, or that the verb is a continuation form with the function of developing an already existing signal.

TABLE 5. Stage-based aspect and appeal in the Biblical Hebrew verbal system

	Defaults for full appeal	**Marked for reduced appeal**
Progressive	*qotel*	*yiqtol*-L
Resultative	*qatal*	*yiqtol*-S

As directives with reduced appeal, the *yiqtol*-forms contrast also with the imperative. The directive functions of the *yiqtol*-forms are derived from the future (*yiqtol*-L) and the optative (*yiqtol*-S) meanings of the forms and can be classified as different kinds of indirect requests, as opposed to the direct form of request performed by the imperative. Besides the function of requesting something of the listener, the indirect request also aims at maintaining a certain understanding of the social conditions surrounding the utterance, which makes them less efficient as signals and, hence, reduces the appeal.

The prohibitive jussive replaces the imperative in negative commands and can have full appeal, but since it is always marked as a command form by means of the negation *'al*, it is syntactically distinct from the other *yiqtol*-forms and should be considered as a form on its own.

By way of synthesis, the two basic semantic factors stage-based aspect and appeal are presented in table 5 (with the reservation that *yiqtol*-S has only been shown to be resultative in *wayyiqtol*).

The question of how the semantic factor of reduced appeal relates to the temporal meanings of the forms can be viewed from both a diachronic and a synchronic perspective. In the diachronic perspective, it can be assumed that reduced appeal becomes a semantic feature in progressive and resultative forms as a consequence of their increased use with nonprototypical meanings, such as the temporalized meanings. When new forms become grammaticalized enough to enter into paradigmatic contrast with the older forms, the latter may become semantically marked for reduced appeal, since they are used relatively less often as prototypical signals in comparison with the new forms. Accordingly, while the temporalized past and future meanings of the Biblical Hebrew forms do not distinguish the *yiqtol*-forms semantically from *qotel* and *qatal*, it is likely that the frequent use of those meanings contributed to the emergence of the semantic feature of reduced appeal in the *yiqtol*-forms.

On a more speculative note, one may ask whether reduced appeal, once it becomes semantically marked, affects the further semantic development of the forms in any way. In this regard, it is pertinent to note that forms marked for reduced appeal may retain real present uses provided that they lack some condition for full appeal, as, for instance, in the case of clauses that refer to common ground or develop a given theme. Such uses may still be felt to convey more of the original appeal to action than the temporalized uses do, since the events that they represent are less detached from the situation at the time of speech. For instance, the real present *Why is the wolf coming* may evoke a stronger sense of the urgency of the situation than the futural *Why will the wolf come*, even though both clauses refer to common ground. Against this background, one may speculate that a semantically marked reduced appeal works against such uses, too, thereby contributing to a relatively higher frequency of temporalized meanings in the forms. But behind such developments there is probably also a push effect from the new forms, since new forms are bound to intrude on the areas of their predecessors by the internal logic of their semantics.

In the synchronic perspective, semantically marked reduced appeal should have the effect of facilitating the successful interpretation of temporalized meanings of the forms by eliminating the option of present tense meaning in some contexts where such meanings would otherwise have been possible.

In conclusion, reduced appeal can be regarded as an additional semantic factor affecting the temporal meanings of the Biblical Hebrew verbal forms besides stage-based aspect.

BIBLIOGRAPHY

Agrell, Sigurd. 1908. *Aspektänderung und Aktionsartbildung beim polnischen Zeitworte: Ein Beitrag zum Studium der indogermanischen Präverbia und ihrer Bedeutungsfunktionen*. Lunds Universitets Årsskrift 4.2. Lund: Håkan Ohlssons Buchdruckerei.
Alter, Robert. 1985. *The Art of Biblical Poetry*. New York: Basic Books.
Andersen, T. David. 2000. "The Evolution of the Hebrew Verbal System." *Zeitschrift für Althebraistik* 13:1–66.
Andrason, Alexander. 2010a. "The Akkadian *Iprus* from the Unidirectional Perspective. *Journal of Semitic Studies* 55: 323–45. doi: 10.1093/jss/fgq001.
———. 2010b. "The Panchronic Yiqtol: Functionally Consistent and Cognitively Plausible." *Journal of Hebrew Scriptures* 10:1–41. doi: 10.5508/jhs.2010.v10.a10.
———. 2011a. "The Biblical Hebrew Verbal System in Light of Grammaticalization: The Second Generation." *Hebrew Studies* 52:19–51. doi: 10.1353/hbr.2011.0010.
———. 2011b. "Biblical Hebrew *Wayyiqtol*: A Dynamic Definition." *Journal of Hebrew Scriptures* 11:2–58. doi: 10.5508/jhs.2011.v11.a8.
———. 2012a. "Cognitive Foundations of the Old Babylonian Iparras." *Journal of Semitic Studies* 57:1–23. doi: 10.1093/jss/fgr030.
———. 2012b. "The Dynamic Short Yiqtol." *Journal for Semitics* 21:308–39.
———. 2012c. "The Gnomic *qatal*." *Orientalia Suecana* 61:5–53.
———. 2012d. "Making It Sound—The Performative Qatal and Its Explanation." *Journal of Hebrew Scriptures* 12:1–58. doi: 10.5508/jhs.2012.v12.a8.
———. 2013a. "Against Floccinaucinihilipilification of the Counterfactual Sense of the BH Suffix Conjugation—or an Explanation of Why the 'Indicative' Qatal Expresses Conditions, Hypotheses and Wishes." *Old Testament Essays* 24:20–65. http://www.scielo.org.za.
———. 2013b. "An Optative Indicative? A Real Factual Past? Toward a Cognitive-Typological Approach to the Precative Qatal." *Journal of Hebrew Scriptures* 13:1–41. doi: 10.5508/jhs.2013.v13.a4.
Andrason, Alexander, and Christo H. J. van der Merwe. 2015. "The Semantic Potential of Verbal Conjugations as a Set of Polysemous Senses: The Qatal in Genesis." *Hebrew Studies* 56:71–88. doi: 10.1353/hbr.2015.0030.
Apollonios Dyskolos. 1981. *The Syntax of Apollonius Dyscolus*. Translated, and with commentary by Fred W. Householder. Studies in the History of Linguistics 23. Amsterdam: John Benjamins.

Baayen, R. Harald. 1997. "The Pragmatics of the 'Tenses' in Biblical Hebrew." *Studies in Language* 21:245–85.
Bache, Carl. 1994. "Verbal Categories: Form-Meaning Relationships and the Perfect." Pages 43–60 in *Tense, Aspect, and Action: Empirical and Theoretical Contributions to Language Typology*. Edited by Carl Bache, Hans Basbøll, and Carl-Erik Lindberg. Empirical Approaches to Language Typology 12. Berlin: de Gruyter.
Baranowski, Krzysztof. 2016. "The Biblical Hebrew *Wayyiqtol* and the Evidence of the Amarna Letters from Canaan." *Journal of Hebrew Scriptures* 16:1–18. doi: 10.5508/jhs.2016.v16.3.
Bartelmus, Rüdiger. 1982. *HYH, Bedeutung und Funktion eines althebräischen "Allerweltswortes": Zugleich ein Beitrag zur Frage des hebräischen Tempussystems*. St. Ottilien: EOS-Verlag.
Benveniste, Émile. (1963) 1966a. "Coup d'œil sur le développement de la linguistique." Pages 18–31 in *Problèmes de linguistique générale*. Bibliothèque des Sciences humaines. Paris: Gallimard.
———. 1966b. "Les relations de temps dans le verbe français." Pages 237–50 in *Problèmes de linguistique générale*. Bibliothèque des Sciences Humaines. Paris: Gallimard.
Bergsträsser, Gotthelf. 1929. *Hebräische Grammatik*. Leipzig: Hinrichs.
Bergström, Ulf. 2015. "The Progressive-Imperfective Path from Standard to Late Biblical Hebrew." *Old Testament Essays* 28:606–35.
———. 2016. "The Progressive in Archaic Biblical Hebrew and the Origin of the Hebrew Participial Predicate." *Journal for Semitics* 25:199–234.
Berlin, Adele. 1985. *The Dynamics of Biblical Parallelism*. Bloomington: Indiana University Press.
Bertinetto, Pier Marco, and Denis Delfitto. 2000. "Aspect and Actionality: Why They Should Be Kept Apart." Pages 189–226 in *Tense and Aspect in the Languages of Europe*. Edited by Östen Dahl. Empirical Approaches to Language Typology 20.6. Berlin: de Gruyter.
Bertinetto, Pier Marco, Karen H. Ebert, and Casper deGroot. 2000. "The Progressive in Europe." Pages 517–58 in *Tense and Aspect in the Languages of Europe*. Edited by Östen Dahl. Empirical Approaches to Language Typology 20.6. Berlin: de Gruyter.
Bertinetto, Pier Marco, and Alessandro Lenci. 2012. "Habituality, Pluractionality, and Imperfectivity." Pages 852–80 in *The Oxford Handbook of Tense and Aspect*. Oxford: Oxford University Press.
Binnick, Robert I. 1991. *Time and the Verb: A Guide to Tense and Aspect*. New York: Oxford University Press.
———. 2006. "Aspect and Aspectuality." Pages 244–68 in *The Handbook of English Linguistics*. Edited by Bas Aarts and April McMahon. Blackwell Handbooks in Linguistics. Malden, MA: Blackwell.
Blau, Joshua. 1976. *A Grammar of Biblical Hebrew*. Porta Linguarum Orientalium N.S., 12. Wiesbaden: Harrassowitz.
———. 2010. *Phonology and Morphology of Biblical Hebrew: An Introduction*. Linguistic Studies in Ancient West Semitic 2. Winona Lake, IN: Eisenbrauns.
Bloch, Yigal. 2009. "The Prefixed Perfective and the Dating of Early Hebrew Poetry—a Re-Evaluation." *Vetus Testamentum* 59:34–70. doi: 10.1163/156853308X377851.

Bohnemeyer, Jürgen. 2014. "Aspect vs. Relative Tense: The Case Reopened." *Natural Language and Linguistic Theory* 32:917–54.

Bondarko, Aleksandr Vladimirovič. 1991. *Functional Grammar: A Field Approach.* Linguistic and Literary Studies in Eastern Europe 35. Philadelphia: John Benjamins.

Bordreuil, Pierre, and Dennis Pardee. 2009. *A Manual of Ugaritic.* English ed. Linguistic Studies in Ancient West Semitic 3. Winona Lake, IN: Eisenbrauns.

Borik, Olga. 2006. *Aspect and Reference Time.* Oxford Studies in Theoretical Linguistics 13. Oxford: Oxford University Press.

Bréal, Michel. 1964. *Semantics: Studies in the Science of Meaning.* Dover Language Books and Records. New York: Dover.

Brockelmann, Carl. 1951. "Die 'Tempora' des Semitischen." *Zeitschrift für Phonetik und allgemeine Sprachwissenshaft* 5:133–54.

Brugmann, Karl, and Berthold Delbrück. 1913. *Grundriss der Vergleichenden Grammatik der indogermanischen Sprachen: Kurzgefasste Darstellung der Geschichte des Altindischen, Altiranischen (Avestischen u. Altpersischen), Altarmenischen, Altgriechischen, Albanesischen, Lateinischen, Oskisch-Umbrischen, Altirischen, Gotischen, Althochdeutschen, Litauischen und Altkirchenslavischen.* Bd. 2, *Lehre von den Wortformen und ihrem Gebrauch.* T. 3, *Vorbemerkungen.* 2nd ed. Strassburg: Trübner.

Bühler, Karl. 1965. *Sprachtheorie: Die Darstellungsfunktion der Sprache.* 2nd ed. Stuttgart: Gustav Fischer.

Bybee, Joan L., Revere Perkins, and William Pagliuca. 1994. *The Evolution of Grammar: Tense, Aspect, and Modality in the Languages of the World.* Chicago: University of Chicago Press.

Carlson, Gregory N. 2012. "Habitual and Generic Aspect." Pages 828–51 in *The Oxford Handbook of Tense and Aspect.* Edited by Robert I. Binnick. Oxford: Oxford University Press.

Cassirer, Ernst. 1944. *An Essay on Man: An Introduction to a Philosophy of Human Culture.* New Haven: Yale University Press.

Clark, Herbert H. *Arenas of Language Use.* 1992. Chicago: University of Chicago Press.

Clark, Herbert H., and Dale H. Schunk. 1980. "Polite Responses to Polite Requests." *Cognition* 8:111–43.

Cohen, David. 1989. *L'aspect verbal: Linguistique nouvelle.* Paris: Presses universitaires de France.

Cohen, Marcel. 1924. *Le système verbal sémitique et l'expression du temps.* Publications de l'École des langues orientales vivantes 5.11. Paris: Éd. Ernest Leroux.

Comrie, Bernard. 1976. *Aspect: An Introduction to the Study of Verbal Aspect and Related Problems.* Cambridge Textbooks in Linguistics. Cambridge: Cambridge University Press.

———. 1985. *Tense.* Cambridge Textbooks in Linguistics. Cambridge: Cambridge University Press.

Cook, John A. 2002. "The Biblical Hebrew Verbal System: A Grammaticalization Approach." PhD diss, University of Wisconsin-Madison.

———. 2006. "The Finite Verbal Forms in Biblical Hebrew Do Express Aspect." *Journal of the Ancient Near Eastern Society* 3:21–35.

———. 2012. *Time and the Biblical Hebrew Verb: The Expression of Tense, Aspect, and Modality in Biblical Hebrew*. Linguistic Studies in Ancient West Semitic 7. Winona Lake, IN: Eisenbrauns.

Curtius, Georg. 1875. *Erläuterungen zu meiner griechischen Schulgrammatik*. 3rd ed. Prague: Tempsky.

Dahl, Östen. 1975. "On Generics." Pages 99–111 in *Formal Semantics of Natural Language*. Edited by Edward L. Keenan. Cambridge: Cambridge University Press.

———. 1985. *Tense and Aspect Systems*. Oxford: Blackwell.

———. 1994. "Aspect." Pages 240–47 in *The Encyclopedia of Language and Linguistics*. Edited by R.E. Asher. Oxford: Pergamon.

———. 2000a. "The Grammar of Future Time Reference in European Languages." Pages 309–28 in *Tense and Aspect in the Languages of Europe*. Edited by Östen Dahl. Empirical Approaches to Language Typology 20.6. Berlin: de Gruyter.

———. 2000b. "The Tense and Aspect Systems of European Languages in a Typological Perspective." Pages 3–25 in *Tense and Aspect in the Languages of Europe*. Edited by Östen Dahl. Empirical Approaches to Language Typology 20.6. Berlin: de Gruyter.

———. 2001. "Languages Without Tense and Aspect." Pages 159–72 in *Aktionsart and Aspectotemporality in Non-European Languages*. Edited by Karen H. Ebert and Fernando Zúñiga. Arbeiten des Seminars für allgemeine Sprachwissenschaft der Universität Zürich 16. Zürich: Universität Zürich, Seminar für allgemeine Sprachwissenschaft.

Dahl, Östen, and Eva Hedin. 2000. "Current Relevance and Event Reference." Pages 385–401 in *Tense and Aspect in the Languages of Europe*. Edited by Östen Dahl. Empirical Approaches to Language Typology 20.6. Berlin: de Gruyter.

Dahlgren, Sven-Olof. 2008. "The Relevance of Tense and Aspect in Semitic Languages. The Case of Hebrew and Arabic." Pages 221–48 in *Interdependence of Diachronic and Synchronic Analyses*. Edited by Folke Josephson and Ingmar Söhrman. Amsterdam: John Benjamins.

Daiber, Thomas. 1992. *Die Darstellung des Zeitworts in ostslavischen Grammatiken von den Anfängen bis zum ausgehenden 18. Jahrhundert*. Monumenta Linguae Slavicae Dialecti Veteris 32. Freiburg im Breisgau: Weiher.

Dallaire, Hélène. 2014. *The Syntax of Volitives in Biblical Hebrew and Amarna Canaanite Prose*. Linguistic Studies in Ancient West Semitic 9. Winona Lake, IN: Eisenbrauns.

Davis, Steven. 1991. "Introduction." Pages 3–13 in *Pragmatics: A Reader*. Edited by Steven Davis. New York: Oxford University Press.

DeCaen, Vincent Joseph John. 1995. *On the Placement and Interpretation of the Verb in Standard Biblical Hebrew Prose*. PhD diss, University of Chicago.

Declerck, Renaat. 1986. "From Reichenbach (1947) to Comrie (1985) and Beyond: Towards a Theory of Tense." *Lingua* 70:305–64. doi: 10.1016/0024-3841(86)90048-3.

———. 2006. *The Grammar of the English Tense System*. In collaboration with Susan Reed and Bert Cappelle. Berlin: de Gruyter.

Detges, Ulrich. 2006. "Aspect and Pragmatics. The Passé Composé in Old French and the Old Spanish Perfecto Compuesto." Pages 47–72 in *Change in Verbal Systems: Issues on Explanation*. Edited by Kerstin Eksell and Thora Vinther. Frankfurt am Main: Peter Lang.

Dik, Simon C. 1997. *The Theory of Functional Grammar: The Structure of the Clause.* Vol. 1. Berlin: de Gruyter.

Dionysios Thrax. 1989. *La grammaire de Denys le Thrace.* Translated, and with commentary by Jean Lallot. Sciences du Langage. Paris: Éditions du Centre national de la recherche scientifique.

Dobbs-Allsopp, F. W. 2000. "Biblical Hebrew Statives and Situation Aspect." *Journal of Semitic Studies* 45:21–53. doi: 10.1093/jss/XLV.1.21.

Dombrovszky, J. 1961. "Contribution à l'étude de la genèse des aspects verbaux slaves." *Slavica* 1:7–30.

Driver, S. R. 1892. *A Treatise on the Use of the Tenses in Hebrew and Some Other Syntactical Questions.* 3rd ed. The Biblical Resource Series. London: Oxford University Press.

Ebert, Karen H. 1995. "Ambiguous Perfect-Progressive Forms Across Languages." Pages 185–203 in *Typological Perspectives.* Vol 2 of *Temporal Reference, Aspect and Actionality.* Edited by Pier Marco Bertinetto. Turin: Rosenberg & Sellier.

Ehrensvärd, Martin. 2003. "Linguistic Dating of Biblical Texts." Pages 164–88 in *Biblical Hebrew: Studies in Chronology and Typology.* Edited by Ian Young. London: T&T Clark.

Endo, Yoshinobu. 1996. *The Verbal System of Classical Hebrew in the Joseph Story: An Approach from Discourse Analysis.* Studia Semitica Neerlandica 32. Assen: Van Gorcum.

Eskhult, Mats. 1990. *Studies in Verbal Aspect and Narrative Technique in Biblical Hebrew Prose.* Studia Semitica Upsaliensia 12. Stockholm: Almqvist & Wiksell.

———. 2000. "Verbal Syntax in Late Biblical Hebrew." Pages 84–93 in *Diggers at the Well: Proceedings of a Third International Symposium on the Hebrew of the Dead Sea Scrolls and Ben Sira.* Edited by Takamitsu Muraoka and John F Elwolde. Leiden: Brill.

Evans, Christopher S., and Peter Marler. 1995. "Language and Animal Communication: Parallels and Contrasts." Pages 341–82 in *Comparative Approaches to Cognitive Science.* Edited by Herbert L. Roitblat and Jean-Arcady Meyer. Cambridge, MA: MIT Press.

Ewald, Georg Heinrich August. 1870. *Ausführliches Lehrbuch der hebräischen Sprache des alten Bundes.* Göttingen: Dieterich.

Fensham, F. Charles. 1978. "The Use of the Suffix Conjugation and the Prefix Conjugation in a Few Old Hebrew Poems." *Journal of Northwest Semitic Languages* 6:9–18.

Fleischman, Suzanne. 1982. *The Future in Thought and Language: Diachronic Evidence from Romance.* Cambridge Studies in Linguistics 36. Cambridge: Cambridge University Press.

———. 1990. *Tense and Narrativity: From Medieval Performance to Modern Fiction.* Croom Helm Romance Linguistics Series. London: Routledge.

Forsyth, James. 1970. *A Grammar of Aspect: Usage and Meaning in the Russian Verb.* Studies in the Modern Russian Language Extra Volume. London: Cambridge University Press.

Friedman, Victor A. 2012. "Language Contact." Pages 398–427 in *The Oxford Handbook of Tense and Aspect.* Edited by Robert I. Binnick. Oxford: Oxford University Press.

Furuli, Rolf. 2006. *New Understanding of the Verbal System of Classical Hebrew: An Attempt to Distinguish Between Semantic and Pragmatic Factors.* Oslo: Awatu.

Garey, Howard B. 1957. "Verbal Aspect in French." *Language* 33:91–110.

Garr, W. Randall. 1998. "Drivers Treatise and the Study of Hebrew: Then and Now." Introduction to *A Treatise on the Use of the Tenses in Hebrew and Some Other Syntactical Questions* by S. R Driver (1892), xviii–lxxxvi. 3rd ed. The Biblical Resource Series. London: Oxford University Press.

Geiger, Gregor. 2012. *Das hebräische Partizip in den Texten aus der judäischen Wüste.* Studies on the Texts of the Desert of Judah 101. Leiden: Brill.

Gentry, Peter J. 1998. "The System of the Finite Verb in Classical Biblical Hebrew." *Hebrew Studies* 39:7–39.

Gibbs, Raymond W., Jr. 1983. "Do People Always Process the Literal Meanings of Indirect Requests?" *Journal of Experimental Psychology: Learning, Memory, and Cognition* 9:524–533.

Gibson, John C. L, and A. B Davidson. 1994. *Davidson's Introductory Hebrew Grammar: Syntax.* Edinburgh: T&T Clark.

Goldfajn, Tal. 1998. *Word Order and Time in Biblical Hebrew Narrative.* Oxford Theological Monographs. Oxford: Clarendon.

Goodwin, William Watson. 1891. *A Greek Grammar.* London.

Gordon, Cyrus H. 1955. *Ugaritic Manual*, rev. ed. Analecta Orientalia 35. Rome: Pontificium Institutum Biblicum.

Greč, Nikolaj I. 1828. *Grammaire raisonnée de la langue russe.* Translated into French by Ch. Ph. Reiff. Sankt Peterburg: Impr. de N. Gretsch.

Greenstein, Edward L. 1988. "On the Prefixed Preterite in Biblical Hebrew." *Hebrew Studies* 29:7–17.

———. 2006. "Forms and Functions of the Finite Verb in Ugaritic Narrative Verse." Pages 75–102 in *Biblical Hebrew in Its Northwest Semitic Setting: Typological and Historical Perspectives.* Edited by Steven Ellis Fassberg and Avi Hurvitz. Publication of the Institute for Advanced Studies, the Hebrew University of Jerusalem 1. Jerusalem: Hebrew University Magnes Press.

Gross, Walter. 1976. *Verbform und Funktion: Wayyiqtol für die Gegenwart?* Ein Beitrag zur Syntax poetischer althäbräischer Texte. Arbeiten zu Text und Sprache im Alten Testament 1. St. Ottilien: EOS-Verlag.

Hackett, Jo Ann. 2012. "Yaqtul and a Ugaritic Incantation Text." Pages 111–18 in *Language and Nature: Papers Presented to John Huehnergard on the Occasion of His 60th Birthday.* Edited by Rebecca Hasselbach and Naama Pat-El. Chicago: The Oriental Institute of the University of Chicago.

Harder, Peter, and Kasper Boye. 2011. "Grammaticalization and Functional Linguistics." Pages 56–68 in *The Oxford Handbook of Grammaticalization.* Edited by Heiko Narrog and Bernd Heine. Oxford: Oxford University Press.

Haspelmath, Martin. 1998. "The Semantic Development of Old Presents: New Futures and Subjunctives Without Grammaticalization." *Diachronica* 15:29–62.

Hatav, Galia. 1997. *The Semantics of Aspect and Modality: Evidence from English and Biblical Hebrew.* Studies in Language Companion Series 34. Philadelpia: Benjamins.

Hatcher, Anna Granville. 1951. "The Use of the Progressive Form in English: A New Approach." *Language* 27:254–280.

Heine, Bernd, Ulrike Claudi, and Friedrieke Hünnemeyer. 1991. *Grammaticalization: A Conceptual Framework.* Chicago: University of Chicago Press.

Heine, Bernd, and Tania Kuteva. 2002. *World Lexicon of Grammaticalization*. Cambridge: Cambridge University Press.

Hendel, Ronald S. 1996. "In the Margins of the Hebrew Verbal System." *Zeitschrift für Althebraistik* 9:152–81.

Hengenveld, Kees. 2011. "The Grammaticalization of Tense and Aspect." Pages 580–94 in *The Oxford Handbook of Grammaticalization*. Edited by Heiko Narrog and Bernd Heine. Oxford: Oxford University Press.

Hermann, Eduard. 1927. "Objektive und subjektive *Aktionsart*." *Indogermanishe Forschungen* 45:207–28.

Hetzron, Robert. 1987. "Hebrew." Pages 686–704 in *The World's Major Languages*. Edited by Bernard Comrie. London: Croom Helm.

Hockett, Charles F. 1960. "The Origin of Speech." *Scientific American* 203:88–111.

Holst, Søren. 2008. *Verbs and War Scroll: Studies in the Hebrew Verbal System and the Qumran War Scroll*. Studia Semitica Upsaliensia 25. Uppsala: Acta Universitatis Upsaliensis.

Homer. 1924. *The Iliad*. Translated by A. T. Murray. Loeb Classical Library. Cambridge: Harvard University Press.

Hopper, Paul J., and Elizabeth Closs Traugott. 2003. *Grammaticalization*. 2nd ed. Cambridge Textbooks in Linguistics. Cambridge: Cambridge University Press.

Huehnergard, John. 1997. *A Grammar of Akkadian*. Harvard Semitic Studies 45. Atlanta: Scholars Press.

Hughes, James A. 1970. "Another Look at the Hebrew Tenses." *Journal of Near Eastern Studies* 29:12–24. doi: 10.2307/543567.

Isaksson, Bo. 2013. "Subordination: Biblical Hebrew." Pages 657–64 in *Encyclopedia of Hebrew Language and Linguistics*. Edited by G. Khan. Leiden: Brill.

Jacobsohn, Hermann. 1926. "Review of: Vorlesungen über Syntax by Jacob Wackernagel." *Gnomon* 2:369–95. doi: 10.2307/27673473.

Jakobson, Roman. 1971. "Shifters, Verbal Categories, and the Russian Verb." Pages 130–47 in *Word and Language*. Vol. 2 of *Selected Writings*. Roman Jakobson. The Hague: Mouton.

Jepsen, Alfred. 1977. "Ḥāzāh." *Theologishers Wörterbuch zum Alten Testament* 2:822–35. Stuttgart: Kohlhammer.

Johanson, Lars. 2000. "Viewpoint Operators in European Languages." Pages 27–187 in *Tense and Aspect in the Languages of Europe*. Edited by Östen Dahl. Empirical Approaches to Language Typology 20.6. Berlin: de Gruyter.

———. 2001. "The Aspectually Neutral Situation Type." Pages 7–13 in *Aktionsart and Aspectotemporality in Non-European Languages*. Edited by Karen H. Ebert and Fernando Zúñiga. Zürich: Universität Zürich, Seminar für allgemeine Sprachwissenchaft.

Johnson, Bo. 1979. *Hebräisches Perfekt und Imperfekt mit vorangehendem w^e*. Coniectanea Biblica 13. Lund: Gleerup.

Johnson, Marion. 1981. "A Unified Temporal Theory of Tense and Aspect." Pages 145–76 in *Tense and Aspect*. Edited by Philip J. Tedeschi and Annie Zaenen. Syntax and Semantics 14. New York: Academic Press.

Joosten, Jan. 1997. "The Indicative System of the Biblical Hebrew Verb." Pages 51–71 in *Narrative Syntax and the Hebrew Bible: Papers of the Tilburg Conference 1996*. Edited by E.J. van Wolde. Biblical Interpretation Series 29. Leiden: Brill.

———. 2002. "Do the Finite Verbal Forms in Biblical Hebrew Express Aspect?" *Journal of the Ancient Near Eastern Society* 29:49–70.

———. 2006. "The Disappearance of Iterative WEQATAL in the Biblical Hebrew Verbal System." Pages 135–147 in *Biblical Hebrew in Its Northwest Semitic Setting: Typological and Historical Perspectives*. Edited by Steven Ellis Fassberg and Avi Hurvitz. Publication of the Institute for Advanced Studies, the Hebrew University of Jerusalem 1. Jerusalem: Hebrew University Magnes Press.

———. 2012. *The Verbal System of Biblical Hebrew: A New Synthesis Elaborated on the Basis of Classical Prose*. Jerusalem Biblical Studies 10. Jerusalem: Simor.

Joüon, Paul. 1923. *Grammaire de l'hébreu biblique*. Rome: Pontifical Biblical Institute.

Joüon, Paul, and Takamitsu Muraoka. 2009. *A Grammar of Biblical Hebrew*. 2nd repr. of the 2nd ed., with corrections. Subsidia Biblica 27. Rome: Pontifical Biblical Institute.

Karadžić, Vuk Stefanović. 1824. *Kleine serbische Grammatik verdeutscht und mit einer Vorrede von Jacob Grimm*. Leipzig: Reimer.

Katz, Graham. 2003. "On the Stativity of the English Perfect." Pages 205–34 in *Perfect Explorations*. Edited by Artemis Alexiadou, Monika Rathert, and Arnim von Stechow. Interface Explorations 2. Berlin: de Gruyter.

Kautsch, Emil. 1909. *Gesenius' Hebrew Grammar*. 2nd ed. Translated by A. E. Cowley. Oxford: Clarendon.

Klein, Wolfgang. 1994. *Time in Language*. Germanic Linguistics. London: Routledge.

Koschmieder, Erwin. 1971. *Zeitbezug und Sprache: Ein Beitrag zur Aspekt- und Tempusfrage*. Reihe "Libelli" 329. Darmstadt: Wissenschaftliche Buchgesellschaft.

Kozinceva, Natalia A. 1988. "Resultative, Passive and Perfect in Armenian." Pages 449–58 in *Typology of Resultative Constructions*. Typological Studies in Language 12. Amsterdam: John Benjamins.

Krifka, Manfred, Francis Jeffry Pelletier, Gregory N. Carlson, Alice ter Meulen, Gennaro Chierchia, and Godehard Link. 1995. "Genericity: An Introduction." Pages 1–124 in *The Generic Book*. Edited by Gregory N. Carlson and Francis Jeffry Pelletier. Chicago: The University of Chicago Press.

Kuryłowicz, Jerzy. 1972. *Studies in Semitic Grammar and Metrics*. Prace Językoznawcze 67. Wrocław: Ossolineum.

———. 1973. "Verbal Aspect in Semitic." *Orientalia*. 42:114–20.

Kustár, Péter. 1972. "Aspekt im Hebräischen." Theologische Dissertationen 9. PhD diss., University of Basel.

Kutscher, Eduard Yechezkel. 1982. *A History of the Hebrew Language*. Jerusalem: Magnes.

Lambrecht, Knud. 1994. *Information Structure and Sentence Form: Topic, Focus, and the Mental Representations of Discourse Referents*. Cambridge Studies in Linguistics 71. Cambridge: Cambridge University Press.

Langacker, Ronald W. 2011. "Grammaticalization and Cognitive Grammar." Pages 79–91 in *The Oxford Handbook of Grammaticalization*. Oxford: Oxford University Press.

Larcher, Pierre. 2012. *Le système verbal de l'arabe classique*. 2nd ed. Collection Didactilangue. Aix-en-Provence: Publications de l'université de Provence.

Lehman, Christian. DATE. "Grammaticalization and Linguistic Typology." *General Linguistics* 26:3–23.

Lindstedt, Jouko. 1985. *On the Semantics of Tense and Aspect in Bulgarian*. Slavica Helsingiensia 4. Helsinki: University of Helsinki.

———. 2000. "The Perfect—Aspectual, Temporal and Evidential." Pages 356–83 in *Tense and Aspect in the Languages of Europe*. Edited by Östen Dahl. Empirical Approaches to Language Typology 20.6. Berlin: de Gruyter.

Lipiński, Edward. 1997. *Semitic Languages: Outline of a Comparative Grammar*. Orientalia Lovaniensia Analecta 80. Leuven: Peeters.

Lyons, John. 1977. *Semantics*. Vol. 1. Cambridge: Cambridge University Press.

Maslov, Jurij S. 1988. "Resultative, Perfect, and Aspect." Pages 63–86 in *Typology of Resultative Constructions*. Edited by Vladimir P. Nedjalkov. Typological Studies in Language 12. Amsterdam: John Benjamins.

McAninch, Andrew, Grant Goodrich, and Colin Allen. 2009. "Animal Communication and Neo-Expressivism." Pages 128–44 in *The Philosophy of Animal Minds*. Edited by Robert W. Lurz. Cambridge: Cambridge University Press.

McFall, Leslie. 1982. *The Enigma of the Hebrew Verbal System: Solutions from Ewald to the Present Day*. Historic Texts and Interpreters in Biblical Scholarship 2. Sheffield: Almond.

Meid, Wolfgang. 1971. *Das germanische Praeteritum: Indogermanische Grundlagen und Ausbreitung im Germanischen*. Innsbrucker Beiträge zur Sprachwissenschaft 3. Innsbruck: Institut für Vergleichende Sprachwissenschaft der Universität Innsbruck.

Meyer, Rudolf. 1972. *Satzlehre*. Vol. 3 in *Hebräische Grammatik*. Sammlung Göschen 5765. Berlin: de Gruyter.

Michel, Diethelm. 1960. *Tempora und Satzstellung in den Psalmen*. Abhandlungen zur evangelischen Theologie 1. Bonn.

Moens, Marc, and Mark Steedman. 1988. "Temporal Ontology and Temporal Reference." *Computational Linguistics* 14:3–14.

Moran, William L. 2003. "A Syntactical Study of the Dialect of Byblos as Reflected in the Amarna Tablets." Pages 1–130 in *Amarna Studies: Collected Writings by William L. Moran*. Edited by John Huehnergard and Shlomo Izre'el. Winona Lake, IN: Eisenbrauns.

Morris, Charles W. [1938] 1971a. "Foundations of the Theory of Signs." Pages 17–71 in *Writings on the General Theory of Signs*. Approaches to Semiotics 16. The Hague: Mouton.

———. [1946] 1971b. "Signs, Language, and Behavior." Pages 79–397 in *Writings on the General Theory of Signs*. Approaches to Semiotics 16. The Hague: Mouton.

Müller, Hans-Peter. 1988. "Das Bedeutungspotential der Afformativkonjugation." *Zeitschrift für Althebraistik* 1:74–98, 159–90.

Musan, Renate. 2002. *The German Perfect: Its Semantic Composition and Its Interactions with Temporal Adverbials*. Studies in Linguistics and Philosophy 78. Dordrecht: Kluwer Academic.

Narrog, H. 2005. "Modality, Mood, and Change of Modal Meanings: A New Perspective." *Cognitive Linguistics* 16:677–731.

Nedjalkov, Vladimir P. 1988. *Resultative, Passive and Perfect in German*. Pages 411–32 in Typology of Resultative Constructions. Edited by Vladimir P. Nedjalkov. Typological Studies in Language 12. Amsterdam: John Benjamins.

Nedjalkov, Vladimir P., and Sergej J. Jaxontov. 1988. "The Typology of Resultative Constructions." Pages 3–62 in *Typology of Resultative Constructions*. Edited by Vladimir P. Nedjalkov. Typological Studies in Language 12. Amsterdam: John Benjamins.

Niccacci, Alviero. 1990. *The Syntax of the Verb in Classical Hebrew Prose*. Journal for the Study of the Old Testament, Supplement Series 86. Sheffield: JSOT Press.

———. 1994. "On the Hebrew Verbal System." Pages 117–37 in *Biblical Hebrew and Discourse Linguistics*. Edited by Robert D. Bergen. Dallas: Summer Institute of Linguistics.

———. 1997. "Analysing Biblical Hebrew Poetry." *Journal for the Study of the Old Testament* 22:77–93. doi: 10.1177/030908929702207404.

———. 2006. "The Biblical Hebrew Verbal System in Poetry." Pages 247–68 in *Biblical Hebrew in Its Northwest Semitic Setting: Typological and Historical Perspectives*. Edited by Steven E. Fassberg and Avi Hurvitz. Publication of the Institute for Advanced Studies, the Hebrew University of Jerusalem 1. Jerusalem: Hebrew University Magnes Press.

Notarius, Tania. 2010. "The Active Predicative Participle in Archaic and Classical Biblical Poetry: A Typological and Historical Investigation." *Ancient Near Eastern Studies* 47:241–269.

———. 2013. *The Verb in Archaic Biblical Poetry: A Discursive, Typological, and Historical Investigation of the Tense System*. Leiden: Brill.

Nöth, Winfried. 2000. *Handbuch der Semiotik*. 2nd ed. Stuttgart: Metzler.

Nyberg, H. S. 1952. *Hebreisk grammatik*. Stockholm: Almqvist & Wiksell.

Olsen, Mari Broman. 1997. *A Semantic and Pragmatic Model of Lexical and Grammatical Aspect*. Outstanding Dissertations in Linguistics. New York: Garland.

Palmer, Frank Robert. 1981. *Semantics*. 2nd ed. Cambridge: Cambridge University Press.

———. 2001. *Mood and Modality*. 2nd ed. Cambridge Textbooks in Linguistics. Cambridge: Cambridge University Press.

Pérez Fernández, Miguel. 1999. *An Introductory Grammar of Rabbinic Hebrew*. Leiden: Brill.

Pinborg, Jan. 1975. "Classical Antiquity: Greece." Pages 69–126 in *Historiography of Linguistics*. Edited by Thomas A. Sebeok and Hans Aarsleff. Vol. 1. Current Trends in Linguistics 13. The Hague: Mouton.

Porzig, Walter. 1927. "Zur Aktionsart indogermanischen Präsenzbildungen." *Indogermanishe Forschungen* 45:152–67.

Prior, Arthur N. 1967. *Past, Present and Future*. Oxford: Oxford University Press.

Priscian. 1855. *Prisciani: Institutionum grammaticarum libri I–XII*. Edited by Heinrich Keil and Martin Julius Hertz. Vol. 2 of *Grammatici Latini*. Edited by Heinrich Keil. Leipzig: Teubner.

Rabinowitz, Isaac. 1984. "'*Āz* Followed by Imperfect Verb-Form in Preterite Contexts: A Redactional Device in Biblical Hebrew." *Vetus Testamentum* 34:53–62.

Rassudova, Ol'ga Petrovna. 1984. *Aspectual Usage in Modern Russian*. Moscow: Russky yazyk.

Recanati, François. 2004. "Pragmatics and Semantics." Pages 442–62 in *The Handbook of Pragmatics*. Edited by Laurence R. Horn and Gregory Ward. Blackwell Handbooks in Linguistics 16. Malden, MA: Blackwell.

Regnéll, Carl Göran. 1944. *Über den Ursprung des slavischen Verbalaspektes*. Lund: Gleerup.

Reichenbach, Hans. 1947. *Elements of Symbolic Logic*. New York: Macmillan.

Rendall, Drew, and Michael J. Owren. 2002. "Animal Vocal Communication: Say What?" Pages 307–14 in *The Cognitive Animal: Empirical and Theoretical*

Perspectives on Animal Cognition. Edited by Marc Bekoff, Colin Allen, and Gordon M. Burghardt. Cambridge MA: MIT Press.
Robar, Elizabeth. 2014. *The Verb and the Paragraph in Biblical Hebrew: A Cognitive-Linguistic Approach*. Studies in Semitic Languages and Linguistics 78. Leiden: Brill.
Robins, Robert Henry. 1990. *A Short History of Linguistics*. 3rd ed. Longman Linguistics Library. London: Longman.
Rogland, Max Frederick. 2003. *Alleged Non-past Uses of Qatal in Classical Hebrew*. Studia Semitica Neerlandica 44. Assen: Van Gorcum.
Rundgren, Frithiof. 1959. *Intensiv und Aspektkorrelation: Studien zur äthiopischen und akkadischen Verbalstammbildung*. Uppsala: Uppsala Universitets Årsskrift 1959.
———. 1961. *Das althebräische Verbum: Abriss der Aspektlehre*. Stockholm: Almqvist & Wiksell.
Ruytenbeek, Nicolas. 2017. "The Comprehension of Indirect Requests: Previous Work and Future Directions." Pages 293–322 in *Semantics and Pragmatics: Drawing a Line*. Edited by Ilse Depraetere and Raphael Salkie. Logic, Argumentation and Reasoning 11. Springer. doi: 10.1007/978-3-319-32247-6_17.
Sáenz-Badillos, Ángel. 1996. *A History of the Hebrew Language*. Cambridge: Cambridge University Press.
Saussure, Ferdinand de. 1987. *Cours de linguistique générale*. Edited by Charles Bally and Albert Sechehaye, with a critical commentary of Tullio De Mauro. Bibliothèque Scientifique. Paris: Payot.
Schneider, Wolfgang. 2001. *Grammatik des biblischen Hebräisch: Ein Lehrbuch*. Munich: Claudius.
Sebeok, Thomas A. 2001. *Signs: An Introduction to Semiotics*. Toronto: University of Toronto Press.
Sempere-Martinez, Juan A. 2008. "Cultural and Psychological Factors for the Present Perfect in British English and American English." *International Journal of Arts Education* 6:123–39.
Silverman, Michael H. 1973. "Syntactic Notes on the Waw-Consecutive." Pages 167–75 in *Orient and Occident: Essays Presented to Cyrus H. Gordon on the Occasion of His Sixty-Fifth Birthday*. Edited by Harry A. Hoffner Jr. Alter Orient und Altes Testament 22. Neukirchen-Vluyn: Neukirchener Verlag.
Slobodchikoff, C. N, Bianca S. Perla, and Jennifer L. Verdolin. 2009. *Prairie Dogs: Communication and Community in an Animal Society*. Cambridge: Harvard University Press.
Smith, Carlota S. 1997. *The Parameter of Aspect*. 2nd ed. Studies in Linguistics and Philosophy 43. Dordrecht: Springer.
———. 2008. "Time with and Without Tense." Pages 227–49 in *Time and Modality*. Edited by Jacqueline Guéron and Jacqueline Lecarme. Studies in Natural Language and Linguistic Theory 75. Dordrecht: Springer.
Smith, Mark S. 1991. *The Origins and Development of the Waw-Consecutive: Northwest Semitic Evidence from Ugarit to Qumran*. Harvard Semitic Studies 39. Atlanta: Scholars Press.
———. 1994. *Introduction with Text, Translation and Commentary of KTU 1.1–1.2*. Vol. 1 of *The Ugaritic Baal Cycle*. Supplements to Vetus Testamentum 15. Leiden: Brill.
———. 1999. "Grammatically Speaking: The Participle as a Main Verb of Clauses (Predicative Participle) in Direct Discourse and Narrative in Pre-Mishnaic

Hebrew." Pages 278–332 in *Sirach, Scrolls, and Sages: Proceedings of a Second International Symposium on the Hebrew of the Dead Sea Scrolls, Ben Sira, and the Mishnah*. Edited by Takamitsu Muraoka and J.F. Elwolde. Studies on the Texts of the Desert of Judah 33. Leiden: Brill.

Soga, Matsuo. 1983. *Tense and Aspect in Modern Colloquial Japanese*. Vancouver: University of British Columbia Press.

Sørensen, Hans Christian. 1943. "Om definitionerne av verbets aspekter." Pages 221–33 in *In Memoriam Kr. Sandfeld: Udgivet paa 70-aarsdagen for hans fødsel*. Edited by Rosally Brøndal. Copenhagen: Gyldendal.

Sperber, Alexander. 1966. *A Historical Grammar of Biblical Hebrew: A Presentation of Problems with Suggestions to Their Solution*. Leiden: Brill.

Streitberg, Wilhelm. 1943. *Urgermanische Grammatik: Einführung in das vergleichende Studium der altgermanischen Dialekte*. Heidelberg: Winter.

Stutterheim, Christiane von, Mary Caroll, and Wolfgang Klein. 2009. "New Perspectives in Analyzing Aspectual Distinctions Across Languages." Pages 195–216 in *The Expression of Time*. Edited by Wolfgang Klein and Ping Li. The Expression of Cognitive Categories 3. Berlin: de Gruyter.

Talstra, Eep. 1997. "Tense, Mood, Aspect and Clause Connections in Biblical Hebrew. A Textual Approach." *Journal of Northwest Semitic Languages* 23:81–103.

Testen, David Douglas. 1998. *Parallels in Semitic Linguistics: The La- in Arabic and Related Semitic Particles*. Studies in Semitic Languages and Linguistics 26. Leiden: Brill.

Thelin, Nils B. 1978. *Towards a Theory of Aspect, Tense and Actionality in Slavic*. Studia Slavica Upsaliensia 18. Stockholm: Almqvist & Wiksell.

———. 1991. "Aspect, Tense or Taxis? The Perfect Meaning Reconsidered." Pages 421–31 in *"Words Are Physicians for an Ailing Mind": Orgēs nosousēs eisin iatroi logoi*. Edited by Maciej Grochowski and Daniel Weiss. Sagners Slavistische Sammlung 17. Munich: Sagner.

Tomasello, Michael. 2008. *Origins of Human Communication*. The Jean Nicod Lectures. Cambridge: MIT Press.

Torres Cacoullos, Rena. 2000. *Grammaticization, Synchronic Variation, and Language Contact: A Study of Spanish Progressive -ndo Constructions*. Studies in Language Companion Series 52. Amsterdam: John Benjamins.

Tov, Emanuel. 1992. *Textual Criticism of the Hebrew Bible*. 2nd ed. Minneapolis: Fortress.

Trask, R. L. 1999. *Key Concepts in Language and Linguistics*. Key Concepts Series. London: Routledge.

Tropper, Josef. 1998. "Althebräisches und semitisches Aspektsystem." *Zeitschrift für Althebraistik* 11:153–90.

———. 2000. *Ugaritische Grammatik*. Alter Orient und Altes Testament 273. Münster: Ugarit-Verlag.

———. 2012. *Ugaritische Grammatik*, 2nd rev. ed. Alter Orient und Altes Testament 273. Münster: Ugarit-Verlag.

Tropper, Josef, and Juan-Pablo Vita. 2010. *Kanaano-akkadische der Amarnazeit*. Lehrbücher orientalischer Sprachen, Section I: Cuneiform Languages 1. Münster: Ugarit.

Tyler, Andrea, and Vyvyan Evans. 2003. *The Semantics of English Prepositions: Spatial Scenes, Embodied Meaning, and Cognition*. Cambridge: Cambridge University Press.

Van de Sande, Axel. 2008. *Nouvelle perspective sur le système verbal de l'hébreu ancien: Les formes *qatala, *yaqtul et *yaqtulu*. Publications de l'Institut Orientaliste de Louvain 57. Louvain: Peeters; Louvain-la-Neuve: Institut orientaliste de l'Université catholique de Louvain.

Varro, Marcus Terentius. 1938. *On the Latin Language*. 2 vols. Translated by Roland G. Kent. Loeb Classical Library. Cambridge: Harvard University Press.

Vauclair, Jacques. 2003. "Would Humans without Language Be Apes?" Pages 9–26 in *Cultural Guidance in the Development of the Human Mind: Advances in Child Development Within Culturally Structured Environments*. Westport, CT: Ablex.

Versteegh, C. H. M. 1980. "The Stoic Verbal System." *Hermes* 108:338–57. doi: 10.2307/4476172.

Vlach, Frank. 1981. "The Semantics of the Progressive." Pages 271–92 in *Tense and Aspect*. Edited by Philip J. Tedeschi and Annie Zaenen. Syntax and Semantics 14. New York: Academic Press.

Volodin, Alexander P. 1988. "Resultative and Perfect Passive in Finnish." Pages 469–77 in *Typology of Resultative Constructions*. Edited by Vladimir P. Nedjalkov. Typological Studies in Language 12. Amsterdam: John Benjamins.

Waltke, Bruce K., and M. O'Connor. 1990. *An Introduction to Biblical Hebrew Syntax*. Winona Lake, IN: Eisenbrauns.

Watson, Wilfred G. E. 1994. *Traditional Techniques in Classical Hebrew Verse*. JSOT Supplement Series 170. Sheffield: Sheffield Academic Press.

Weingreen, Jacob. 1959. *A Practical Grammar for Classical Hebrew*. 2nd ed. Oxford: Clarendon.

Weinrich, Harald. 1964. *Tempus: Besprochene und erzählte Welt*. 1st ed. Sprache und Literatur 16. Stuttgart: Kohlhammer.

———. 1977. *Tempus: Besprochene und erzählte Welt*. 3rd ed. Stuttgart: Kohlhammer.

Whitney, William Dwight. 1875. *Life and Growth of Language*. The International Scientific Series 16. London: Henry S. King.

Wikander, Ola. 2010. "The Hebrew Consecutive Waw as a North West Semitic 'Augment': A Typological Comparison with Indo-European." *Vetus Testamentum* 60:260–70.

Wildgen, Wolfgang. 2004. *The Evolution of Human Language: Scenarios, Principles, and Cultural Dynamics*. Advances in Consciousness Research 57. Amsterdam: John Benjamins.

Young, Ian. 2003. "Introduction: The Origin of the Problem." Pages 1–7 in *Biblical Hebrew: Studies in Chronology and Typology*. Edited by Ian Young. JSOT Supplement Series 369. London: T&T Clark.

Zevit, Ziony. 1988. "Talking Funny in Biblical Henglish and Solving a Problem of the Yaqtul Past Tense." *Hebrew Studies* 29:26–32.

Zuber, Beat. 1986. *Das Tempussystem des biblischen Hebräisch: Eine Untersuchung am Text*. Beiheft zur Zeitschrift für die alttestamentliche Wissenschaft 164. Berlin: de Gruyter.

INDEX

accomplishments, 81, 83, 92
achievements, 38–40, 80, 83, 85, 86n53, 91
activities, 77–78, 81, 83, 114, 132
Aktionsart. *See also* atelicity; durativity; dynamicity; punctuality; stativity; telicity
  explanation of, 66–69
  fiens as, 48
  Leipzig school on, 34, 47
  limit-based aspect and, 93, 114, 133, 155
  perfect as, 37
  progressive aspect and, 10, 76
  resultative aspect and, 54
  stage-based aspect and, 81–84
aorist aspect. *See also* completive aspect; egressive aspect; ingressive aspect
  Ancient grammarians on, 30–31
  in Biblical Hebrew (see under *qatal*; *qotel*; *weqatalti*; *yiqtol*-L; *yiqtol*-S, declarative)
  Curtius on, 35–37
  Driver on, 46
  limit-based description of, 38–42, 42
  perfective aspect and, 36
  progressive aspect and, 41, 87–89, 95
  resultative aspect and, 87–89, 95
appeal. *See* communicative appeal
Archaic Biblical Hebrew, 18–19, 98n1
Aspect. *See also* aorist aspect; completive aspect; egressive aspect; imperfective aspect; ingressive aspect; perfect meaning; perfective aspect; preparative aspect; progressive aspect; prospective aspect; resultative aspect
  Aktionsart and, 69
  Aktionsart as, 33–34
  Bohnemeyer on, 86n53
  completed, 3, 29–32, 33, 36, 62
  definition of, 41–42, 70–71, 94, 189
  external-vs.-internal approach to, 36–42, 47
  fiens and stative, 3, 48
  grammatical aspect, 69n12
  Greč on, 32–33
  in Greek, 31
  Hebraists on, 2n11, 3, 28, 45–48, 60–61
  Johanson on, 39
  Klein on, 40
  in Latin, 31
  limit-based, 38–42, 48, 60, 84–87, 94–95
  vs. relative tense, 5, 24–26
  in Russian, 33, 38n56
  sequence aspect, 3, 48
  situation aspect, 69n12
  Smith on, 86, 12
  stage-based (*see also* preparative aspect; progressive aspect; resultative aspect): *Aktionsart* and, 81–84; explanation of, 71–81, 94, 189–90; vs. limit-based aspect, 84–89; temporalization of (*see* temporalization)
  temporal succession/sequentiality and, 48, 93, 100, 149

Aspect (*continued*)
  uncompleted, 3, 29, 31–32, 33, 36, 62
  Vater on, 32n28
  vid, 32–33
  viewpoint aspect, 69n12
atelicity
  completive aspect and, 114–15, 149
  extended event and, 83–84
  imperfective aspect and, 114, 150, 155
  ingressive aspect and, 131–32, 149
  progressive aspect and, 69, 76
  preparative aspect and, 92
  resultative aspect and, 71–74
  of semelfactives, 81
  telic/atelic ambiguity, 39, 105
  telic phrases with atelic verbs, 67
  temporalization and, 92
  of verbs and events, 67

basic meaning, 9–12, 61, 75, 92, 156, 192
  original meaning and, 11–12, 59, 159, 188
Biblical Hebrew. *See* Archaic Biblical Hebrew; Late Biblical Hebrew; Standard Biblical Hebrew

cohortative. See *yiqtol*-S, volitive
communicative appeal. *See also* signal
  in Biblical Hebrew (see under *qatal*; *qotel*; *yiqtol*-L; *yiqtol*-S, declarative; *yiqtol*-S, volitive)
  Bühler on, 6, 158–59
  criterion of efficiency, 165–69
  criterion of imminence, 162–63
  criterion of nonexpectancy, 163–65
  diachronic pathways and, 170, 187, 191, 192
  full and reduced, 160
  in grammar, 161, 170, 186
  linguistic attitude and, 161
  relative, 172–73
  in semantics, 7
  temporalization and, 174
completive aspect, 42, 87, 89
  in Biblical Hebrew (see under *qatal*; *qotel*; *weqatalti*; *yiqtol*-L; *yiqtol*-S, declarative; *yiqtol*-S, volitive)
continuative, 55, 57

deictic center
  definition of, 24
  other terms for, 43n71
  reference time and, 44–45
  secondary, 24, 134–35
  speech time and, 24, 70, 134
  "still" and, 75–76
  temporalization and, 89
  tense and, 24, 189
  transposition of, 52
deixis, 24
diachronic pathways, 4, 53, 55–58, 162n14, 170, 188
diathesis, 10, 90n61
durativity, 67, 76, 80, 83, 92, 100–102
dynamicity
  as *Aktionsart*, 66–68
  English progressive and, 10
  progressive aspect and, 76–78
  qotel and, 98
  resultative aspect and, 71
  stative *qatal* and, 120
  yiqtol-L and, 110, 179

E/"the point of the event" (Reichenbach). *See* event time: in Reichenbachian tense theory
egressive aspect, 42
event
  definition of, 66–67
  extended, 82–86, 94, 189
  focused content of vs. whole, 70
  nuclear: aspect and, 84, 94; definition of, 82–83; extended event and 83–89, 189; in *qatal*, 121, 132; temporalization and, 8, 93–94, 95, 190; in *yiqtol*-L, 110; in *yiqtol*-S, 150
  tense and (*see* event time)
event time
  aspect and, 42, 60, 70–71, 94
  extended event and, 84–85
  focused time and, 42–45, 70
  nuclear event and, 84–85
  in Reichenbachian tense theory, 42–45
  relative tense and, 25–26, 62
  tense and, 23

fiens. *See* under aspect
focalizing event
  absence of, 88
  Hebrew examples with, 98–99, 110–11, 119, 151, 145
  Hebrew examples without, 100, 114, 115, 133, 155
  in nonpresent settings, 70, 93
  in present settings, 70, 98–99, 110–11, 119
focused time/focused content of the event
  aspect and, 41–42, 70–71, 76, 78–79, 84–87
  in Biblical Hebrew, 103, 113, 143, 150
  definition of, 70, 189
  temporalization and, 89, 190
  tense (absolute and relative) and, 24–26, 43–45, 189
frame, 70, 88, 100
frequentatives, 55–58, 63
future in the past. *See* relative tense: relative future
future tense, 31–32
  in Biblical Hebrew (see under *qatal*; *qotel*; *weqataltí*; *yiqtol*-L; *yiqtol*-S, declarative)
  for commands, 56, 166–67
  communicative appeal and, 163, 166–67
  linguistic attitude and, 52
  modality and, 49–51
  non-aspectual sources for, 12, 56, 132n14
  preparative/prospective sources for, 10, 79, 89–93, 156, 188, 190
  progressive sources for, 4, 81, 188

generalizing meanings, 49–50, 56, 62, 68–69, 77–78, 95. *See also* generic meaning; gnomic aorist; gnomic meaning; habitual meaning
generic meaning, 13, 49, 68, 95, 111
gnomic aorist, 121
gnomic meaning. See *qatal*, *yiqtol*-S
grammaticalization, 3, 21, 49, 53–61, 63, 162n114. *See also* diachronic path(ways)

habitual meaning, 49–50, 53, 55–58, 77, 78, 82
  in Biblical Hebrew (see under *qatal*; *qotel*; *weqataltí*; *yiqtol*-L; *yiqtol*-S, declarative)

imperative, 6–7, 15n46, 30n22, 186. *See also* imperative, Biblical Hebrew
  communicative appeal of, 6–7, 158, 160, 162, 166
imperative, Biblical Hebrew, 127, 129–30, 140, 149
  communicative appeal of, 180–81, 182–83, 185–86, 192
imperfect, 30-31, 35, 81. See also *yiqtol*, *yiqtol*-L
  consecutive. See *yiqtol*-S, declarative
imperfective aspect. *See also* aspect: uncompleted
  Aktionsart and, 34
  in Biblical Hebrew (see under *qatal*; *qotel*; *weqataltí*; *yiqtol*-L; *yiqtol*-S, declarative; *yiqtol*-S, volitive)
  definitions of, 36, 38, 42
  diachronic pathways of, 53, 55
  Ewald on, 46
  future, 32
  Johnson on, 81
  as limit-based aspect category, 38–42
  as *paratasis*, 41
  progressive aspect and, 86–87, 93–94
  resultative imperfective, 40n66
  in Russian, 33, 38n56, 39
ingressive aspect, 35–42
  in Biblical Hebrew (see under *qatal*; *qotel*; *weqataltí*; *yiqtol*-S, declarative)
invariance
  aspectual, 95
  in Biblical Hebrew, 98–102, 108–13, 119–32, 142–48, 191
  criteria for, 9–11, 59
iterative, 33, 34, 55–58, 63

jussive. See *yiqtol*-S, volitive
Late Biblical Hebrew, 18–19, 99, 101, 110, 156

linguistic attitude ("Sprechhaltung"), 51–53, 62–63, 161–62, 191

macroevent, 68, 81, 131
meaning. *See* basic meaning; diachronic pathways; invariance; pragmatic meaning; reanalysis; semantic meaning
microevent/microlevel, 68, 106, 131
modality, 49–51, 55–56, 115–17, 128–29, 139, 185
mood, 6–7, 30, 33, 129–30, 158

participle, active. See *qotel*
participle, passive. See *qatul*
past in the past/past preterite. *See* relative tense: relative past
past tense
 in Biblical Hebrew (see under *qatal*; *qotel*; *weqataltí*; *yiqtol*-L; *yiqtol*-S, declarative)
 communicative appeal and, 163, 167–69
 definition of, 23–24
 modality and, 50, 139
 perfect and, 43–44
 resultative sources for, 4, 74–75, 89–90, 92–93, 190
path(way). *See* diachronic pathway
perfective aspect 33, 34, 35–38
perfect meaning
 in Biblical Hebrew (see under *qatal*; *yiqtol*-S, declarative)
 completed aspect and, 30–32, 36–37
 Declerck on, 43n71
 definitions of, 37, 42, 84, 86n53
 diachronic pathway of, 4, 53
 experiential perfect and, 74, 120–21
 in Greek, 31
 Hengenveld on, 90n61
 as imperfective, 40, 48
 inchoative meaning and, 72n16
 in Latin, 31
 as limit-based aspect category, 38–42, 42, 84, 94
 perfect of persistent situation and, 74, 120–21
 Reichenbach on, 42

 vs. relative past (past in the past), 24–26, 43–45, 62, 189
 as resultative, 71–76, 95
 tense and, 43n71, 75, 90n61
perfect progressive, 26, 72
performative speech acts, 87–88, 121, 146, 167, 170, 190
pluractionality, 68, 82, 84, 98, 101
posteriority. *See* relative tense: relative future
pragmatic meaning
 Andrason on, 59–60, 63
 in Biblical Hebrew, 16, 115, 131, 156, 183, 191
 criteria for, 8–9
 explanation of, 7–8
preparative aspect
 communicative appeal of, 180
 emergent 89n59
 explanation of, 79–81, 189, 190
 extended event and, 84–85
 future meaning and, 89, 95
 as progressive/preparative (overlapping meanings), 79–81, 91, 95, 190
 prospective aspect and, 79
present tense, 24, 34, 88
 aorist aspect and, 41, 88
 in Biblical Hebrew (see under *qatal*; *qotel*; *weqataltí*; *yiqtol*-L; *yiqtol*-S, declarative)
 communicative appeal and, 163, 170–71, 173, 177
 historic, 50, 65
 imperfective aspect and, 87
 linguistic attitude and, 52–53
 modality and, 50
 perfect aspect and, 24, 25, 43n77, 44, 65
 performative (*see* performative speech acts)
 poetic use of, 20
 prospective/preparative aspect and, 10, 24, 25, 79–80
 reportive, 41, 88, 95
preterite. *See* past tense
progressive aspect
 Aktionsart and, 81–82
 atelicity and, 69, 71

in Biblical Hebrew (see under *qatal*;
    qotel; *weqataltí*; *yiqtol*-L)
communicative appeal and, 170–72,
    176–80
continuous, 86–87, 95
continuous verbal type and, 58n126
diachronic pathway of, 4, 55, 57–58
emergent, 41, 89
in English, 10, 22
explanation of, 76–78, 94, 189–90
extended event and, 84–86
future meaning originating from, 4, 10,
    53, 90–92, 95, 190
imperfective aspect and, 86–87, 93–94
limit-based aspect and, 86–87, 95
nuclear event and, 84–86
as progressive/preparative aspect (over-
    lapping meanings), 79–81, 91, 95, 190
resultative-progressive ambiguity, 39,
    54
transient, 87–89, 95, 190
prospective aspect
    as limit-based aspect category, 38, 40,
        42, 84
    as preparative, 79
    temporalization and, 10, 90n61, 93, 190
punctuality, 80, 81, 83, 89, 92

qatal. See also *weqataltí*
    'āz and, 152
    adjectival, 118, 141
    aorist, 121–32, 46, 132–35
    communicative appeal of, 173–75, 192
    completive, 121, 131, 133
    consecutive (see also *weqataltí*): asyn-
        detic, 130–31
    counterfactual, 138–41, 156
    diachronic pathway of, 4, 21, 53, 54,
        188–89
    experiential, 120
    future, 119, 122–23, 147
    generalizing, 131, 135 (see also *qatal*:
        gnomic)
    gnomic, 121, 146
    indicative, 49
    ingressive, 131–32, 133
    linguistic attitude and, 2
    optative, 138–39

past, 27, 28n12, 119, 123–24, 143–44
perfect, 13, 45–46, 119–20, 142–44
perfective, 1n9, 54, 61
performative, 121
pluractional, 133
poetic usage of, 20
precative, 140
present, 119–21
present-past ambiguity, 133–34, 174
prophetic, 122–23, 147
relative past, 28, 134
reportive, 88n58
resultative, 119–32, 190, 192
stative, 120, 141–42
temporalized, 132–41
weqatal (nonconsecutive), 15, 135–38
qatul, 73n21, 104
qotel
    'āz and, 152–53
    aorist, 100–101 (see also *qotel*:
        completive)
    in Archaic Biblical Hebrew, 18, 98n1
    communicative appeal of, 176–77, 186,
        192
    completive, 103, 106
    definition of, 98
    diachronic pathway of, 4, 21, 53, 188–89
    of duration, 100–101
    future, 98–99, 103, 104
    generalizing, 99, 101, 108
    habitual, 99
    imperfective, 98–100, 152
    ingressive, 101
    in Late Biblical Hebrew, 99, 101
    nominal, 104–8
    past, 98–99, 102, 103, 104, 107
    periphrasis with *hāyâ*, 19, 101
    preparative, 81, 102, 103–4
    present, 27, 98, 99–100, 101n4, 102
    progressive, 13, 98–102, 111, 142, 156, 192
    resultative, 104–5
    stative, 99, 106, 141–42
    temporalized, 103–4, 156
    of vivid narration, 101n4

reanalysis, 9–12, 89–90, 103, 141, 190, 191
reference time, 24, 29, 42–45, 48, 60,
    90n61

relative tense
  aspect vs., 25–27, 44–45, 62, 189
  definition of, 24
  relative future (posteriority), 26, 28, 115
  relative past (anteriority), 3, 26, 28, 134
  simultaneity, 1, 25, 28, 89
resultative aspect
  atelicity and, 74
  in Biblical Hebrew (see under *qatal*; *qotel*; *weqataltí*; *yiqtol*-S, declarative)
  communicative appeal and, 173–76, 191
  continuous, 87, 95
  diachronic pathways of, 4, 21, 53, 84–86
  diathesis and, 90n61
  emergent, 88, 89, 95, 190
  explanation of, 71–76, 189
  extended event and, 84–85
  limit-based aspect and, 87–89, 95
  past meaning originating from, 65, 75, 89, 92–93, 95, 195
  perfect aspect as, 10, 72–76
  resultative-progressive ambiguity, 39, 54, 142
  telicity and, 69, 71

semantic meaning
  Andrason on, 58–60
  in the Biblical Hebrew verbal system, 192
  communicative appeal and, 170, 186
  criteria for, 2, 8–13
  explanation of, 6–8
semelfactive, 33, 81–82, 85
sign, 158–59, 191. See also signal
signal, 158–60, 163–69, 191–92
speech time (S/time of speech)
  communicative appeal and, 163, 170–71
  imperfective aspect and, 46
  perfect aspect and, 74, 142
  performatives and, 87
  progressives and, 76
  temporalization and, 89
  tense and, 23–29, 42–45, 81, 103
Standard Biblical Hebrew, 18–19, 28–29, 101
stativity
  in Biblical Hebrew (see under *qatal*; *qotel*; *yiqtol*-L; *yiqtol*-S, declarative)

  communicative appeal and, 163
  definition of, 67
  extended event and, 83
  progressive aspect and, 10, 68, 77–78
  resultative aspect and, 72
  by stativization, 68–69, 98, 108, 187, 190
TAM 1, 23
taxis, 26
telicity/*telos*. See also telicity/*telos* and completive aspect
  atelic-telic ambiguity, 39–40, 105–6, 142
  definition of, 34, 67
  extended event and, 83–84
  nuclear event and, 82
  progressive aspect and, 79, 82
  resultative aspect and, 69, 71, 73–74
telicity/*telos* and completive aspect
  performatives and, 88
  in *qatal*, 121, 131, 133
  in *qotel*, 103, 106
  in *yiqtol*-L, 114, 115
  in *yiqtol*-S, 155
temporalization, 10, 74–75, 89–94, 95, 174, 187
tense. See also future tense; past tense; present tense; relative tense
  absolute, 24, 27
  adverbial sources for, 161–62
  communicative appeal and, 163, 167–69, 171, 192–93
  definition of, 23–24, 42–43, 60, 70, 95, 189
  Hebraists on, 27–29
  linguistic attitude and, 52
  non-semantic factors indicating, 64–66
  perfect verbal form and, 24, 43n71
  poetic license and, 20
  preterite (*see* past tense)
  prospective aspect and, 24
time of speech. See speech time

verb, function of, 66
wayyiqtol. See *yiqtol*-S, declarative
weqataltí
  aorist, 131, 190
  cohortative and, 127–28

completive, 131
in conditional sentences, 125–26
diathesis in, 125, 128
future, 1n3, 27, 126–27
habitual, 15, 19, 126–27
imperative and, 127–30
imperfective, 131
ingressive, 131–32
jussive and, 127–28
in Late Biblical Hebrew, 19
modal, 49
origin of, 125
progressive, 54
qotel (nominal) and, 128–29
in Qumran Hebrew, 19n59
resultative, 124–31
same form as *qatal*, 15–16, 125, 130–31, 156
for sequential/successive events, 15, 27
vs. *weqatal* (nonconsecutive), 135–38
yiqtol-L and, 126–27

yiqtol, 1–2, 4, 13, 45–47. See also *yiqtol*-L; *yiqtol*-S, declarative; *yiqtol*-S, volitive
yiqtol-L
aorist, 112, 114, 154n86 (see also *yiqtol*-L: completive)
communicative appeal of, 178–79, 181–83, 186–87, 191–92
completive, 114, 115
definition of, 98
diachronic pathway of, 4, 21, 53, 55, 188–89
future, 13, 27, 114, 122
future in the past, 115
generalizing, 110–11 (see also *yiqtol*-L: generic; *yiqtol*-L: habitual)
generic, 13, 111
habitual, 13, 55–58, 110–11
imperfective, 61, 109–10, 114, 117
modal, 49–51, 55–56, 115–18, 156, 191
past, 110–11, 112, 113, 115
pluractional, 110
preparative/prospective, 112–13

present, 108–10, 112, 118, 178–79
progressive, 98n1, 108–11, 178–79, 190, 192
relative future (see *yiqtol*-L: future in the past)
stative, 110
temporalized, 114–18
weqatalti, semantic difference from, 131
yiqtol-S, declarative
ʾāz and, 152
aorist, 145–46, 151–54 (see also *yiqtol*-S; completive; *yiqtol*-S; ingressive)
apocopated, 13–14, 18, 151–52
communicative appeal of, 175–76, 187, 192
definition of, 13–14
diachronic pathway of, 4, 21, 53, 188–89
free-standing (asyndetic), 14–15, 151–54
future, 147
generalizing (see *yiqtol*-S, declarative: gnomic; *yiqtol*-S, declarative: habitual)
gnomic, 146, 153
habitual, 147, 151
imperfective, 150–51
ingressive, 149
past, 13, 27, 142–45, 149–51
perfect, 142–45, 146
performative, 146–47
present, 143–47
resultative, 142–48
stative, 144–45, 151, 171
temporalized, 149–54
wayyiqtol, morphology of 14, 17–18
in *weqatalti*-chain, 147–48
yiqtol-S, volitive
cohortative, 14, 46n78, 49, 142, 185
communicative appeal of, 183–86, 192
completive, 155
definition of, 13–14
imperfective, 155
jussive, 14, 155–56, 183–86, 192
unmarked for resultative aspect 155–56